IN SEARCH *of* SILVER

IN SEARCH *of* SILVER

THE GREATEST WRITING ON ATLANTIC SALMON FISHING

EDITORS: CHARLES GAINES AND MONTE BURKE

Published in association with the Atlantic Salmon Federation

DUNCAN BAIRD PUBLISHERS

LONDON

In Search of Silver
Charles Gaines and Monte Burke

First published in the United Kingdom and Ireland in 2001 by
Duncan Baird Publishers Ltd
Sixth Floor
Castle House
75–76 Wells Street
London W1T 3QH

Created and designed by Duncan Baird Publishers

Managing Editor: Judy Barratt
Editor: Charles Rangeley-Wilson
Designer: Tim Foster
Picture Researcher: Cee Weston-Baker
Commissioned Photography: David Murray
Editorial Assistant: Louise Nixon

British Library Cataloguing-in-Publication Data:
A CIP record for this book is available from the British Library.

ISBN: 1-903296-33-1

10 9 8 7 6 5 4 3 2 1

Typeset in Stempel Garamond 10.5/16
Colour reproduction by Scanhouse, Malaysia
Printed and bound in Singapore by Imago

PUBLISHERS' NOTES

The captions in this book are by Charles Gaines and Monte Burke.

There are three accepted spellings of the word gillie (also ghillie and gilly), a word
which derives from 17th-century Scottish Gaelic, meaning boy or servant. The
Editors have used the former in their captions, but in order to retain the character
of each article have preserved the various spellings in the original stories.

The inside front and back covers (endpapers) of this book show a map illustrating
the principal migratory routes of the Atlantic salmon. (Map © Atlantic Salmon
Federation.)

CONTENTS

FOREWORD

THE WILD ATLANTIC SALMON has enthralled man for centuries. More than 15,000 years ago, European cave dwellers painted pictures of Atlantic salmon on their walls and carved the fish's sleek, muscular shape into pieces of bone and antler. When the legions of Julius Caesar invaded Gaul, in the Rhine Valley they reported great fish leaping in the rivers and named them *salar*, Latin for "the leaper." More than 2000 years later, Izaak Walton, the father of modern-day angling, crowned the Atlantic salmon "the King of Gamefish" in his 1653 treatise *The Compleat Angler*. Our fascination with the Atlantic salmon continues to grow and never have we celebrated the salmon's world – the fish's beauty, strength and perseverance, the magnificent rivers where it begins and often ends its miraculous life journey, and the traditions surrounding our sport – more eloquently than in this book.

Wild Atlantic salmon are a defining element of the North Atlantic. They represent the very essence of her wild, free-flowing rivers. From the clear northern waters of Canada to pastoral Iceland and the wild unexplored rivers of Russia, to the dramatic fjords of Scandinavia and the historic rivers of Europe, the Atlantic salmon is a symbol of the North Atlantic. Like the canary in the coalmine, their presence in our rivers is a signal of the health of our own world.

This book is a celebration of wild Atlantic salmon and their rivers. No fish, nor sport, has as rich a literature as the Atlantic salmon. Charles Gaines and Monte Burke have gathered together for the first time ever the finest writing, art and photography, providing a rare and beautiful window into the wondrous world of the Atlantic salmon.

The pursuit of Atlantic salmon is the pinnacle of the sport of fly-fishing. The challenge of enticing an Atlantic salmon – a fish that refuses to eat upon entering its native river from the sea – to take a free-floating fly requires skill, patience and luck. The "fish of ten thousand casts" as the Atlantic salmon is often called, is a title that is well earned and rarely disputed. These poignant stories and poems, together with stunning photography from around the North Atlantic, reveal the essence of that which draws us to the salmon.

To watch an Atlantic salmon savagely swirl behind a swinging wet fly, or rise with purpose to a dry fly, are among the most exciting experiences in all of fly-fishing. When we feel the surge of energy and power of a fresh-run Atlantic salmon as it races across a cold, clear river at dawn, mist hanging over a fragrant spruce forest alive with birds and wildlife, we feel a connection to the wilderness itself. And when we finally cradle the salmon gently in our hands, carefully pointing its head into the oxygen-rich current before releasing it back to the river, we feel the very pulse of the wilderness through a creature that has been to the far corners of the vast North Atlantic Ocean and survived countless obstacles and predators to rise and take our fly in the very river where it was born.

The Atlantic Salmon Federation is honoured to be associated with this important book and the distinguished writers, photographers, and artists, both past and present, who have generously contributed to this landmark project. The days of abundance that Henry Van Dyke wrote about more than a hundred years ago in his wonderful story "The Ristigouche From a Horse-Yacht" are gone, maybe forever. Today the Atlantic salmon's future hangs in the balance.

ASF president Bill Taylor fishes Little Indian Pool on the St Jean River, Quebec.

The rivers and ocean where it lives are under siege. But while the threats to its survival are many, the salmon is not without its friends. The Atlantic Salmon Federation is working with our partners throughout the North Atlantic to safeguard the species, and to protect and restore its habitat so that our children and grandchildren will have the opportunity to share and enjoy this extraordinary creature. It is my hope that this book will arouse and inspire all who share the Atlantic Salmon Federation's quest for clean rivers filled with healthy runs of wild salmon to rise up and join in our conservation crusade.

Bill Taylor

Bill Taylor, President, Atlantic Salmon Federation, St Andrews, New Brunswick, Canada. November, 2000.

INTRODUCTION

A NOTABLE THING about Atlantic salmon is how richly and variously they have caused human beings over the centuries to feel in response to them. And the expressions of that feeling have been equally rich and various: For more than 15,000 years men have made Atlantic salmon the treasured subject of carvings, paintings, and songs, as well as enough first-rate poems, stories, and books to comprise – second only to the writing on trout – the finest and largest body of literature there is on a particular fish.

If my collaborator, Monte Burke, and I had no idea how extensive that literature was when we dreamed up the idea for an anthology of the best writing we could find from around the world on Atlantic salmon, we certainly do now. In fact, there is one hell of a lot of it – so much, and so much of that of high quality, that it astonishes us that such an anthology, so far as we know, has never before been put together.

Wherever and whenever men have coexisted with Atlantic salmon, it seems, more than a few of those men have been moved to write passionately about angling for the fish. It has been my and Monte's great pleasure over the past few months to read dozens of examples of that writing from or about North America, Russia, Scandinavia, Germany, Spain, France, Great Britain, Ireland, Greenland, and Iceland – some of it dating back more than two centuries; some of it, poignantly, having to do with salmon stocks that no longer exist.

During that reading, as I say, we were struck with the range and intensity of feeling that the Atlantic salmon elicits among its chroniclers – the lust and awe it inspires in virtually everyone who writes about it, and the mythic proportions it is given in story

after story. Almost entirely – in my reading, at least – trout, bass, bonefish, tarpon, even billfish (with the notable exception of the blue marlin in Hemingway's *The Old Man and the Sea*) are written about, however respectfully or fondly, as prey, unfreighted for the great part with symbolism. But Atlantic salmon writers, almost to a man, are Santiagos – being caught over and over again by fish that are as much dream and legend as they are flesh and bone.

In this volume, the Norway-based excerpt from William Bromley-Davenport's 1884 book, *Sport*, and W. Earl Hodgson's 1904 Scottish story, "The 'Whustler'" are prime examples of that convention – with their heroic language, their great verve and thirst for battle against dragons with fins. So are Ernie Schwiebert's more contemporary account of a phenomenal day on the Alta, "The Night of the Gytefisk," and the excerpt from *The Spawning Run*, William Humphrey's *non-pareil* treatise on the socio-sexual similarities between salmon and humans. So too, in a darker, more ironic color, is Andrew Lang's Scottish tale, "The Lady or the Salmon?" in which a hooked and lost terror of a salmon costs an angler first his marriage to the wonderfully named Olive Dunne, and then, indirectly, his life.

Within this overall convention of writing about the Atlantic salmon as a sort of conduit to the noble testings that lie in wait beneath the surface of life, one discovers a number of distinct and time-tested categories for dealing with the subject. Roland Pertwee's "The River God," John Cole's "Robinsonville, NB" and Art Lee's "Rotation" are *initiation stories* – about mentors and hard knocks, and about the humiliations,

Opposite: *A lone angler on a Nova Scotia spate river.*

8

confusions, and dawning joys of stumbling for the first time into the great, ancient ceremony of Atlantic salmon fishing, rather like a bushman into a Vivaldi concert.

Once initiated, the salmon fisher tends to become highly sensitized to both the victories and defeats of the sport, and to want to tell you considerably more about the former than the latter. *Banner day stories*, in which the dragon appears to be conquered for the last time, are well represented here by A.H. Chaytor's 1908 "One of Our Best Days" and Romilly Fedden's "An Autumn Fishing," as well as by the Hodgson, Bromley-Davenport, and Schwiebert pieces.

The *tall tale*, a sort of *banner day story* with a wink, is another popular convention in Atlantic salmon writing, perhaps because of the heavy demands the fish has always made on hyperbole. The charming, utterly Irish story, "The Rajah's Rock," by

Paul Hyde Bonner is a best of breed in this category. Tom McGuane's "Fly-Fishing the Evil Empire," with its perfectly poised writing, its sophisticated sense of humor, and its howling "Mr Duff" is another, by a modern master of angling stories with attitude.

The McGuane piece – along with "The Night of the Gytefisk" and the excerpts from *Sport* and *The Spawning Run* – is also a *quest story*, wherein an angler sallies forth to a distant land to bring back reports not only of great fish fought but of the peculiar life, customs, and people met there. Two other energetic examples of that hoariest of approaches to writing about salmon fishing are the incomparable Roderick Haig-Brown's piece on Iceland, "Salmon of the Vatnsdalsa," and Henry Van Dyke's "The Ristigouche from a Horse-Yacht," a chipper, turn-of-the-century account of upper-class adventuring along Canada's Restigouche River.

A great deal of Atlantic salmon literature is, of course, from and about the upper classes, and many of its salliers are given to writing with fondness and humor about the Sancho Panzas who accompany and attend them on their quests. Thus the *gillie story*, in which the man with the net, or behind the paddle or oars, takes on mythic proportions himself – as in "The Rajah's Rock," or John Alden Knight's delightful "Spare the Rod" – or all-too-human ones, as in "The 'Whustler.'"

Monte Burke and I considered how-to writing on salmon angling to be outside the scope of this collection, although we are both suckers for the form when it is done well (as in Melville and Hemingway, for example). But we are happy that Lee Wulff's fine memoir piece, "Fifty Years of Dry-Fly Salmon," has as much of that convention in it as it does – enough, in fact, to make it the best how-to story on Atlantic salmon fishing we know about. And the best piece of writing we know about on the natural history of the Atlantic salmon is the excerpt from *Fishing Atlantic Salmon* by Joseph Bates and Pamela Bates Richards, that leads off this volume with a complete and vivid description of the subject.

Good poems always make their own conventions. The two in this collection, "Photograph" by John Engels, and "October Salmon" by the late Poet Laureate Ted Hughes, come at their material from very different directions, yet share a certain *tristesse* over loss that the Atlantic salmon, in the silver perfection of its transitory peak, has often moved writers to feel.

Finally, loss is also the subject of Monte Burke's closing essay here, "The Dying of the Light" – specifically what of this planet's once virtually inexhaustible Atlantic salmon resources we have blundered into losing already, and what is left to lose.

The stories and poems that follow testify to how profoundly, variously, and perennially Atlantic salmon have meant something to human beings, and to how much of the best of us has been coaxed forward into expression by their strident indomitability. It is the editors' hope that the writings collected here, in addition to providing armchair pleasure, might remind their readers of the overwhelming preciousness and importance of what is left to lose, and move them to feel this too about Atlantic salmon: that loss simply must not be allowed to happen.

Charles Gaines

Charles Gaines,
"Seafields",
Nova Scotia,
Canada.
January, 2001.

PROLOGUE

"THE STRENGTH AND DETERMINATION OF SALMON RUNNING
UPRIVER IS QUITE A SIGHT, ESPECIALLY WHEN LARGE NUMBERS
OF THEM ARE NEGOTIATING AN OBSTACLE SUCH AS A WATER-
FALL OR A DAM. IN HIS BOOK "THE SALMON", DR J.W. JONES
DESCRIBES A SALMON LEAPING 11 FEET FOUR INCHES OVER A
PERPENDICULAR WATERFALL AT A VERTICAL SPEED OF 20
MILES PER HOUR. THE FISH WILL TRY AGAIN AND AGAIN UNTIL
THE LEAP IS ACCOMPLISHED. IN ONE PLACE, WHERE THE CUR-
RENT OF A SMALL STREAM SWEPT DOWNWARD OVER A ROCKY
CHUTE CAUSED BY AN INCLINED LEDGE, THE SALMON WERE
SMART ENOUGH NOT TO TRY TO SWIM THE CHUTE. INSTEAD,
THEY SELECTED THE THIN, SLOWER WATER AT THE EDGE OF
THE LEDGE, AND SLITHERED UPWARD OVER IT EASILY IN
WATER INSUFFICIENT TO FLOAT THEM."

From "The Lives of the Salmon" by Joseph D. Bates Jr and
Pamela Bates Richards, 1996

THE LIVES OF THE SALMON

by Joseph D. Bates Jr and Pamela Bates Richards, 1996

"There is a lesser and greater reward in the catching of salmon; one relates to the mastery of skill, but the greater lies in cherishing the fish and knowing humility in the face of its saga." – *Orri Vigfússon.*

DEEP DOWN in the gravel of salmon river tributaries, there occurs each year an age-old ritual. In the fall, instincts guide the salmon through the laying of eggs in scattered beds more than six inches deep. To defend them from the depredations of insect larvae and hungry fish and birds, instincts also warn the salmon to separate and carefully cover her selected nests until her job is completed and, exhausted, she returns to the rehabilitating vigor of the sea.

Later, when the warming water of early spring trickles through chinks in the gravel, the eggs, soft, orange-pink, and little larger than buckshot, quiver with life. Fishlike heads and tails soon emerge, leaving suspended from the belly the yolk sac that will nourish the tiny salmon until it can wriggle freely and feed on microscopic life in the water. No more than half an inch long, these baby salmon are called *alevins.*

Salmon, in their several stages of development, are given various names. When the alevin has absorbed its yolk sac, it is called a *fry.* Longer than an inch but still less than fingersize, it is known as a *fingerling.* Exceeding finger length, it develops a dark back and lighter belly, with vertical bars called *parr marks* along its sides; in this stage, it is termed a *parr*

The spawning run: Salmo salar *leaping a cascade at Buchanty Spout on the River Almond in Perthshire, Scotland.*

A handsome grilse. From the Reverend W. Houghton's British Freshwater Fishes, *1879.*

and closely resembles a small brook trout, except primarily for its deeply forked tail.

The life of the parr in the river is a precarious one. Over the period they stay in the river, their chances of survival are less than one in a thousand. As they subsist and grow, devouring nymphs, insects, and later-born alevins, their numbers are constantly depleted by larger fish and diving birds. Depending on environmental factors, the little parr remain in the river for two to six years before they go to sea.

The avidity of the parr for insects is well known to anglers who go fly-fishing for salmon. Very often a hungry parr catches its little mouth around the hook and gives the line a slight tap. Then the angler must carefully draw in the baby fish, lift it by the hook, turn the barb over, and let the parr wriggle off – usually with an invitation for it to return when it grows up!

As the parr reaches the river's estuary, it gradually takes on a silvery color, which hides the parr marks and indicates that it is almost ready to go to sea. In this stage, the brightly shining fish is called a *smolt.* Its age at this point is generally three years, occasionally more or less, depending on environmental conditions. In Labrador, for example, they are five or six years of age at the time of this transition. Never free from the dangers of nature and man, the smolts that survive school together, often in tremendous numbers, awaiting by instinct the tide that is to take them to sea.

During the springtime change from parr to smolt, the vertical bars and troutlike spots are obscured by a deposit of silvery guanine in the skin. This camouflage coat is created by an excretory substance and indicates internal physiological changes that are taking place to enable the baby salmon to transfer from its freshwater environment to the marine one in which it will grow. As the smolt journeys downstream, its memory is miraculously imprinted with the atmosphere of the native river that will guide its return to its birthplace to spawn. On its return, its silvered "armor" is spectacularly brilliant, but it gradu-

Salmon must negotiate the hazards of estuarial and tidewater nets like the Balcary fishery salmon trap (shown here), Auchencairn, Dumfries and Galloway, Scotland.

ally fades in fresh water – hence, one can distinguish fish that have recently returned from the sea from those that have been in the river some time.

Where the salmon go while they grow to adulthood in the sea is somewhat of a mystery. Research tells us that large numbers of salmon from both sides of the Atlantic migrate to waters off southwestern Greenland, while others travel to lesser-known feeding grounds. There they mature rapidly, dining on the bounty the sea offers – unless they become the bounty. After one or more years in the salt water, the surviving salmon return to their rivers. That they almost all return to the rivers of their birth (as learned from the tagging of smolts and other research), and even to the very tributary wherein they were born, is astonishing: The return of the Atlantic salmon to their native river may span thousands of miles of open ocean, not unlike the unerring migrations of butterflies and birds.

When the salmon return to the region of their rivers and travel up or down the coast to identify the rivers of their birth, they must survive a new set of dangers. Their strength and swiftness may enable them to avoid predators such as seals, porpoises, and lampreys, but they are no match for the maze of nets and weirs that block many estuaries. Then, for the salmon that make it past the hazards of the estuarial and tidewater nets, there are dams to leap, fishways to negotiate, and, too often, the nets of poachers.

Scientists have concluded that when instinct brings the salmon back to its native territory, memory of the characteristics of the river of its birth guides the fish into it. The presumption is that every river has an identifying combination of chemical composition, odor, water pressure, taste, and perhaps temperature, and that salmon remember these characteristics and can follow them home.

Salmon may spend one, two, three, or even four years in the sea, growing bigger year by year. A salmon returning after its first year at sea is called a *grilse* and normally weighs between two and eight pounds; a salmon that spends two or more winters at sea is called a *multi-sea-winter-salmon* (MSW). Those that have been at sea two winters usually weigh eight to 15 pounds, and three-winter salmon and repeat spawners can weigh 20 to 30 pounds or more.

When the salmon first arrive in the river, they are in their prime – bright, fat, and strong – and a joy to observe or pursue. But as they do not feed to any appreciable extent after entering the river, their beauty and strength gradually diminish. As their appearance wanes, certain internal systems degenerate in favor of the development of their reproductive systems. During this time, the males' body cavities fill with sperm, or *milt,* and the females' with eggs or *roe.* The male salmon also develop a hook in their lower jaw, called a *kype.* Their minds are no longer on feeding, although fortunately for anglers, they will by instinct take insects occasionally, and sometimes other things. They are totally occupied with their primal quest and are determined to reach their nuptial gravel beds as

"WHETHER OR NOT SALMON FEED IN FRESH WATER AND, IF SO, HOW MUCH ARE QUESTIONS DEBATED OVER MANY DECADES."

quickly as possible.

Whether or not salmon feed in fresh water and, if so, how much are questions debated over many decades. These questions are of particular interest to anglers because of the connection with what fly (or other lure) to use, what size, when, and why. Feeding is not mere swallowing of material; it is the digestion, absorption, and use of the material by the body. The studies on this subject generally conclude that salmon will ingest a great variety of food, but they will not metabolize it.

Among others, the writings of Malloch, Chaytor, LaBranche, McFarland, Waddington, and Jones report that salmon will often readily take insects or flies floating in the water very much in the manner of trout – that, although what the salmon has ingested is often found in its mouth and gullet, it is not found in the stomach. Waddington, in 1948, reported, "The average salmon may 'swallow food' in the river but it can derive no nourishment from it. He does not take

A grilse from the Eagle River in Labrador, Canada. Labrador is a province known for an abundance of one-sea-winter salmon.

Salmon holding in a pool on the Dartmouth River on Quebec's Gaspé Peninsula.

it because he is hungry; he is not, in fact, feeding." Collectively, these studies can be summed up by saying that, of a combined total of nearly five thousand salmon whose stomachs were studied, food remains were found in only nine.

Then why do salmon take flies? Once again, instinct seems to be the common denominator. Baby salmon in the parr stage of growth not only look like tiny brook trout, but feed like them, too. Except in the coldest climates, they thrive principally on insects, which are represented by artificial flies, or on much smaller fish, which may be represented by sparse wet flies. If, after one or more years at sea, a salmon can return from its wanderings and remember its own river, why can't it remember what it used to eat there? The returning salmon isn't hungry, but its mind may be imprinted with what it used to do in the river as a parr – that is, to sip in flies.

Lee Wulff, as a result of his vast experience, said, "I believe the main reason an Atlantic salmon takes a fly is due to its long stream life as a parr. As with young trout in the streams, the parr's food is mainly underwater insect forms. A salmon parr has a long (three years and over) river life and a long feeding period to remember … . In spite of the wide variety of flies that may work, I still think the basic urge to rise comes from a salmon's insect-feeding memories as a parr." It would follow, then, that this same instinct would extend to larger bait for larger and older fish, such as minnows and elvers.

Second, most creatures are curious and selective. Babies and puppies frequently mouth and reject items that capture their interest, or try to drive away objects that irritate them. The strike of an angry salmon is quite different from the casual rise and sipping caused by remembered behavior or curiosity. It is a savage attack that makes both the water and the blood of the angler boil. Thus, when a salmon sees a fly floating down on the surface or drifting or swing- ing in the current, it may rise because of residual memory, curiosity, or anger – all of which are ele- ments of instinct.

If salmon will take such diverse items as bugs, insects, berries, sweets, worms, and even cigarette butts, why should we be so fussy about offering them carefully dressed artificial flies in particular colors, shapes, and sizes selected to suit the conditions of the water, temperature, and so on? There are simply no pat answers – the variables are too numerous and the species too unpredictable. This is fortunate, because conclusive answers about fly selection and presenta- tion methods would diminish the fun of fishing. The best one can do is to try to deal with varying condi- tions and likely response, and enjoy the challenge of discovery. Years of personal experience and reading the extensive angling literature can provide valuable insight.

Salmon may enter their rivers at any time of the year, although there are peak periods. Their runs upriver in spring, summer, and fall vary from river to river and depend on the conditions of the rivers. Thus, by their peak periods, rivers may be known as spring, summer, or autumn rivers. By knowing when the runs of the fish should occur, anglers can visit one river after another and expect good fishing through- out the season.

Grilse habitually ascend different rivers at differ- ent times. If you fish the Matapedia in early July, for example, you will almost always take salmon. But if you go there later in the season, you will take a larger proportion of grilse. People who have observed a few salmon and many more grilse in a pool say that the grilse will nearly always go for the fly first. Whether you are allowed (or expected) to release the fish or not varies from river to river; however, there is a two- fish limit on many Canadian rivers, and it can be

Yvon Chouinard cracks a cast across a pool on Canada's Southwest Miramichi.

disappointing to hook and land two grilse and have to stop fishing for the day, particularly when you have traveled far, at considerable expense, in the expectation of catching large salmon.

Often the size of the salmon is proportionate to the size of the river, but not always. Thirty-pounders occasionally are caught on the Miramichi, but they are fairly common on the Matapedia, a river of about the same size. Forty-pounders, or even larger, are taken on bigger rivers, such as the Restigouche and the Grand Cascapedia. In his excellent book *The Atlantic Salmon*, Anthony Netboy says, "No generalizations are possible about the size of adult salmon, although some countries like Norway and Scotland seem to breed heavier fish than others. Salmon weighing up to 70 pounds and more have been taken in these lands."

It is also believed that salmon, just like people, exist within different cultures. Simply put, all salmon

do not behave the same way, and all rivers do not fish the same way. Salmon indigenous to specific rivers have certain characteristics in common. These characteristics include the general appearance of the fish as well as behavior patterns, such as when they rest and when they move.

The strength and determination of salmon running upriver is quite a sight, especially when large numbers of them are negotiating an obstacle such as a waterfall or a dam. In his book *The Salmon*, Dr J.W. Jones describes a salmon leaping 11 feet four inches over a perpendicular waterfall at a vertical speed of 20 miles per hour. The fish will try again and again until the leap is accomplished. In one place, where the current of a small stream swept downward over a rocky chute caused by an inclined ledge, the salmon were smart enough not to try to swim the chute. Instead, they selected the thin, slower water at the edge of the ledge, and slithered upward over it easily in water

Why do salmon take flies? Instinct? Aggression? Curiosity? There are many theories.

insufficient to float them.

For one reason or another, salmon move mostly during the night or during the hours approaching night or daylight. During the day, or when the flow is insufficient for travel, they rest in pools. A pool devoid of salmon one day or even one hour may be full of them the next.

The trip up the river to the nesting areas in the tributary streams may take several weeks, delayed perhaps by low water or possibly because the fish do not want to reach their destinations until they are almost ready to spawn. The males and females spend considerable time resting in the pools at either end of the spawning bed, although the dominant male will frequently prod a female with his snout, push against her, or bully other males. The next stage is the movement of a female out of the pool and over the gravel. There she will select and cut her nests, called *redds*, in the river-bed by using strong thrusts of her tail to make saucerlike depressions about six inches deep.

A spawned-out Atlantic salmon on the River Almond, a tributary of the famous River Tay, Perthshire, Scotland.

In most spawnings, the eggs are ejected into the cracks between the stones at the bottom of the bed, where they are difficult to see and reasonably well sheltered from the shower of gravel the female sends down after the eggs are fertilized by the milt of the male. The "covering up" is usually continued at the beginning of the next spawning sequence. As many as eight such sequences, each farther upstream than the previous one, may be carried out before the female has deposited all her eggs.

A female salmon will lay about eight hundred eggs per pound of body weight, and repeat spawners may produce up to 50 percent more eggs than maiden fish.

Interestingly, a male salmon may fertilize the eggs of several females. The reproductive functions of living things are wonderful in many ways. In the case of salmon, for example, nature has ensured that when a ripe female and a spent or nearly spent male are together, the female's eggs may be successfully fertilized even if insufficient milt remains in the male. Instances are recorded of male parr – weighing only fractions of an ounce – invading the beds of giant salmon while the male salmon is too occupied to drive them away (or perhaps he doesn't notice that one or two of the neighborhood boys are getting into the act!). The little parr, with their tiny vents close to the big one of the large female, instinctively deposit their milt over the eggs at the proper time.

This disparity in sizes, somewhat like a dinghy next to an ocean liner, may seem ludicrous, but scientific experiments in observation tanks prove otherwise: Small parr, sharing a tank with sterilized adult male salmon, can effectively fertilize the eggs of the female.

After spawning in the late fall or early winter, the salmon, exhausted by their efforts and the lack of food, are emaciated and are called *kelts* (or "spent fish" or "black salmon"). Some die of disease; others (unlike the Pacific salmon, which die after a single spawning) drift downriver to the sea, where they can feed or regenerate and perhaps return, as beautiful as before and larger than ever, to spawn again or perhaps to provide superlative sport to the angler with his fly rod and fly.

An integral part of fishing for salmon is understanding the remarkable lives of the fish – lives that are predicated on instinct and heredity. Understanding the various periods in their development, and knowing something about their habitats and why they are in rivers at some times and not others, will enable you to fish more successfully. Then, when one of this noble species suddenly boils up to slam at your fly, the thrill of the fishing will be greater than it could have been before!

Another of the many satisfactions in salmon fishing can be the safe release of the catch. The practice of catch and release is a relatively recent advance among conservation-minded anglers. Heated debate has long raged as to whether salmon caught by anglers should be released. Many government officials and anglers look unfavorably upon it – some anglers even comment that "one should not play with one's food." Others argue strongly in its favor for conservation reasons, especially releasing the larger females, unless the fish has been bleeding or is otherwise injured. The Atlantic Salmon Federation, in co-operation with Dr Bruce Tufts of Queens University and the New Brunswick and Canadian governments, spent several years researching the effects of catch and release on

Atlantic salmon, and they determined that virtually every salmon carefully played, handled, and released will survive to spawn successfully.

One authority who recommends releasing seemingly healthy fish is Dr Wilfred M. Carter, president emeritus of the Atlantic Salmon Federation, who provided the instructions: "Keeping the net in the water, grasp the fish firmly just ahead of the tail, exerting a circular pressure. Usually the salmon will then lie quietly, allowing you to complete the release. Remove the hook with small pointed pliers (or forceps), or use your thumb and forefinger to shake it loose. (The use of barbless hooks employed by many conscientious anglers makes this job easier.) Now remove the salmon from the net, continuing to support it in an upright position (keeping it in the water and taking great care not to touch the gill area) while you face it into the current for a minute or two to circulate water through the gills until it regains enough strength to swim away."

Then let it go and rejoice in the time you had together in the river.

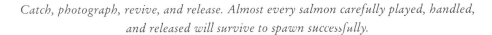

Catch, photograph, revive, and release. Almost every salmon carefully played, handled, and released will survive to spawn successfully.

FIFTY YEARS OF DRY-FLY SALMON

by Lee Wulff, 1983

THE MOMENT was etched so indelibly in my memory that even today, a half-century later, I can see the silvery shape, the black spots on its gill covers, the slow drift through crystal water up to the surface to take the Grizzly Bivisible and the swift turnaway and leap when the hook sank home. The memory stays, although the Hut Pool on Nova Scotia's Margaree River, where that first salmon of mine took a dry fly, has disappeared with the river's meanderings. The intervening years have been filled with the rises of thousands of other Atlantic salmon.

That year, 1933, started me on a career of casting flies, preferably of the floating type, on the salmon rivers of the North Atlantic.

Dry-fly fishing for salmon was so new at the time that only two patterns were being used to any extent: the Pink Lady, which was George LaBranche's favorite, and the Bivisibles that Ed Hewitt had designed. My own dries of the Wulff series – high floaters with heavier than usual bodies and bucktail wings and tails – were more insectlike and they, the White Wulff in particular, would become the favored dry flies for salmon.

But their acceptance and that of surface flies for salmon in general didn't come overnight. I would give away my Wulff patterns to anglers I fished with and then, when I'd meet them again on the river a year later, I'd find the fly tucked away in a corner of their fly box where they'd put it the year before, pristine, unused. It is hard to believe how traditional the salmon anglers of that day were. Like Henry Ford, who believed that any color was fine for a car as long as it was black, salmon anglers seemed to feel that any fly was OK as long as it was a Jock Scott or one of their other very few trusted traditional wet flies. I used dry flies to bring delight and surprise to the anglers and guides I fished with, and my memories are filled with examples of their angling wonder.

Perhaps the best example was with Jack Young of Georges Bay, Newfoundland. Jack was the finest guide I have ever known. I watched and helped him build a log cabin on a salmon river without his using a single nail or any other hardware. His only tools were his axe and his hunting knife. When the cabin was finished it had walls of peeled spruce and fir logs, a leakproof roof of birch bark covered with sod that immediately started to grow, a door that swung on wooden pins, and four bunks well mattressed with spruce bough tips. Jack was a most courteous man and thoroughly knowledgeable about Newfoundland's hunting and fishing. Besides all that, he could make the finest English muffin-type biscuits that ever

Fishing a misty autumn morning out of Keith Wilson's fine camp on the Miramichi, one of Canada's most celebrated Atlantic salmon rivers.

came from a campfire.

Jack had never seen a dry fly fished before he guided me on the Serpentine River in 1940. He started out as a disbeliever, then became a convert.

Jack stood beside me on our last day as I fished the Governor's Pool, working over a large salmon we had seen porpoise there a few minutes before. His eyes were on my dry-fly floats as doggedly as were my own. That salmon's first rise was a test of my maturity as a dry-fly angler and, fortunately, I passed it. The big White Wulff had floated time after time over the salmon's lie. Suddenly we saw him materialize under it ... saw the white of his open mouth and followed the head-and-tail rise through its deliberate pattern. But I saw, too, that although he opened his mouth as the fly came near, the fly was still floating and passing his eye

as his mouth closed. My arm was tense, cocked to lift the rod and set the hook, but I held it still and let the fly drift on to drown in the wash of the swirl his tail made as he sank to his lie again.

Had I whipped the fly away from the salmon's head as it drifted by, I'm sure he would never have risen again. But a few casts later he did, and this time I could see the white fly disappear into his mouth and his jaws close. He was a wild fish, a big male that leaped and leaped, 22 times in all, before he came to the tailer and warmed our hearts with the dry fly's success. It was then that Jack Young stated succinctly what many of us have felt over the years.

"Mr Wulff," he said, "I don't think there's anything more beautiful in all the world than a salmon's rise to a dry fly."

Then there was Sam Shinnix of River of Ponds. It was 1941, and that isolated spot – Sam and his family made up more than half the souls in the town – had seen few salmon fishermen except for the Royal Navy officers who came to fish on their time off when their ships were near, and a few anglers from Hawke Bay, which had its own two salmon rivers, nine miles down the shore. Sam was the patriarch of River of Ponds, the political boss if politics there were, the best fiddler at the square dances, the best salmon fisherman and the head guide.

He became my guide, for he had first whack at any job that developed in his bailiwick. He was a positive man, infallible in the eyes of his peers. He was a canny man, too, and when I took out a size-4 White Wulff to tie on my leader, his face took on a shocked expression. Then he laughed. "They'd as soon take a seagull, sir," was his comment.

"I don't think there's anything more beautiful in all the world than a salmon's rise to a dry fly."

I handed Sam the fly and he looked at it curiously. "You mean it, sir?" he asked. "You're going to fish with that?" He laughed again as if humoring a small boy.

We moved to the head of the tidal pool just above his house. Later I was to have fishing camps on that river and would come to know it well. It rose in the high, rocky, and barren country in the middle of Newfoundland's northern peninsula. The salmon liked dry flies well enough when the water was normal or in low flow, but it was hard to bring a salmon to a dry fly when the river was high and dark and stained with the peat-bog drainoffs. The river, although dropping, was high – and still as dark as bitter tea.

A silvery 16-pounder rolled to the surface just above where we stopped to fish. I began casting the

Opposite: A grilse from the St Jean River on Quebec's Gaspé Peninsula, caught on a skated dry fly.

big White Wulff over him. The sun was low and conditions were, I thought, ideal. The fish rolled up again between two casts but for 20 minutes ignored the fly. Then we saw the silver of his side as he came up under the fly; but he didn't break the surface.

Encouraged, I continued casting for another 20 minutes without a response. The cook from our launch came up to say that supper was ready to go on the table. I made a few desperation casts, and on the last one as the fly passed over the salmon's back, for some strange reason I twitched the rod, sank the fly, and let it drift on, a white blur just under the surface.

There was a great splash and the salmon was hooked.

"There's some live rocks out there," Sam yelled. "Don't let him get to the far side!"

But the warning came too late. The fish reached the submerged rocks, passed between two of them and headed back toward the sea, snapping the leader and leaping derisively immediately afterward.

I think Sam was more surprised that the salmon took that "God-awful thing" underwater – where everyone *knew* you needed one of the standard English patterns to catch a fish – than if he had taken it from the surface. I was nearly as surprised as Sam at the maneuver that had drawn the rise. From that time I have never left a reluctant fish without dunking the fly over his back for an underwater drift. Salmon have made some gymnastic rises to reach my fly from that position. It seems to surprise them, as much as that first wild rise surprised Sam and me.

The next day five grilse and two good salmon were caught on that big white fly and Sam Shinnix was converted.

A host of memories of the River of Ponds in normal flow crowd in on me as I write. Once I climbed out on a big rock in the middle of one of the upper pools. I slid up from the downstream side and, as I got to my knees, I saw two salmon move away upstream from the area just above the rock. I moved up and sat on the rock's upstream face, feet dangling in the flow.

I began to cast to the good-looking spots within range, working each one carefully and covering the water with several flies. No salmon rose to my offerings but, as I glanced down to see how I would slide off the rock and wade on upstream, I saw that one of the salmon had returned to his previous lie. I watched the fish while continuing to make my 50-foot casts. Finally, I let my line swing around downstream and

reeled in until my leader was halfway into the guides. Slowly I swung the rod forward and danced the fly on the surface. The third time my fly touched the water the salmon lifted up and took it.

Salmon are gifted with amazing speed. Even though I was watching that fish closely, at a distance of not more than eight feet, his move was so fast that he had taken the fly before I realized he'd left his position near the streambed.

This bit of learning has stood me in good stead many times since. Now, in clear rivers, especially the

Few rivers in the world are as perfect for fishing the dry fly as the emerald green St Jean River.

larger ones, when I wade deep or fish from a canoe, I'll drop anchor or take a wading position and then look carefully over all the water I can see. When I spot fish that are reasonably close I purposely ignore them while first fishing farther water where I think salmon may lie. After 15 minutes or more, when the fish have accepted my presence as something harmless that drifted down the river and took hold there, I start to fish for the closest salmon. They're used to my presence and my casting action, whereas a cast over them when I first arrived would have had no chance of success.

I drop a big fly over a salmon's head and watch for a reaction. If in the first few casts he shows any sign of interest or moves at all as the fly passes over him, I change to a smaller fly and drift that down to him. Very often the smaller fly will bring a rise. If it doesn't, I go back to the big fly then vary my presentation through a number of dry-fly categories and sizes. It is rare when such a salmon moves at all under the fly that he cannot be brought to the fly. All casts must be careful, all movements smooth and easy. Because the fish is close and visible it is possible to make each cast perfect and to make sure your fly has drifted beyond his vision or point of interest before it is picked up for the next presentation.

It was on the upper River of Ponds at about a four-foot depth that I found one of my most memorable dry-fly salmon. The fish had risen to my fly while I was casting my way up through the pool. I knew by the character of the rise that it was a good fish.

I moved closer to his lie. At about 35 feet I guessed that I could see him: a dark shadow lying over some dark rocks. My position was dead across the current, a spot from which I would be able to see him best, from which the casting would take a minimum of effort and where my line and leader would not come nearer to him than the fly. I didn't feel I'd come close enough to alarm him, and after a few minutes I continued casting, using a Gray Wulff size-8, the same fly to which he had originally risen.

For almost two hours we played a game, that salmon and I. I'd long before learned never to strike till I was sure as I could be that my fly was inside the salmon's mouth. Within a dozen casts he came up again. I watched his long silvery shape move up under the fly; I saw his nose break the surface and come up out of the water with my fly riding on top of it; then I watched as he slid back downward to let the fly float on a foot or two behind him before I lifted it out of the water.

Then he ignored the fly. A few casts with a White Wulff brought him up again for another look. He turned down again without breaking the surface and the fly danced on the little push waves he made. Then he showed no more interest in that fly.

A Surface Stonefly, usually my ace-in-the-hole,

> **"FOR ALMOST TWO HOURS WE PLAYED A GAME, THAT SALMON AND I."**

Popular Canadian flies (top to bottom):
Blue Charm, Green Machine, Glitter Bug,
Dungarven Spey, and Thunder and Lightning.

was next. The salmon came up under the first float, allowed the fly to pass over and sank it precisely with a well-aimed flick of his tail. Then quiet again.

A Gray Wulff drifted over him again brought another close look with as many as 15 investigative rises until finally he paid no attention to any flies. There were other salmon to fish for. I knew his location, and I thought it might be wise to let him rest until later in the evening.

Before I left I followed another of my "rules" or patterns of salmon fishing: I put the original Gray Wulff over him again in as near a replica as I could of the cast that brought the first rise. I make it a point never to leave a fish that has risen but not been pricked without one last cast or two with the fly that triggered the first rise. I had little hope he'd take it; the cast and the effort were perfunctory. I dropped the fly just over his nose. Up he came, pushing his big head half out of the water to take it. He was a good fish, about 20 pounds. More than that, he was the most interesting dry-fly salmon I'd ever fished for.

A beginning Atlantic salmon fisherman's greatest dilemma can be knowing when to set the hook while fishing with a dry fly. He knows that he must set the hook for his line is slack to the dry fly and salmon taking it will rarely hook themselves. If he is an accomplished trout fisherman the dilemma may be even greater than normal. The thing that throws most anglers off – if they aren't sharp-eyed, cool, calm, and collected – is that, in the excitement, they are sure the salmon has come to take their fly. He's a swift, *sure* fish: Why should he miss it?

They strike, and the fly comes sailing back to them untouched.

Naturally, many an angler is hurried by his excitement at seeing so large a fish coming to the fly and doesn't wait long enough for the salmon to close his mouth on it. Others are so paralyzed by their excitement they fail to strike until the fish has ejected the fly. But many, many times the fish did not actually take the fly. He may come up for just a look, and that look may bring him within a couple of feet, a foot or just a few inches.

Advice to a trout fisherman is usually to strike deliberately, as he would with a big brown trout. How big is big? How many have really hooked and caught five-pound trout or better on a dry fly? There is only one time to strike and that is when the salmon takes the fly out of sight into his mouth – or the fly goes out of sight in splashing or swirling water and you *think* it's in his mouth. Striking well with the dry fly requires an intentness and control few anglers have developed, and even the wisest must puzzle now and then over why he failed to hook a salmon.

I had one like that on the Grand Cascapedia in Quebec recently.

We had anchored the canoe close to a very large salmon, fished the far-away fish for 15 minutes before casting to him. He lay in a slight depression with a fish half his size some ten feet closer to us. A Bomber over him made him move. The next ten casts passing over left him unmoved.

I changed to a Surface Stonefly, and on the first cast he came savagely to the fly, jaws agape, spray flying. I lifted the rod, and the fly sailed back through the air over my head. I still don't know why I failed to hook that salmon.

Awaiting battle: two Bogdans and a Hardy take a break on the Eagle River, Labrador.

I think it is wise to rest a fish a bit after a particularly vicious rise so, without thinking much about it, I let my next cast drop the fly well short of the big fish but, as it happened, close enough to the smallest salmon. He rose deliberately and took the fly. Reflecting on it later, I should have taken the fly away from the smaller fish. After I'd landed that ten-pounder, moving the canoe to a shore eddy to do it, we went back to the same anchorage. But the large salmon

– which I'm sure could have been coaxed into another rise after a suitable wait – was no longer there.

One of my finest dry-fly memories came on the River Dee in Scotland where George LaBranche had tried and failed to bring a salmon to the dry fly, although Arthur H.E. Wood, who owned the water, was catching them by the dozens on his famous greased-line method with wet flies. I was there to fish competitively with "Jock Scott" (pen name of Donald

Rudd), premier salmon-fishing writer of Britain. It was my six-foot, one-and-three-quarters-ounce split cane against his sixteen-and-a-half-foot greenheart; he had indicated that my rod was a toy rather than a capable fishing tool. I was there to prove it wasn't. I caught one more fish than he did, and that fish took a dry fly.

The night before, Captain Tommy Edwards, long-time British casting champ, had stopped by our hotel.

After looking at my rod he declared it wouldn't cast 60 feet ("twenty yards" as he put it) and wouldn't even reach most salmon. He was standing on the bank when I cast out a size-8 White Wulff. Seeing the rise he cried: "Hah! A sea trout."

But it proved to be a salmon of ten pounds, one that hadn't read the book that British salmon don't take dry flies.

What about dry flies in the rain? Will salmon take them? They will! They will! I've taken a good many dry-fly salmon in the rain. The clincher was back in 1946, one August evening on the Lower Humber. I was waist-deep in a swift and steady flow at Shellbird Island Pool. No salmon were moving. I had fished a size-8 Gray Wulff for half an hour without response. I'd seen one fish leap as I walked down to the pool, so I knew there was at least one salmon in the water I was fishing.

It began to sprinkle. A few drops, big drops, far apart, and I put on my rain jacket. I switched to a size-4 White Wulff, something easier for both the salmon and myself to see against the dark water under a darkening sky. By the time I had made the fly change, the storm was sweeping over the limestone cliffs that façade the river. Thunder roared and lightning flashed. Rain pelted down so heavily I could barely make out the white fly at the end of a 50-foot cast. Rain ran down my neck, it soaked my casting arm up to the elbow and collected there. I thought to myself: "You darn fool – you haven't got sense enough to go in out of the rain!"

Then a big Humber salmon came up under my fly in a dramatic rise. His head came up out of the water followed by half his body. I set the hook and half an hour later had a 30-pounder lying on the grass of the shore. I was thoroughly soaked and thoroughly happy. That fish has since given me hope and kept me fishing through weather that would have driven me

The long, late twilight of Labrador in summer is a magical time to go fishing for salmon.

ashore before the Humber experience.

Is a fine leader necessary for the fishing of a dry fly? I like to use one. It makes me feel I'm separating my fly from me as much as possible, and I feel quite comfortable in playing salmon on leaders of six-pound test. But heavy leaders do catch fish. The first year I fished Newfoundland (1935), I watched my friend Vic Coty make the sloppiest cast I'd ever seen him make. His big dry fly popped down in a tangled mess of line and leader. A 20-pounder, our largest of that trip, rose up into the mess, took his fly and hooked himself.

Nothing is impossible or even improbable in salmon fishing. Still, I pattern myself on the basis of my experiences and fish according to certain precepts. I never forget that each salmon has a mind of its own and can be most unorthodox and contrary.

When I flew down to Newfoundland in 1947 with my J3 Piper Cub on floats, it was the first non-government, non-military plane to be based there. I could fly back into the wild country of that island and Labrador where no one had ever fished for salmon before and find fabulous fishing. One of those places was the inlet to Big Blue Lake. I came over it on a sunny afternoon at about 750 feet and looked down at the inlet and the shallow water around it with an eye for salmon. The water was only lightly peat-stained, and from that altitude I could see rocks and large things on the bottom. I looked for individual salmon but saw none. There were a couple of long, dark rock ledges stretching out from the mouth; I made a mental note that they would probably be slippery if I waded out on them.

I circled to look for any obstacles that might interfere with my landing or taxiing into shore. As the plane's shadow crossed the ledges, my heart came up into my throat. The ledges disintegrated into hundreds of salmon that scattered in all directions. There were more Atlantic salmon there than I'd ever seen in one place. I circled again, landed and taxied to shore.

> **"Nothing is impossible or even improbable in salmon fishing."**

I wore waders when I flew and my six-foot rod was always set up in the plane beside me. I slipped into my vest and waded carefully out through the shallows to the area where the "ledges" had been.

There was no wind. The lake was mirror still. Breaking the surface here and there were little black triangles which, as I drew closer, I could identify as the tips of salmon's tails. They hardly moved which meant that the fish were hanging just below the surface in a slightly head-down attitude. I moved out with the slight flow of the incoming water so as to send out a minimum of wading-waves. The rod as I'd taken it from its hangers in the plane carried a dry fly at the end of the leader – a size-6 White Wulff, my searching fly. I cast five feet in front of the nearest tail.

The fly dropped gently and a tail disappeared. I waited, not moving the fly. I set the hook and the salmon raced away amid the swirls and splashes of that great spreading school.

I brought him to where I stood, knee deep, and picked him up by the tail. He would weigh about 12 pounds: a trim and beautiful fish. I worked the hook free and slid him back into the lake. One after another I caught salmon from the school, never changing my fly. Sometimes I made it twitch when I became impatient, but it didn't seem to make much difference. I just cast it out and let it lie most of the time. There were so many salmon there I don't believe *any* fly could have landed without being in sight of at least one. I caught a dozen fish, releasing them all. And then, satisfied, I flew back to camp. (Had I stayed, I think I might have caught a hundred.)

Several times that year I took special friends there to fish, and each time the number of catchable fish seemed endless. Sometimes on dead calm days the drifting tails were there to see. Those salmon were making their endless wait for spawning time, and I believe most of them spawned at the mouth, in the great gravel bar that spread around it, as the inlet was small and a quarter of the fish would have filled it. The country was opening up. The paper company was making roads; word of the concentration of fish leaked out. The inlet could be reached by dogsled over an early snow, and spawning salmon were often killed for dog food. It could also be reached by long portages up the river and through its chain of lakes. In a year or two there were only a very few salmon where there had been so many. How glad I am to have seen it when I did.

Perhaps the most exciting dry-fly fishing of all is the attempt for big salmon with the smallest of dry flies. In 1964 a group of us decided to try for a salmon of more than 20 pounds on a size-16. In order to tie the biggest possible fly on a size-16 hook I designed the Prefontaine. It is essentially a Bivisible with a long bucktail snoot and a tail of its own hackle tips. The snoot makes it flop and wobble when skated on the surface in retrieve, the only fly I know that has an action of its own. To see a salmon of over 20 pounds charge such a tiny fly is a sight to remember.

Only a few anglers have taken Atlantic salmon of 20 pounds or more on a single size-16 hook. One lucky afternoon on the Moisie two great fish, each weighing in at 24 pounds, took my Prefontaine five casts apart and were brought in to where I could hand-tail and carry them ashore.

The playing of so great a fish on so small a fly calls for sensitivity and judgment. Size-16 hooks

> " PERHAPS THE MOST EXCITING DRY-FLY FISHING OF ALL IS THE ATTEMPT FOR BIG SALMON WITH THE SMALLEST OF DRY FLIES. "

A colorful group of traditional autumn patterns. Salmon flies are often as attractive to fishermen as to fish.

either break or bend at a pull of four pounds; the fine wire can cut through flesh on even a four-pound pressure. Most big fish on such small hooks are lost because of tactical errors early in the struggle. A little too much pressure at the start can slightly loosen the hook's hold. Then, in the final moments of playing, the already weakened flesh gives away.

I have a feeling when playing an over-20-pounder on a size-16 that I can sense the varying urgency in his runs and leaps, and I do my best to accommodate him with suitable pressure or lack of it. I must urge him on when I can handle his runs and try to coax him into relaxing when I cannot and need time to reposition. It is almost as if I must sense his heartbeats and measure constantly his remaining strength. It is a challenge worthy of the finest fishermen; those who succeed enter a charmed circle of salmon anglers.

After 50 years of experience I have found there is no fishing in the world quite like dry-fly fishing for Atlantic salmon. Not all salmon will take a dry fly well, particularly those in Europe. Fortunately, most of the salmon of this continent's [North America] rivers are as addicted to dry flies as the anglers are, and that makes for wonderful sport.

SCOTLAND

"THEN I GENTLY LIFTED THE LINE, AND VERY ELABORATELY TESTED EVERY LINK OF THE POWERFUL CASTING-LINE. THEN I GAVE HIM TEN MINUTES BY MY WATCH; NEXT, WITH UNSPEAKABLE EMOTION, I STEPPED INTO THE STREAM AND REPEATED THE CAST. JUST AT THE SAME SPOT HE CAME UP AGAIN; THE HUGE ROD BENT LIKE A SWITCH, AND THE SALMON RUSHED STRAIGHT DOWN THE POOL, AS IF HE MEANT TO MAKE FOR THE SEA. I STAGGERED ON TO DRY LAND TO FOLLOW HIM THE EASIER, AND DRAGGED AT MY WATCH TO TIME THE FISH; A QUARTER TO EIGHT. BUT THE SLIM CHAIN HAD BROKEN, AND THE WATCH, AS I HASTILY THRUST IT BACK, MISSED MY POCKET AND FELL INTO THE WATER. THERE WAS NO TIME TO STOOP FOR IT; THE FISH STARTED AFRESH, TORE UP THE POOL AS FAST AS HE HAD GONE DOWN IT, AND, RUSHING BEHIND THE TORRENT, INTO THE EDDY AT THE TOP, LEAPED CLEAN OUT OF THE WATER. HE WAS 70 POUNDS IF HE WAS AN OUNCE."

From "The Lady or the Salmon?" by Andrew Lang, 1891

THE LADY OR THE SALMON?

by Andrew Lang, 1891

THE CIRCUMSTANCES which attended and caused the death of the Hon. Houghton Grannom have not long been known to me, and it is only now that, by the decease of his father, Lord Whitchurch, and the extinction of his noble family, I am permitted to divulge the facts. That the true tale of my unhappy friend will touch different chords in different breasts, I am well aware. The sportsman, I think, will hesitate to approve him; the fair, I hope will absolve. Who are we to scrutinise human motives, and to award our blame to actions which, perhaps, might have been our own, had opportunity beset and temptation beguiled us? There is a certain point at which the keenest sense of honour, the most chivalrous affection and devotion, cannot bear the strain, but breaks like a salmon line under a masterful stress. That my friend succumbed, I admit; that he was his own judge, the severest, and passed and executed sentence on himself, I have now to show.

I shall never forget the shock with which I read in *The Scotsman,* under "Angling", the following paragraph:

"Tweed. – Strange Death of an Angler. – An unfortunate event has cast a gloom over fishers in this district. As

Mr K., keeper on the B–water, was busy angling yesterday, his attention was caught by some object floating on the stream. He cast his flies over it, and landed a soft felt hat, the ribbon stuck full of salmon flies. Mr K. at once hurried upstream, filled with the most lively apprehensions. These were soon justified. In a shallow, below the narrow, deep and dangerous rapids called 'The Trows', Mr K. saw a salmon leaping in a very curious manner. On a closer examination, he found that the fish was attached to a line. About 70 yards higher he found, in shallow water, the body of a man, the hand still grasping in death the butt of the rod, to which the salmon was fast, all the line being run out. Mr K. at once rushed into the stream, and dragged out the body, in which he recognised with horror the Hon. Houghton Grannom, to whom the water was lately let. Life had been for some minutes extinct, and although Mr K. instantly hurried for Dr – , that gentleman could only attest the melancholy fact. The wading in 'The Trows' is extremely dangerous and difficult, and Mr Grannom, who was fond of fishing without an attendant, must have lost his balance, slipped, and

"The Falls and Cemetery Pool – River Cassley" by William Garfit. The River Cassley flows into the Dornoch Firth, Scotland, along with the famous Rivers Oykel and Carron.

had been dragged down by the weight of his waders. The recent breaking off of the hon. gentleman's contemplated marriage on the very wedding-day will be fresh in the memory of our readers."

This was the story which I had read in the newspaper during breakfast one morning in November. I was deeply grieved, rather than astonished, for I have often remonstrated with poor Grannom on the recklessness of his wading. It was with some surprise that I received, in the course of the day, a letter from him, in which he spoke only of indifferent matters, of the fishing which he had taken, and so forth. The letter was accompanied, however, by a parcel. Tearing off the outer cover, I found a sealed document addressed to me, with the superscription, "Not to be opened

until after my father's decease". This injunction, of course, I have scrupulously obeyed. The death of Lord Whitchurch, the last of the Grannoms, now gives me liberty to publish my friend's *Apologia pro morte et vita sua.*

"Dear Smith" (the document begins), "Before you read this – long before I hope – I shall have solved the great mystery – if, indeed, we solve it. If the water runs down tomorrow, and there is every prospect that it will do so, I must have the opportunity of making such an end as even malignity cannot suspect of being voluntary. There are plenty of fish in the water; if I hook one in 'The Trows', I shall let myself go whither the current takes me. Life has for weeks been odious to me; for what is life without

honour, without love, and coupled with shame and remorse? Repentance I cannot call the emotion which gnaws me at the heart, for in similar circumstances (unlikely as these are to occur) I feel that I would do the same thing again.

"Are we but automata, worked by springs, moved by the stronger impulse, and unable to choose for ourselves which impulse that shall be? Even now, in decreeing my own destruction, do I exercise free-will, or am I the sport of hereditary tendencies, of mistaken views of honour, a seeming self-sacrifice, which, perhaps, is but selfishness in disguise? I blight my unfortunate father's old age; I destroy the last of an ancient house; but I remove from the path of Olive Dunne the shadow that must rest upon the sunshine of what will eventually, I trust, be a happy life, unvexed by memories of one who loved her passionately. Dear Olive! how pure, how ardent was my devotion to her none knows better than you. But Olive had, I will not say a fault, although I suffer from

it, but a quality, or rather two qualities, which have completed my misery. Lightly as she floats on the stream of society, the most casual observer, and even the enamoured beholder, can see that Olive Dunne has great pride, and no sense of humour. Her dignity is her idol. What makes her, even for a moment, the possible theme of ridicule is, in her eyes, an unpardonable sin. This sin, I must with penitence confess, I did indeed commit. Another woman might have forgiven me. I know not how that may be; I throw myself on the mercy of the court. But, if another could pity and pardon, to Olive this was impossible. I have never seen her since that fatal moment when, paler than her orange blossoms, she swept through the porch of the church, while I, dishevelled, mud-stained, half-drowned – ah! That memory will torture me if memory at all remains. And yet, fool,

maniac, that I was, I could not resist the wild, mad impulse to laugh, which shook the rustic spectators, and which in my case was due, I trust, to hysterical but *not* unmanly emotion. If any woman, any bride, could forgive such an apparent but most unintentional insult, Olive Dunne, I knew, was not that woman. My abject letters of explanation, my appeals of mercy, were returned unopened. Her parents pitied me, perhaps had reasons for being on my side, but Olive was of marble. It is not only myself that she cannot pardon, she will never, I know, forgive herself while my existence reminds her of what she had to endure. When she receives the intelligence of my demise, no suspicion will occur to her; she will not say 'He is fitly punished'; but her peace of mind will gradually return.

"It is for this, mainly, that I sacrifice myself, but also because I cannot endure the dishonour of a laggard in love and a recreant bridegroom.

"So much for my motives: now to my tale.

"The day before our wedding-day had been the happiest in my life. Never had I felt so certain of Olive's affections, never so fortunate in my own. We parted in the soft moonlight; she, no doubt, to finish her nuptial preparations; I, to seek my couch in the little rural inn above the roaring waters of the Budon.*

'Move eastward, happy earth, and leave
   Yon orange sunset fading slow;
   From fringes of the faded eve
   Oh, happy planet, eastward go,'
I murmured, although the atmospheric conditions were not really those described by the poet.

'Ah, bear me with thee, smoothly borne,
   Dip forward under starry light,
And move me to my marriage morn,
   And round again to – '

*From motives of delicacy I suppress the true name of the river.

"'River in grand order, sir,' said the voice of Robins, the keeper, who recognised me in the moonlight. 'There's a regular monster in the Ashweil,' he added, naming a favourite cast; 'never saw nor heard of such a fish in the water before.'

"'Mr Dick must catch him, Robins,' I answered; 'no fishing for me tomorrow.'

"'No, sir,' said Robins, affably. 'Wish you joy, sir, and Miss Olive, too. It's a pity, though! Master Dick, he throws a fine fly, but he gets flurried with a big fish, being young. And this one is a topper.'

"With that he gave me goodnight, and I went to bed, but not to sleep. I was fevered with happiness; the past and future reeled before my wakeful vision. I heard every clock strike; the sounds of morning were astir, and still I could not sleep. The ceremony, for reasons connected with our long journey to my father's place in Hampshire, was to be early – half-past ten was the hour. I looked at my watch; it was seven of the clock, and then I looked out of the window: it was a fine, soft, grey morning, with a south wind tossing the yellowing boughs. I got up, dressed in a hasty way, and thought I would just take a look at the river. It was, indeed, in glorious order, lapping over the top of the sharp stone which we regarded as a measure of the due size of water.

"The morning was young, sleep was out of the question; I could not settle my mind to read. Why should I not take a farewell cast, alone, of course? I always disliked the attendance of a gillie. I took my salmon rod out of its case, rigged it up, and started for the stream, which flowed within a couple of hundred yards of my quarters. There it raced under the ash tree, a pale delicate brown, perhaps a little thing too coloured. I therefore put on a large Silver Doctor, and began steadily fishing down the ash-tree cast. What if I should wipe Dick's eye, I thought, when, just where the rough and smooth water meet, there boiled up a

> "I stooped to seize him. The frayed and overworn gut broke at the knot, and with a loose roll he dropped back towards the deep."

head and shoulders such as I had never seen on any fish. My heart leaped and stood still, but there came no sensation from the rod, and I finished the cast, my knees actually trembling beneath me. Then I gently lifted the line, and very elaborately tested every link of the powerful casting-line. Then I gave him ten minutes by my watch; next, with unspeakable emotion, I stepped into the stream and repeated the cast. Just at the same spot he came up again; the huge rod bent like a switch, and the salmon rushed straight down the pool, as if he meant to make for the sea. I staggered on to dry land to follow him the easier, and dragged at my watch to time the fish; a quarter to eight. But the slim chain had broken, and the watch, as I hastily thrust it back, missed my pocket and fell into the water. There was no time to stoop for it; the fish started afresh, tore up the pool as fast as he had gone down it, and, rushing behind the torrent, into the eddy at the top, leaped clean out of the water. He was 70 pounds if he was an ounce. Here he slackened a little, dropping back, and I got in some line. Now he sulked so intensely that I thought he had got the line around a rock. It might be broken, might be holding fast to a sunken stone, for aught that I could tell; and the time was passing, I knew not how rapidly. I tried all known methods, tugging at him, tapping the butt, and slackening line on him. At last the top of the rod was slightly agitated, and then, back flew the long line in my face. Gone! I reeled with a sigh, but the line tightened again. He had made a sudden rush under my bank, but there he lay again like a stone. How long? Ah! I cannot tell how long! I heard the church clock strike, but missed the number of the strokes. Soon he started again downstream into the shallows, leaping at the end of his rush – the monster. Then he came slowly up, and 'jiggered' savagely at the line. It seemed impossible that any tackle could stand these short violent jerks. Soon he showed signs of

Mature salmon "drawn from nature" by A.F. Lydon, 1879.

weakening. Once his huge silver side appeared for a moment near the surface, but he retreated to his old fastness. I was in a tremor of delight and despair. I should have thrown down my rod, and flown on the wings of love to Olive and the altar. But I hoped that there was still time – that it was not so very late! At length he was failing. I heard ten o'clock strike. He came up and lumbered on the surface of the pool. Gradually I drew him, plunging ponderously, to the gravel beach, where I meant to 'tail' him. He yielded to the strain, he was in the shallows, the line was shortened. I stooped to seize him. The frayed and overworn gut broke at the knot, and with a loose roll he dropped back towards the deep. I sprang at him, stumbled, fell on him, struggled with him, but he slipped from my arms. In that moment I knew more than the anguish of Orpheus. Orpheus! Had I, too, lost my Eurydice? I rushed from the stream, up the steep bank, along to my rooms. I passed the church door. Olive, pale as her orange blossoms, was issuing from the porch. The clock pointed to 10.45. I was ruined, I knew it, and I laughed. I laughed like a lost spirit. She swept past me, and, amidst the amazement of the gentle and simple, I sped wildly away. Ask no more. The rest is silence."

Thus ends my hapless friend's narrative. I leave it to the judgement of women and of men. Ladies, would you have acted as Olive Dunne acted? Would pride, or pardon, or mirth have ridden sparkling in your eyes? Men, my brethren, would ye have deserted the salmon for the lady, or the lady for the salmon? I know what I would have done had I been fair Olive Dunne. What I would have done had I been Houghton Grannom I may not venture to divulge. For this narrative, then, as for another, "Let every man read it as he will, and every woman as the Gods have given her wit."*

*After this paper was in print, an angler actually drowned while engaged in playing a salmon. This unfortunate circumstance followed, and did not suggest the composition of the story.

THE "WHUSTLER"

by W. Earl Hodgson, 1904

WHEN RONALD AND I set out on Loch Voil, the weather was unusually promising. In the morning there had been squalls charged with rain; but now, just after luncheon, the wind was steady. Surveying the hillsides of the glen in which the water lies, one could now and then see a patch of heather or of bracken gently gleaming in the sunshine. That showed the clouds to be thin and airy. At length, apparently, we were to have a good day. Anglers will know what that means. Others will regard it as an unimportant remark, and will perhaps say that fishermen, like farmers, are always grumbling. Those who are neither fishermen nor farmers are strangely ignorant about the weather. The outstanding facts are plain to them; but they are not conscious of the gradations and other subtleties. They know when there's rain, or heat, or cold, or a gale; but when they go forth to business of a morning feeling chilled a little they say, "Ah! An east wind again," although probably it is from the west, and are unaware that the force of the wind varies from minute to minute. The knowledge which they lack is possessed by anglers; and that is why, having a strange story to tell, I begin about the weather. It is all-important. If the wind is strong, the boat drifts so quickly that in playing one trout you pass over places in which others might be expected. If

"The Old Ghillie" by Erskine Nicol, 1875; like many gillies, faithful but contrary.

it is of the fitful, gusty kind that sometimes comes when there's thunder lurking about, the fish are sulky and don't rise. If there is no wind at all, what are you to do? The boat won't move unless you pull it. .

The last-mentioned predicament befell Ronald and me. We had not been five minutes afloat before our soft breeze drooped and died. We had intended to go to the head of the loch, where there is a large sand-and-pebble shallow, just the place where sport is to be hoped for in a good wind; but, now that the breeze has passed, there was no use going. Indeed, was it any use going anywhere? I put it to Ronald frankly, but with chagrin.

"'Deed, ay, sir!" said the gamekeeper reassuringly. "Ye have to throw the flees lichtly in a dead calm like this; but if ye manage that ye often raise a troot."

This I knew. In a smooth stream a dead calm does not put a stop to one's sport: why should it render hopeless fishing on a lake? Only because the flies and the gut which one uses on a lake are as a rule heavier than those which one uses on a stream. The cast I had on was not at all a thin one; it was stout enough, indeed, to hold as big a trout as could be expected; still, there would be no harm in trying. Perhaps the wind would be back ere long.

Out on the deep, then, Ronald slowly rowed, and

*Dusk silhouettes a sport and his gillie, a relationship as old
and accustomed as Scotch and water.*

I kept casting as we went along. Not a trout moved. The water was so still that the scenery was reflected on it with bewitching minuteness of detail. As you gazed steadfastly, there seemed to be no water at all, but only space, with two ranges of hills converging downwards, downwards, until, very far down indeed, they were standing on their snow-capped heads. It was a spectacle the paradoxical fascination of which made one giddy.

"There's a rise, sir," said Ronald: "wull I pu' to't?"

It was a relief thus to be recalled from looking upon the Highlands upside-down. We pulled towards the rise, the expanding ring of which lingered on the water; but, although the flies fell lightly over where the trout was, the trout remained below. So it was with a good many other trials. Like hunting the fugitive ripple when the air is faint, stalking the rising fish is sometimes a fruitful occupation; but it was of no use that particular afternoon.

Ere long we reached the head of the loch. "Wull we try Doine noo?" Ronald asked. Lying to the west, Loch Doine is connected with Loch Voil by a short, deep, slowly moving river. I was not sure whether it would be well to go into Doine. If the wind, when it rose again, should be from the east, we should be favourably situated as regards Doine, having only to slip through the river, with a drift the whole length of the loch before us. On the other hand, if the breeze should come from the west, we should be equally well-placed on Voil. So I answered:

"Let's wait a little, and see where the breeze is to come from. It will probably be either from the east or from the west."

"Ay: that's so," said the gillie. "There's never a north or a sooth wind on the lochs. The cloud-carry may be frae ane o' they airts; but the hills block the wind, and it aye soops up or doon the glen."

I laid aside the rod, and prepared to smoke.

"That's a dainty bit wand," said Ronald, taking up the rod and making a gingerly cast. "Nae mair than nine feet long, I'se warrant; and as licht as a heron's feather."

"Only five ounces, without the reel," I answered proudly. "It is a present from America. Built-cane, you see, and quite strong – the friend who gave it to me says there's not a trout fit to break it in this over-rated island."

"No?" said Ronald, who during this brief dialogue had been testing the casting power of the little rod. "Guidsake, what's that?"

It was for him, rather than for me, to say; although out of the corner of an eye, as I was screening with my hands the flame of a match, I saw a disturbance just where the flies had fallen. It was a sudden surge in the water and a furrow heaving outwards.

"She's a whustler, whatever," said Ronald eagerly. "Tak' the rod, sir?"

"No, no Ronald: your bird, you know. Does he feel heavy?"

"Vera," said he in quiet wonderment. "A whustler beyond a doobt."

"Whustler" means big and fierce fish, probably so-called from the peculiarly agreeable tune which the reel plays as the line is run off. Thus, Ronald's statement was very cheering.

"Michty me, look at that! Tak' the rod sir – tak' the rod! We'll ha'e to pu'oot."

"That" was a large dorsal fin and half of a majestic tail angrily protruding, and then a long dark-blue back, as the whustler, now 30 yards off, cleft his way.

Ronald handed me the rod imperiously, and sat down to the oars, pushing outwards stern-first. There were about 40 yards of line left on the reel, and these I was yielding foot by foot. Ronald's most vigorous efforts with the back-watering oars were scarcely sufficient to prevent disaster. If I paid out no line at all, something would break; if I let it go freely I should soon, with the same result, be at the end of the tether. My legs began to tremble: they did not seem to be based on anything substantial. Still, I contrived to speak with admirable composure;

"What's to be done, Ronald?"

"Am thinkin', sir, ye'll better step over to the bow. Then I'll turn the boat, and be able to follow her faster. Canny, canny!" he added, as I stumbled across the thwarts. "If ye let her slack a second she'll slip off, and if ye're too tight she'll break ye!"

Thus admonished, I found myself standing with dignity at the prow, gazing out on the mysterious deep, somewhere in which the whustler was still unmistakably on. He showed as yet no violent

> **" 'WHUSTLER' MEANS BIG AND FIERCE FISH, PROBABLY SO-CALLED FROM THE PECULIARLY AGREEABLE TUNE WHICH THE REEL PLAYS AS THE LINE IS RUN OFF. "**

The eerie gloaming of "Loch Calladale." Oil painting by William Garfit.

excitement: only, away he went, steadily, unrelentingly, the boat in pursuit as quickly as Ronald could drive it. Within ten minutes we were halfway across the loch, which is much less broad than long. Suddenly the strain yielded. To my horror, I found that I could reel in without resistance. Sick at heart, I turned and looked at Ronald. He was rowing with might and main.

"Stop, Ronald."

He looked at me, over his shoulder, in apprehensive interrogation: clearly he meant, "Is she off?"

"I think so," said I; and was beginning to assure him that I had really made no mistake, when the sound of a heavy splash just behind caused me to wheel round to attention at the prow once more. To the left, not more than ten yards off, was a circle of writhing water.

"I saw her," Ronald was exclaiming in low tones; "and she's no' off yet. Reel up, sir; reel up like the tevil when ye've got the chance."

Obeying, in less than a minute I had the happiness of discovering that Ronald was right. The whustler was not off. He had merely changed his tactics. Perhaps he had leapt to snap the line; perhaps ...

This was no time for conjectures. The fish was running down the loch at a very rapid pace. Like a living thing on lightsome wing, the boat sped before the oars as it never sped before; yet the reel was screeching. Just as the end-of-the-tether crisis was at hand, the whustler slowed down a little: indeed, it was possible to recover a few yards of the line.

"That's richt, sir," said Ronald encouragingly, but rowing as hard as ever.

"Aye reel up when ye can. It pits off the evil hour."

The evil hour! At times of excitement the imagination is alert, active; and Ronald's words started a new train of thought. When was the evil hour to come? Already it seemed a long time since the whustler had made his presence felt. Already we had gone anxiously after him through the little bay lying to the south of the river from Loch Doine; thence we had crossed the mouth of the Monachyle Burn: these were landmarks on the northward course. On the way down the loch, Monachyle Mhor was already far behind; we were now flying past Rhuveag, a pretty cottage from whose chimneys the blue smoke of wood fires was lingering opalescent among the dark-green pines in the background; soon we should be at Craigruie Point, off which the loch is unnavigable when the west winds are out in earnest. The evil hour! Were not we in pretty evil case already?

Ronald himself seemed to think so.

"This," he said, "looks like a long job. She'll no' tire for a while. Ye needna' gi'e her the butt – the bit wand would just bend and she wudna feel it. Am no'

muckle in favour o' they newfangled split-cane toys. Gi'e me an auld-fashioned greenheart – something ye can hud on by. That fish micht vera near as weel be free a'thegither. It's no' us that's caught her – it's her that's nabbit us."

This seemed true. As far as I could make out, we were no nearer capturing the whustler than we had been before he took the fly. He was not now tearing through the water quite so fiercely; but I had no confidence that he was without reserve of strength. Certainly he was full of resource. He had turned to the right, as if to pay a call at Muirlagan Bay, and was apparently wagging his head from side to side. I felt that the gut might give way to one of his uncomfortable tugs.

"What do you think he is, Ronald? A big trout?"

"Na."

"A ferox?"

"Ther's nae ferox here. This is a well-bred loch."

"A salmon, then?"

"A salmon sure enough, sir; and a 30-pounder unless am much mista'en. I saw her loupin' when ye turned roond thinkin' she was off."

"But what did she take the fly for, Ronald? Salmon don't feed in fresh water – so they say nowadays."

"That's a' damisht nonsense. What for should they starve in fresh water, sir? Because ye never finds flees or meennows or onything else in their mouths, or

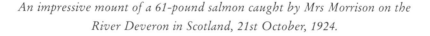

An impressive mount of a 61-pound salmon caught by Mrs Morrison on the River Deveron in Scotland, 21st October, 1924.

inside them, when ye catch ane? As weel say that they dinna' feed in the sea either, for the same reason; and that, thairfore, they pit on four or six pounds weight every year on naething at a'. Whaur's she off tae noo?"

The whustler had again changed his course, and was making for Ledcriech, on the north shore. We followed submissively. Leidcriech Bay is made beautiful in the summer with water-lilies. These were not in blossom just then, so early in the year; but I dared to say that below the surface the stalks were in tough abundance. What if the fish got in among them? Could we ever get him

out? I had misgivings; but I did not like to mention them. Ronald was not in the best of tempers. He seemed to think that we were having an untoward afternoon, and that I was responsible. Among other misfortunes, we had no gaff aboard. I felt that he was thinking of this, and assuring himself that it added to the certainty of the evil hour.

Fortunately, we did not reach the water-lily bay. A considerable time before he could be in sight of the opportunity offered by its harbourage, the fish was cruising down the middle of the loch. It was not at all easy to keep up with him. If I could have spared any sympathy from myself, I should have bestowed it upon Ronald. Although the sun was now sinking behind the western peaks and the evening chill had

Right: *There's nae a grimace to be found on these two jolly Scots, holding the fruits of a peat-stained Scottish river.* Below: *A toast to opening day on the Tay River, 1951.*

come, Ronald was sweating, and, not having foreseen the possibility of this how-d'ye-do, we had set out unprovided with the means of refreshment.

The tension changed. Instead of keeping on the forward path, the whustler seemed to go straight down. Down, down, down he bored, getting leave of the line only because the boat, although Ronald was stopping her, was still going towards the place from which the dive had begun. Down, down, down: when we were practically straight over him he was still diving, taking the line from the reel. Here was a new peril. About this place Loch Voil is at its deepest. If I remembered the chart rightly, the depth was very great indeed. Would the line of the little trout rod suffice? If not, should I supplement it by dipping down rod and arm on the desperate chance that the extra 12 feet thus gained would be enough? At the moment I had no thought for the ludicrousness of the prospective situation. Humour flees from fright.

Much to my relief, the line itself sufficed, and there was even a little to spare. Whether the salmon had gone quite to the bottom or not I cannot say; but, wherever he was, he stopped. He moved neither to right nor to left, neither up nor down; but he was still on. Of that there was no doubt. I had never lost touch with him during the dive; and I felt him still, although he was steadfast; and through the line there ran a tense quivering thrill like that of a telegraph wire. The little rod was trembling as my legs had been at the beginning of the episode. Being now well inured to the crisis, I myself was comparatively at ease.

So, I noticed gladly, was Ronald, resting on his oars after nigh three hours of hard and anxious toil. Five minutes passed; ten; fifteen; and then it dawned upon me that, although tearing over the loch at the truculent will of the whustler had been fearsome work, we were not now very much better off. At least, we were not perceptibly further forward. There

May it be a taking day. The Northwest Highlands of Scotland rear above Turn Pool on the little River Inver.

was no disguising the fact that the enemy had us at a disadvantage. Excepting that I had to keep in constant touch with him and be sure he was still there, we had nothing whatever to do. The shades of night were falling; we were fixed on a cold wilderness of water with neither food nor drink; and it had become evident that we might have to stay there indefinitely unless we were willing to cut the painter and scuttle home defeated and disgraced.

That, of course, was not to be thought of.

"What's to be done, Ronald?"

"That I canna' tell, sir. I've never been in sic a scrape as this before."

"O, surely: it often happens: a salmon often lies doggo."

"Never like this that I've seen; although it's true enough that, exceptin' when I went to the war wi' Lovat's Scouts, I've never been anywhaur else but Glenartney Forest and here."

"I've seen it happen on the Dee."

"Ay; but the Dee's a river, no' a loch."

"On the Dee, when a salmon lies long at the bottom of a pool, the gillie can always get at him and stir him up somehow."

"Nae doot; but the Dee's no' scores o' fathoms deep."

"The gillie sometimes throws big stones at him."

"In this boat there are nae stanes, either big or sma'."

Ronald, with his cold logic, had undoubtedly the

best of the argument, which, indeed, I had initiated less from having anything to say than from a vacuous feeling that silence would seem a confession of helplessness. It was true that I had seen a gillie stoning, and thereby putting to flight, a sulking salmon in the Dee, at Banchory; but I had realised, even as I mentioned this that such an expedient was out of the question on Loch Voil. It is astonishing how a man chatters when in a dilemma. Contemptuously irritated at myself, I turned upon the gillie in wrath and mixed metaphors.

"Chuck it, Ronald," I adjured him. "What's the good of sitting there wise as an owl and depressing as a wet blanket? Buck up. We've got to land this salmon."

"Ha'e we, sir? There's mony a thing we've got to do that we never do."

"Come, come, Ronald. That's no talk for a Lovat Scout."

Ronald was not pleased; but he answered reasonably:

"That wark was naethin' to this, sir. In the war we aye kent that onything was possible, and did it; but in fishin' some things are clean impossible, and this is ane of them. She was a cunnin' man, the Boer; but she was an innocent babe to this fish."

"Dry your eyes, Scout. He'll surrender some time."

"No' she. Ye dinna' seem to understand, sir. D'ye no' see that when she starts again after this long rest she will be quite restorit – just as bad as if we had never run at a'? Wi' that wee toy o' a rod, ye've dune her no harm whatever. If we ever get oot o' this, and ha'e to dance after her again, it will just be as if you had hookit a new salmon, and we'll ha'e the same business a' ower. I see nae end tilt."

Neither did I; but I saw something else. Although the light had almost gone, I saw that there was a ripple on the water at the head of the loch, far away. It was coming towards us rapidly. Soon, too, the sound of the burns on the hillsides began to grow in the volume and the briskness. Hitherto the noises of their falling waters had been soft and hushed, half lost in the immediate still atmosphere absorbing them; but now they were loud, and growing louder, almost harsh. That meant the coming of a wind. Would the wind awake the whustler? Time would tell. It did; and soon.

When the curl on the water reached us Ronald took to the oars again. A very slight breeze is sufficient to set a boat moving; and, of course, the extent of our line allowing next to no latitude, we had to keep, in relation to the whustler until he moved, nearly perpendicular. That was not a task so easy as those who are unused to boats may imagine, and Ronald did not enjoy it. Each minute the air, at first a zephyr, was increasing; and amid such conditions it is impossible to keep a boat exactly where you want. A few yards in any direction would again take us to the end of the tether; and then?

Happily, the need to consider the query was postponed. The whustler moved. Perhaps the ripple attracted him. The surmise was in accord with a theory which I had been cherishing in secret, and for a moment I thought of broaching the argument to Ronald. A discontented gillie, however, is not an appreciative audience for speculative thought; and I held my peace on all save the topic of the hour.

"Well, we're off again," said I, cheerily, hoping to quiz Ronald out of the doldrums.

"Quite so," he answered; "and practically, sir, – practically, mind ye – it's a new salmon we ha'e to deal wi' – just as fresh and ferocious as if she had only this minute risen at the flee." To himself he added, muttering, "And a bonnie time o' nicht to begin the day's sport!"

I could not understand Ronald. As a rule he was the best of gillies, grudging neither time nor trouble in the pursuit of game, keen and joyous as Tim the terrier in a rabbit warren. There are bonnie lasses in Balquhidder; and Ronald is a youthful warworn hero; and perhaps Spring, which, it will be remembered, deals in a livelier iris, –

"Steady, sir, steady! Sit doon!" exclaimed Ronald, interrupting my apologetic reflections. "See yon!" he nodded westward. I turned for a moment to look.

To within a hundred yards of us, all the loch was churned and seething white, and the dark air was grey with sleet.

Having had some little experience of the storms which suddenly descend upon Highland lochs, I did not like the look of things. Indeed, inwardly I began to sympathise with Ronald's view that we should have anticipated the evil hour by cutting ourselves free from the whustler long before. However, the time was not suited to after-thoughts; and I pretended not to understand.

"Right-o, Ronald! The gut, I think, will hold – sound Lochleven."

Meanwhile the whustler had led us a considerable

distance from the place in which he had rested and been refreshed. As it was now impossible to see the shore, or even the point of the rod, I could not say how far we had gone; but I felt in a general manner that we were still on the eastward course. Ploughing industriously on, the fish had been making no undignified display of anger: indeed, I had come to regard him with the familiar affection in which one holds a good retriever, saying to him, as occasion required, "Steady, lass!" or "To heel, you devil!" or other caressing phrases of the field; but with the progress of the storm our relations became strained. He began to leap. We could not see him; but we could hear him well enough amid the short thick thuds of the waves beating on the boat and the baritone boom of the squall. It was, I confess, an alarming sound. At each

leap I expected the performance to be my last. That seems a strange remark; but it is accurate. When he was down in the water and could be felt, I was not without hope; but that was momentary only. Whenever the line slackened I knew he was aloft in the air, and my heart stopped.

Ronald was in similar extremity. The salmon seemed to be aimless in his movements. At any rate, his leap was sometimes on one side of our creaking craft, sometimes on the other; now off the stern, anon off the bow. Thus, Ronald was in perplexity. Sometimes he had to pull away from the fish; sometimes to push towards him. All through this trying time the general drift of things was determined by the wind, which we believed to be still from the west.

"This canna' go on much longer, am thinkin'," said Ronald. "I daurna' pu' either to the north shore or to the sooth, for then we'd be broadside-on and be blawn ower. Forbye, the boat has been lyin' up a' winter, and is brittle. If ane o' they big waves catches her on the side when we're turned to follow the fish, she'll be starved in. I doobt we're by wi't, sir."

Although he had to shout in order to be heard, Ronald delivered this grave opinion in a deliberate, matter-of-fact tone, in which there was no petulance. He was seriously alarmed. Perhaps he had a melancholy satisfaction in the prospect of the evil hour being much worse than he had foreseen.

The hour, however, had not yet struck. Suddenly I realised that we were aground. Our arrival was without violence. As placidly as an express train slips into King's Cross a few minutes after covering full 60 miles an hour, our boat ran up against a shelving bank. I leapt ashore, and renewed my attentions to the whistler. He, too, seemed to realise that the battle had entered into new conditions. He bored about, calmly, almost in a weak manner, as if he were a conger-eel. I reeled the line in, and let it out, according to his comings and goings; but I did not stand still. I had to run about a good deal, and in breaking through the scrub, which came down to the edge of the water, was sorely gashed in hands and face and clothes. Nevertheless, my spirits had gone up with a bound. Even if I had lost the whustler, it was now certain that I should have nothing to be ashamed of in the morning. Besides, the squall had gone as suddenly as it had come. A swell as if of the sea was swishing on the shore; but there was not so much as a puff of air, and behind a vast mass of blackness which I took to be a shoulder of Ben Ledi there was a slowly-rising radiance not unlike the glow that a far-off fire sends upwards to the clouds of London. Soon the source of the gentle illumination appeared above the high horizon. She was covered and uncovered as the wrack floated over her face. She was a welcome visitor, tempting to gaiety.

"Methinks the moon frowns with a watery look," said I, inaccurately endeavouring to recall a snatch of appropriate poesy.

"For Goadsake, sir, dinna' sweer – at this tome o' nicht and in a graveyaird!"

"A graveyard?"

"Ay," said Ronald. "D'ye no' ken whaur ye are? Ye're no' on ordnar' warldly land at a'. Ye're on a sma' island, the buryin-grun' of the Stewarts of Glenbuckie for mair centuries than onybody can remember."

"This is the Inch, then?"

"The same. No' a canny place ava'. There's naething but wraiths here – Popish wraiths, tae. I'll be glad when we're weel awa' frae 't. Hoo's the salmon, sir?"

"Very well, thank you, Ronald. We might get him now if we had a gaff. Just step into the boat and ask

the Minister to lend us his."

Ronald obeyed with alacrity. He had not far to go. This being the Inch, we were only two or three hundred yards from the northeast corner of the loch, and not much more from the Kirkton, a hamlet close by the manse.

The boat gone, the whustler had a chance. If only he had made a rush outwards, he could have snapped the tackle and been free. He did not think of that. Instead, he sauntered to and fro, now and then raising himself so high that I could see his tail slowly waving above the water in the moonlight. It waved sedately, and seemed to be the tail of a tired whustler; but I had no bigotry on that score. Once, by way of rehearsing the final act, which was to go off in acclaim when Ronald brought the gaff, I tried to persuade him to come ashore. I was not successful. Although the rod bent into a semicircle, the whustler paid no heed. He went on his leisurely way as if nothing at all were happening. I had an uneasy thought that he was recruiting his energies in contemplation of a new campaign, and I longed for the return of the boat.

> "Had I not read in some scientific book that salmon travel mainly by moonlight, and at a speed which the best of human engines cannot attain?"

At length I heard the plash of oars and the sound of excited voices. In a few minutes Ronald and the Minister came ashore. I heard the rattle of a chain, and knew that the boat was being fastened.

"Hold hard, Ronald," I called out. "I'm coming aboard whenever I can get him round."

"Takin' her oot to sea again!" said Ronald, aghast. "Mercy on us! What for?"

"To tell you the truth, I don't know. I can't say when we'll get him into the boat; but I am certain we'll never get him into the shore. I've been trying to guide him in; but he won't come. Once or twice he has gone round and round this place, and then it looked as if I were conducting a circus. You wouldn't have me do that all night – in a cemetery, too?

Besides, Ronald, if he bolts more than fifty yards we're done, for I can't follow him through the loch on my feet. We're safer in the boat."

"Vera weel, sir," Ronald answered, turning away with a sigh: "I'll bring her roond."

We were now in a situation that required tact, skill, rapidity of judgement and of action. The whustler could not be expected to pause in his stroll for our convenience. Thus, the boat had to be "brought round" not a few times, and to not a few places, before we were safely seated.

What was to be done next? I thought it would be well to put off gently and await the strategy of the whustler. That came with decision and energy. Apparently rendered suspicious by noticing that the slight strain on him came from a new quarter, he bolted like a torpedo. Helped a little by the reel giving up the line I had recovered, Ronald made a desperate but successful effort. The wild rush was soon over.

Trouble, however, was to come. Obeying some strange instinct, the great fish was making for the Balvaig River into which Loch Voil pours its excess. Inwardly I rebuked myself for having left the comfortable graveyard. There we might have spent a chill and cheerless night, with little hope that the dawn would herald in a brighter day; but if we were hauled or lured into the river the prospect would be nothing less than disquieting. Had I not read in some scientific book that salmon travel mainly by moonlight, and at a speed which the best of human engines cannot attain? True, the man of science had been speaking of salmon when running up the rivers; but he had not said that when running down they go with any less celerity. What, then, if the whustler got into the Balvaig, which was in brawling flood from nearly a week of rain? The river has an almost straight run to the sea. In my startled imagination I beheld our craft, in tow of the whustler, leaving Strathyre within ten

A long line over Middle Rapids on the aptly-named River Awe – well-known for its large salmon.

minutes; Callander within quarter of an hour. Rushing past Doune, ere long we should cross the romantic Allan Water, and be making full-steam-ahead for the Firth of Forth. Perhaps we might look in at St Margaret's Hope or at the Port of Leith. There was no finality to the possibilities with which the situation was charged. Once in the North Sea, if we did not turn into Tweed or Tyne, there would be no reason why we should not run up the Thames and make an involuntary appearance before the Terrace of the House of Commons.

It may be that I overestimated the risks suggested by the broad torrent of the Balvaig glittering in the light of the fuliginous moon. I know not. All I know is that when the potentialities of the case burst upon a mind excited by many hours of struggle and high hope I resolved upon an uncompromising measure. Come what might, the whustler must not enter the Balvaig. He must stay in Voil.

"Stop the boat, Ronald," I said, in commanding voice, when, every inch of the line out, I saw the salmon meandering very near a sandbank over which the water of the loch was in motion towards the river.

Then, instead of holding the rod erect, I held it straight out. Followed a game of pull-devil, pull-baker. The real meaning of this phrase was unknown to me; and even now, recalling the events and the emotions of that night, I am not calm enough to be fastidious in philology. The words seem to express what I wish to convey, which is that when salmon pulled so did I. Above the clean yellow sandbank, in which pebbles were sparkling like diamonds, I saw him poking, poking, poking; moving sideways, about a foot at a time, as if seeking a place at which to dart across the shallows. At length he lost his temper. Ceasing to struggle in what may be called a straight-forward manner, he turned a lateral somersault, and rolled over. Now, cantrips of that kind are sometimes an indication that the game is up, and that practically all is over but the gaffing. On this occasion, however, one had to moderate one's transports. I did so by a mental railing of which I now repent. "O, William F. Fisher, of Colorado Springs and the City of London, why, when you were foolin' around Noo York, didn't you buy me one of them tooboolar-steel telescopic poles, calc'lated fit for tarpon, instead of this five-ounce proposition? A Dago, William F. – that's the kind of hair-pin You are!" It was touch-and-go with the whustler. Within a time which must have been short although it did not seem so, he rolled himself beyond the point, on the hither side of the sandbank, that was in a straight line with the southern

Munro Killer

Gary Dog

Blue Charm

Logie

Alastair

Gold-Bodied Willie Gunn

Roger McPhail's stately rendition of the productive Junction Pool on the River Tweed.

bank of the river, and was once more in the motion-less water of the loch. Along the shore he cruised, slowly, silently, and, I think, sadly. He may have been seeking for some definite thing. Ronald and the Minister thought so. On the other hand, he may have been dazed a little, and wandering at random. That was my belief. At any rate, it is not customary for a salmon to move into a brook in spring. That is what the whustler did. Coming to the mouth of a burn not more than three feet wide, he paused a moment as if pondering, and wriggled up.

Ronald pulled the boat ashore, leaped frantically out, squatted down in the mouth of the burn, took a knife from his pocket, and deliberately cut my line.

"Nabbit, Nabbit!" he cried. "She's nailed at last!"

"Is he?" I asked, nigh dumb with doubt and amazement.

"Ou, ay," said Ronald in a tone of triumphant cer-titude. "The Minister couldna' find the gaff – I didna' like to tell ye that a' at aince. But the salmon's richt noo. Ye see, there's a high waterfall no' twenty yairds up among the trees there. She canna' get past that. Neither can she get doon tae the loch again while I sit here, and that I'll do a' nicht. So she'll ha'e to stop in the pool. If the Minister's man will bring me a hay-fork at the scriegh o' day – it winna' be long noo – I'll bring the whustler to the Big Hoose afore breakfast time."

I pondered while lighting my pipe.

Yes; I would allow Ronald to do as he proposed.

On parting for the night, the Minister and I arranged to forget about the hay-fork. We would be up betimes and go back to the pool unarmed.

FRANCE

"THE DAY TOO WAS WONDERFUL. A WARM DIMNESS LAY OVER ALL THE VALLEY; AN AUTUMNAL STILLNESS, BROKEN FROM TIME TO TIME BY THE CRY OF A PLOUGHMAN BEYOND THE RIVER, OR THE CHINK OF THE CHAINS AS THE HORSES TURNED IN THE HAZE OF THE FURROWED LAND. FAINTER STILL AT INTERVALS CAME THE DISTANT SOUND OF A SHOT GUN; AND NEAR AT HAND THE CONSTANT SWISH OF JEAN PIERRE'S ROD AS HE WORKED DOWN THE GLISTENING FOAM-FLECKED WATERS — THE CLICK OF HIS ANCIENT WOODEN REEL. IT WAS WELL PAST LUNCH-TIME WHEN AT LAST CAME THE HOPED-FOR PULL. A FINAL CAST UNDER THE FAR ALDER-BUSHES RESULTED IN A GROWING AND PURSUING WAVE WHICH BROKE TO LEAVE A BRILLIANT AND FRESH-RUN NINE-POUNDER MADLY SPLASHING."

From "An Autumn Fishing" by Romilly Fedden, 1919

An Autumn Fishing

by Romilly Fedden, 1919

I CALL TO MIND THE FIRST TIME, now many years ago, that Jean Pierre and I together fished for salmon. Earlier lessons had been given along the rough-grown lawn and from the bank at the foot of the curé's garden. It was here, too, that I first learned how to extricate a fly which had become fast among some sunken brushwood in the middle of the river. An old fisherman's dodge this, yet of such value in the snagged and untended waters of Brittany that an attempt at its description is surely worthwhile, if it can help but one brother angler and so save him even a tithe of the trout and salmon flies that the writer has thus retrieved in days gone by. When my fly first caught on the further side of the snag, the position seemed hopeless, as each pull would drive the hook further into the obstruction. But Jean Pierre took my rod, and paying out some yards of slack, he cast the looped line *above* and *beyond* the imprisoned fly. The looped line sank, and was slowly borne down in the current till it reached a point opposite to and *beyond* the snag. Then Jean Pierre struck and the fly jerked free. The pull, be it noted, was now indirect, coming from a new direction – not from the near bank, but from the sunk line close to the far bank. So was the fly plucked *out* from the snag, whereas each tug, direct from the rod, must have embedded it further *in*, till the cast or barb finally gave way.

Below the brushwood pile was good open water. Just the place for practice and instruction. Here the big fish from time to time broke surface, inciting the novice to further efforts. Even after endless attempts to imitate that overhead or the underhanded cast

> "THE WATER SEEMED IN PERFECT CONDITION, JUST TINGED WITH A GOLDEN BROWN WHERE AT THE FOOT OF EACH RUN THE POOLS DEEPENED."

which, in the hands of the master, sent the line with a great serpentine swoop to straighten far out across the river, but in those of the pupil resulted in a violent blow in the small of the back, or a tangled skein which would often fall noisily some yards away from the spot aimed at – even these afflictions were forgotten when the next salmon came up with a resounding boil and flop. Yet never once were my strenuous exertions rewarded by so much as a half-hearted pull. Indeed, Jean Pierre maintains that all the salmon in this reach are "sleeping fish"; that they do not "wake up", or assume that state of consciousness in which they are apt to be attracted by any lure, till they have reached the pools higher up the valley. Be that as it may, it is certain that these fish are quite insensible to every bait. Are they, then, in reality somnambulists, and their noisy plungings simply the tossings of a troubled sleep? An open eye proves nothing – for the salmon must sleep, or rest, wide-eyed – he has no lids to close.

So it was that a certain late autumn morning saw us on our way to the upper water, Jean Pierre with his old greenheart rod while I carried the gaff. The village was soon left behind, our lane winding past swampy fields and through even more muddy farmyards. Scents of baking bread and crushed cider apples followed us, and from each stone doorway the children ran out to greet Jean Pierre. Whole bevies of smiling, freckled little girls, full-skirted and white capped; small boys in precocious trousers and broad-brimmed beaver hats; and all chattering louder than the magpies. There were, in fact, scores of those birds along our way hunting for worms and walnuts and fat slugs,

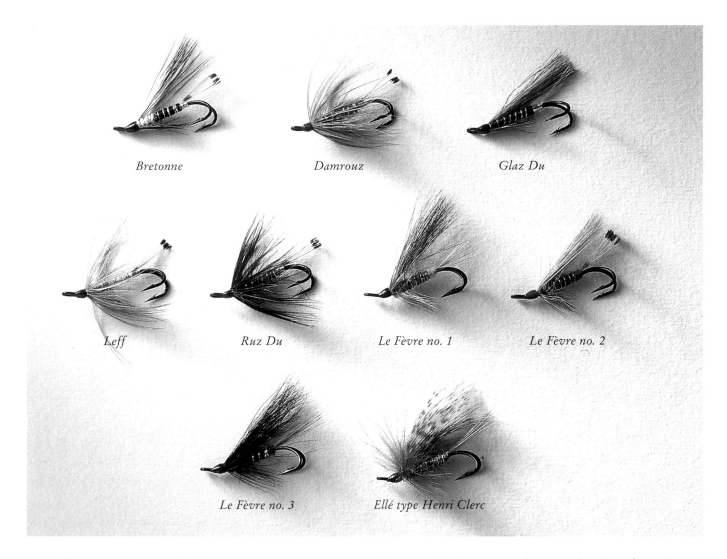

Bretonne *Damrouz* *Glaz Du*

Leff *Ruz Du* *Le Fèvre no. 1* *Le Fèvre no. 2*

Le Fèvre no. 3 *Ellé type Henri Clerc*

and talking as they scratched.

Now when you meet two magpies face-to-face you say "*une pie tant pis; deux pies tant mieux*"; but when you meet a dozen, you cross yourself and bow nine times. We left the children and the *manoir* gates bobbing with deep obeisance.

This great stone pile has mellow walls and tall blue roofs of time-worn tile. It is dead and sightless, its windows are shuttered, its halls are still. In its gardens moss grows everywhere, and by a broken fence you reach a dark pine-wood. In the heart of the wood it was still high summer, but further, at its fringe, you came upon a hint of time and change. There was a thin silver network of gossamer upon the whin-bushes, and a sharp tang in the frost-touched air. But the hill-side's blue and gold was bathed in soft sunlight, and

below us the brown pools were clearing after rain.

The water seemed in perfect condition, just tinged with a golden brown where at the foot of each run the pools deepened. The fish apparently were still "sleepy", for during the whole morning only a single salmon moved, and he came up with an angry boil merely to turn sulkily behind the fly. Yet it was a delight to watch my old friend while he fished, to see that long, clean cast of his – the perfectly pitched fly that searched in every likely nook and corner, or hung exactly, beyond the heavier stream, working in tempting fashion. The day too was wonderful. A warm dimness lay over all the valley; an autumnal stillness, broken from time to time by the cry of a ploughman beyond the river, or the chink of the chains as the horses turned in the haze of the furrowed land. Fainter still at intervals came the distant sound of a shotgun; and near at hand the constant swish of Jean Pierre's rod as he worked down the glistening foam-flecked waters – the click of his ancient wooden reel. It was well past lunch-time when at last came the hoped-for pull. A final cast under the far alder-bushes resulted in a growing and pursuing wave which broke to leave a brilliant and fresh-run nine-pounder madly splashing.

Never before or since have I seen my old friend flustered while he played a fish, but on this occasion he was distinctly nervous. He perspired profusely while the crinkles at the corners of his mouth twitched and deepened. An uncomfortable five minutes followed, in which the lightly hooked salmon plunged and rolled and lashed upon the surface, while Jean stood upon the bank and roundly cursed him in raucous Breton. Here actions did not tally with harsh words; never once did that fish get the butt,

La Dordogne at Argentat in southwest France: once a prolific salmon river.

but only respectful attention, and when he chose to "slither" down the pool, then Jean Pierre "slithered" too. He made wild rushes and appalling leaps just as he felt disposed, and then would pause to shake his head, like a dog who shakes a rat. Twice in sheer hopelessness was the line slackened, but each time it pulled itself together to tentatively coax the floundering fish. At length it chanced that the salmon sheered towards the near bank, and hung motionless for a moment to think matters over. At a sign from Jean Pierre I slipped quietly into the water, and by luck rather than good management gaffed the fish behind the shoulder as he turned … . The fly came away as we carried him up the bank.

We laid him caressingly among the bracken. Jean's hands still trembled as he mopped his forehead and took an ample pinch of snuff, while I had to light a

congratulatory pipe before we could open our bag to get out the *vin rouge* and cold chicken.

Lunch over, Jean Pierre was soon at it again, and his third cast was rewarded by a splendid head and tail rise in mid-stream. This fish was well hooked, and consequently was allowed no undue liberties. Each furious rush was firmly dealt with and eventually checked. Once the salmon tried a somersault, but met only the looped line for his trouble. An attempt at boring in deep water was countered by a steady and relentless side strain. Soon the vibrations of the rod conveyed the message that the struggle was nearly at an end, till at length the fish rolled over on the surface and slowly but surely yielded inch by inch to the winding line and fate. My spring-balance allowed him eleven-and-a-half pounds: a fresh-run fish and as bright as the first. A beautiful pair they made on the bracken side by side, while Jean Pierre fixed the fly afresh and chortled.

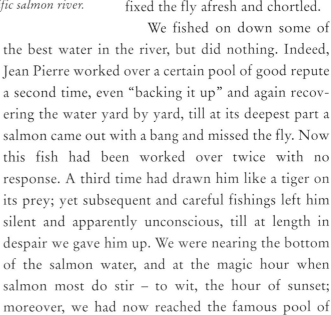

We fished on down some of the best water in the river, but did nothing. Indeed, Jean Pierre worked over a certain pool of good repute a second time, even "backing it up" and again recovering the water yard by yard, till at its deepest part a salmon came out with a bang and missed the fly. Now this fish had been worked over twice with no response. A third time had drawn him like a tiger on its prey; yet subsequent and careful fishings left him silent and apparently unconscious, till at length in despair we gave him up. We were nearing the bottom of the salmon water, and at the magic hour when salmon most do stir – to wit, the hour of sunset; moreover, we had now reached the famous pool of Mary Morgan*, beloved yet feared by every Breton

*Mary Morgans are the Kelpies or river sirens of Brittany. They do not appear to abound, yet there are a few in the district of Morbihan.

poacher. The river at this point is of stately dimensions. The head waters of the pool flow through a long and rocky channel banked by high heather bluff; its tail is bushed and difficult, but in between there is an open space, deep and mysterious. Here Jean Pierre changed to a larger fly and cast it out in the darkening water. He fished the stream to the thicket-edge, then plodded up the bank and began all over again. Halfway down the line tightened and held, buzzing in the heavy current. For some seconds I thought the fly had fouled a sunken rock, till the line slowly began to forge ahead and Jean Pierre's lips to purse and tighten. The pace soon quickened and we could not follow the fish downwards; but eventually he hove-to, some 30 yards below us, hanging dull and heavy in the stream, till the steady strain from the big greenheart rod forced him to move out and up into more tranquil quarters. Here the salmon played deep and sullenly, never coming near the surface; only the taut line was visible, hissing and rippling above dark depths. The salmon pulled up eventually in the deepest hole, and there he lay and sulked. That fish refused to budge; the stout greenheart was unavailing; likewise the heavy stones which we heaved towards his nose and perilously near the strained line only induced him to shift a foot or two, when he would revert once more to the old position. At last in desperation I cut a long hazel stick from the bank, and tying a white pocket handkerchief to its tip waded into the river, prodding with the beflagged branch as near as I dare to where the salmon lay. This suddenly brought him to life again, and while I scrambled ashore he rose noisily to the surface; once there, he commenced a fight which was as strenuous as it was unexpected. The fish had the advantage of twilight in his favour, while for some minutes he pulled and plunged and leapt amongst the boulders. I shall never forget Jean Pierre's sigh of relief when we got him safely up the bank. Here memory whispers that he was not a handsome fish ... . Perhaps he *was* a trifle red – yet might that not have been reflection, for still

the afterglow of sunset lingered in the sky? In any case he scaled a full and heavy 19 pounds Jean Pierre and I were well content as we trudged home. The weight of those three fish seemed good and solid. Such days in Brittany are rare and far between.

In the village the first lights were gleaming. At the inn door we left, below the sprig of mistletoe, our gaff and rod along with two old muzzle-loaders we discovered propped against the wall.

Within was sparkling warmth and hearty greetings – even the old curé was there to see our catch and hear our doings while he sipped his evening cup of *tilleul.* The firelight played upon the dresser's many-coloured bottles, flickering among the black beams overhead, where hung the skins of lard and bunches of dried herbs. Above the chimney's shelf the blue smoke wreathed from numerous dwarfed clay pipes that puffed and drew contentedly, their owners pushing back their chairs to give us place in the convivial circle. There was indeed a large company of *chasseurs* round the fire that night. The village baker who shoots for pleasure, likewise his cousin the schoolmaster, and their friend the notary. Also there were the professional poachers – fascinating people, rough of speech, thriftless, their worn garments patched and sewn with yellow twine, miserably poor, eking a scanty existence with help of caps and rusty powder-horns. They, like their weapons, are old and out of date. They live with Nature under the open skies; they still see visions and at times are "fey", so meet, despite their poverty, some joy upon the road.

We found many friends around the open hearth, not least among them being the tired dogs, who lay with sleepy heads on spattered, steaming paws, before

Père et fils holding an estimated 60-pound salmon, the largest ever caught in France.

the glow; too weary to be roused, they gave us salutation by kindly flaps of tails upon the hearthstone. Only Corantine, the ancient spaniel, came slowly over – grumbling at her rheumatism – to place a wet and friendly nose within my palm. She cast a conscious glance towards the heaped corner where a sleek hare, some brace of birds, and two fat woodcocks lay. Then she crept back to sigh and sleep amongst the wood-ash, to dream of hunting, and while she dreamed she softly whimpered in pursuit.

We heard such talk that night, stories of moonlit expeditions, of trapping wild-boars and how were foxes slain! I learned the weather wisdom of all wildfowl. The advent of the widgeon to the lakes during the time of heavy frosts; the signs which always portend the first great flight of woodcocks to the *landes*; likewise the peculiar voice of snipe that marks the coming of the winter gale. Then the conversation turned to topics of the valley, nearer home, touching upon a certain dipper who for many seasons has built above the mill-pool. You'll find her nest (unless the autumn floods have washed it quite away), a great round dome of moss, framed in the woodwork beneath the broken mill-hatch. In spring it is a house well set in order, with four white, warm and glossy eggs inside. These birds, beloved by all good fishermen, are only shy and wary of the remainder of mankind. The pearl-breasted dipper is, in fact, our patron saint – a pale star that when we go a-fishing flits on ahead, from stone to stone, to guide us to the fat and speckled trout. Always she stays near us, and when we waste our time on likely-looking pools, pillaged by otters overnight, the kindly ousel leaves the river-bed to perch upon the bank; then, with many dips and polished bows, she whispers for us her note of warning – "use-less, use-less".

High on the *landes,* some distance from the river, there is a reed-rimmed lonely pond, wherein dwell eels both fat and succulent. Now it lies brimming, black and deep, but in the droughts of summer the water drops stagnant to the mud. Therefore the frogs enjoy it and talk loudly day and night, but the eels get up and leave the place for fresher and less noisy feeding-grounds. You'll meet them – any dew-drenched moonlight night – *walking upon their tails.*

In the still reach below the mill-dam live many water-spiders. You might suppose on casual acquaintance that they lead an idle water-side existence. But just lie down and watch from the long grass – that little lady there, beside the weed patch, has spent a long and tiring day seeking provisions for her ample household. Now watch her as she hauls upon her rope of web, a tiny submerged handrail leading direct downstairs. A few seconds while she gathers up her parcels, then a frisk and down she goes. You can mark her passage by a wee bead of air that glistens like a diamond. This she carries with her to deposit carefully in her nest as fresh air for the children. Alas! It is a little sparkling lamp which guides the sticklebacks to dinner … . "The *Bon Dieu* was not half asleep when He arranged it all" – this was from old poacher Guerik with a knowing wink. Then: "Monsieur has also doubtless heard how once, not so very long ago, during a time of need, Saint Herbot brought the small red mountain partridges up to our very doors – not one or two as nowadays, but scores and scores, and each one plumper than the last. Likewise in the year of cholera … My father remembered it well … how in the people's need and poverty the Holy Virgin called the salmon up the river. 'Tis said they lay so thick above

The beautiful Gave d'Aspe, for years the home of the Salmon Fishing World Championship.

the bridge of Karn that a full-grown man might walk their backs dry-shod, from bank to bank …"

The old man paused, sucking at his clay pipe. The great logs crackled on the fire; Corantine still slept with tremors in her dreams of hunting, and as the quarry doubled back she gave one sharp, short bark. Then the old poacher turned to me again, speaking in his slow and unaccustomed French. "*Est-ce-que vous avez le même Bon Dieu en Angleterre que nous avons … ici … avec nous?*"

The curé's voice hailed me across the room, where I found Jean Pierre wrapping the larger fish within a dish-cloth, while he explained that the temperature was over-warm. He added in excuse that tobacco smoke was not good for young and fresh-run fish! But we all knew that a wet cloth overnight can work wonders on an elderly ill-coloured salmon. Everyone drew round the table where the great slain hero lay: doubtless he blushed the more beneath his snowy shroud. With brimming glasses raised, we gave the Breton toast to the season's heaviest fish … "*Illa mad.*"*

Now you of Tay and Tweed, of Bann and Shannon, you who may turn the contemptuous lip, boasting of 30-pounders, I'd have you know, ours was a *Breton* salmon … . In any case, don't argue with Jean Pierre. Once roused, you'll find him rough and irrelevant. Only suggest that salmon had a ripe, full-coloured mien, Jean will retort that he does not like *your* face, or quote in Breton counterpart such sentiments as these:

"Your salmon are so fat and red
　　your chicken are so thin and blue;
'Tis plain to see which God has fed,
　　And which was fed by you."

---

* "Good health."

NORWAY

"ITS FISHING HISTORY IS UNIQUE. TWICE IN THE PAST CEN-
TURY, IT SURRENDERED MORE THAN 30 SALMON TO ONE ANGLER
IN A SINGLE NIGHT. BOTH ROXBURGHE AND WESTMINSTER
ACCOMPLISHED THAT FEAT, TAKING FISH THAT AVERAGED 26
POUNDS. SAMPSON FIELD HOLDS THE MODERN RECORD WITH
17 FISH IN A SINGLE NIGHT FROM THE STORIED GARGIA – ALL
TAKEN WITH FLIES AND AVERAGING JUST UNDER 30 POUNDS.
THE RIVER IS THE LEGENDARY ALTA."

From "The Night of the Gytefisk" by Ernest Schwiebert, 1976

FROM "SPORT"

by W. Bromley-Davenport, 1884

"KLOKKEN FEM I MORGEN, OLE!" "Five o'clock tomorrow morning, Ole!" was my last instruction to my faithful boatman and gaffer yesterday evening, and, sure enough, as I jump up instinctively a quarter of an hour before the appointed time, I see him outside my window busying himself with my line to reach the smooth black water, full of submerged eddies, beyond the influence of the force of the torrent, and I begin; once – twice – thrice does the fly perform its allotted circuit and return to me unmolested; but the fourth time, just as I am in the act of withdrawing it from the water for another cast, the bowels of the deep are agitated, and, preceded by a wave impelled and displaced by his own bulk, flounders heavily and half out of the water a mighty salmon. Broad was he, and long to boot, if I may trust an eye not unaccustomed to such apparitions; his white and silvery side betokening his recent arrival from the German Ocean, the slightly roseate hues of his back and shoulders giving unfailing evidence, if corroborative evidence were wanting, after one glimpse of that spade-like tail, of a *Salmo salar* of no common weight and dimensions. My heart – I con-

fess it leaped up to my very mouth – but he has missed the fly, and an anxious palpitating five minutes which I always reluctantly allow must elapse before I try him again. They are gone, and in trembling hope – with exactly the same length of line, and the boat exactly in the same place, Ole having fixed the spot to an inch by some mysterious landmarks on the shore – I commence my second trial. Flounce! There he is not so demonstrative this time – a boil in the water and a slight plash, as the back fin cuts the surface, that's all; but something tells me this is the true attack. A slight, but sharp turn of the wrist certifies the fact, and brings – oh, moment of delight! – my line taut and my rod bent to a delicious curve.

Habet! he has it! Now, Ole! steadily and slowly to the shore! He is quite quiet as yet, and has scarcely discovered the singular nature and properties of the insect he has appropriated, but swims quietly round and round in short circles, wondering no doubt, but so far unalarmed. I am only too thankful for the momentary respite, and treat him with the most respectful gentleness, but a growing though scarcely perceptible increase of the strain on my rod bends it

Salmon fisher's Valhalla: Norway's Alta, regarded as one of the finest big-fish rivers in the world.

gradually lower and lower until the reel begins to give out its first slow music. My fingers are on the line to give it the slight resistance of friction, but the speed increases too rapidly for me to bear them there long, and I withdraw them just in time to save their being cut to the bone in the tremendous rush which follows. Whizz-z-z! up the pool he goes! the line scattering the spray from the surface in a small fountain, like the cut-water of a Thames steamer. And now a thousand fears assail me – should there be one defective strand on my casting-line, one doubtful or rotten portion of my head-line, should anything *kink* or foul, should the hook itself (as sometimes happens) be a bad one – farewell, oh giant of the deep, for ever! *Absit omen!* all is well as yet, the rush is over. He has a terrible length of my line out, but he is in a safe part of the pool and rather disposed to come back to me, which gives me the opportunity, which I seize eagerly, of reeling up my line. The good-tempered, reasonable monster! But steady! there is a limit to his concessions. No further will he obey the rod's gentle dictation. Two rebellious opiniative kicks near-

ly jerk my arms out of the shoulder joints, and then down he goes to the bottom. Deep in the middle of the pool he lies, obdurate, immovable as a stone. There must he not remain! That savage strength must not be husbanded. I re-enter the boat, and am gently rowed towards him, reeling up as I advance. He approves not this, as I expected. He is away again into the very midst of the white water, till I think he means to ascend the foss itself – hesitates irresolute there a moment, then back again down the middle of the stream like a telegraphic message. "Row ashore, Ole! Row for life! for now he means mischief!" Once in the swift water at the tail of the pool he will try not only my reel, but my own wind and condition to boot; for down he *must* go now, weighed he but a poor five pounds; once out of this pool and there is nothing to stop him for 300 yards. We near the shore, and I spring into the shallow water and prance and bound after him with extravagant action, blinding myself with the spray which I dash around me. Ah! well I know and much I fear this rapid! The deep water being on the other side of the river, the fish

69

invariably descend there, and from the wide space intervening, too deep for man to wade in, too shallow for fish to swim in, and too rough for boat to live in, the perturbed fisherman must always find an awful length of line between him and his fish, which, however, he can in no way diminish till he arrives considerably lower down, where the river is narrower. Many a gallant fish has by combination of strength and wile escaped me here. Many a time has my heart stood still to find that my line and reel have suddenly done the same – what means it? In the strength of that mighty torrent can mortal fish rest? Surely, but he must have found a shelter somewhere? Some rock behind which to lie protected from the current! I must try and move him! Try and move the world! A rock is indeed there and the line is round it, glued to it immovably by weight of water. It is *drowned*. But he, the fish! seaward may he now swim half a league away, or at the

bottom of the next pool may be rubbing some favourite fly against the stones. Nay – but see! the line runs out still, with jerks and life-like signs. Hurrah! we have not lost him yet. Oh, dreamer, ever hoping to the last, no more life there than in a galvanised corpse, whose spasmodic actions the line is imitating! It is bellying deep in the stream, quivering and jerking, slacking and pulling as the current dictates, creating movements which, through the glamour of a heated imagination, seem as the struggles of a mighty fish.

That fish, that fly, and perhaps that casting-line shall that fisherman never see again? Such doom and such a result may the gods now avert! My plungings and prancings have brought me to the foot of my wooden bridge – made very high on purpose to avoid

the perils above described (and for the same purpose I keep well behind or upstream of my fish) – which I hurry over with long strides, and many an anxious glance at my 90 or 100 yards of line waving and tossing through the angry breakers encompassed by a hundred dangers. With rod held high and panting lungs I spring from the bridge, and blunder as I best may along the stony and uneven bank for another 100 yards with unabated speed. I am saved! Safe floats the line in the deep but still rapid and stormy water beyond the extremest breaker, and here, fortunately for me, my antagonist slackens his speed, having felt the influence of a back-water which guides him rather back to me, and I advance in a more rational manner, and in short sobs regain the breath of life; but one aching arm must still sustain the rod on high while the other reels up as for very existence. Forward, brave Ole! and have the next boat ready in case the self-willed monster continues his reckless course, which he most surely will; for, lo! in one fiery whizz out goes all the line which that tired right hand had so laboriously reclaimed from the deep, and down, proudly sailing mid-stream, my temporary tyrant recommences his hitherto all triumphant progress. I follow as I best may, but now, having gained the refuge of the boat, a few strokes of Ole's vigorous boat-compelling oars recover me the line I had lost, and land me on the opposite bank, where, with open water before me for some distance, I begin for the first time to realise the possibility of victory. However –

"Much hath been done, but more remains to do," but of a less active, more ponderous, painstaking patience-trying description. The long deep stream of Langhole is before me in which he will hang – does

Norwegian tube flies have become popular on rivers throughout the world.

hang, will sulk – does sulk, and has to be roused by stones cast in above, below, and around him. As yet, I have never seen him since his first rise, but Ole, who has climbed the bank above me, and from thence can see far into the clear bright water, informs me that he gets an occasional glimpse of him, and that he is "*meget meget store*", or very very big. My heart – worn and weary as it is with the alternations of hope and fear – re-flutters at this intelligence, for I know that Ole is usually a fish-decrier or weight-diminisher. All down the length of Langhole, 250 yards by the tale, does he sullenly bore, now and then taking alarming excursions far away to the opposite shore, oftener burying himself deep in the deepest water close at my feet; but at length he resolves on more active operations, and, stimulated by the rapid stream at the tail of Langhole, takes advantage thereof and goes down bodily to the next pool, Tofte. I have no objection to this, even if I had a voice in the matter; I have a flat smooth meadow to race over, the stream has no hidden rocky dangers, so, like swift Camilla, I scour the plain till the deeper and quieter recesses of

Tofte afford an asylum for the fish and breathing time to myself. Here, I hope, but hope in vain, to decide the combat; occasionally I contrive to gain the advantage of a short line, but the instant he perceives the water shoaling away he bores indignant, and spurns the shallow. The engagement has now lasted more than an hour, and my shoulders are beginning to ache, and yet no symptoms of submission on the part of my adversary; on the contrary, he suddenly reassumes the offensive, and with a rush which imparts such rotary motion to my reel as to render the handle not only intangible but actually invisible, he forsakes the delights of Tofte, and continues his course down the river. I must take to the boat again (I have one on every pool) and follow, like a harpooner towed by a whale. The river widens below Tofte, and a short swift shallow leads to the next pool, Langholmen, or Long Island. I have a momentary doubt whether to land on the island or on the opposite side where there is a deeper but swifter pool, towards which the fish is evidently making. I decide at once, but decide wrong – which is better, however, than not deciding at all – and

I land on Langholmen, into whose calm flowing water I had fondly hoped that incipient fatigue would have enticed my fish, and find him far over in the opposite pool with an irreconcilable length of line doubtfully connecting us. It is an awful moment! If he goes up stream now, I am lost – that is to say, my fish is – which in my present frame of mind is the same thing; no line or hook would ever stand the strain of that weight of water. But, no, mighty as he is, he is mortal, and but a fish after all, and even his giant strength is failing him, and inch by inch and foot by foot he drops down the stream, and as he does so the reel gradually gains on him, till at the tail of Langholmen I have the delight of getting, for the first time since he rose, a fair sight of his broad and shining bulk, as he lies drifting sulkily and indolently down the clear shallows. I exult with the savage joy which the gladiator may have felt when he perceived for the first time the growing weakness of his antagonist, and I set no bounds to my estimate of his size. Fifty pounds at least! I proclaim loudly to Ole, is the very minimum of the weight I give him. Ole smiles and shakes his head detractingly. The phlegmatic, unsympathetic, realistic wretch! On I go, however, wading knee-deep over the glancing shingle. The lowest pool, and my last hope before impassable rapids, Lærneset, is before me, and after wading waist deep across the confluent stream at the end of the island, I gain the commanding bank and compel my now amenable monster into the deep, still water, out of the influence of the current. And now, feebler and feebler grow his rushes, shorter and shorter grows the line, till mysterious whirlpools agitate the calm surface, and at last, with a heavy, weary plunge, upheaves the spent giant, and passive, helpless, huge, "lies floating many a rood".

Still even now his *vis inertiæ* is formidable, and much caution and skill have to be exercised in towing that vanquished hull into port, lest with one awkward heavy roll, or one feeble flop of that broad, spreading tail, he may tear away hook or hold, and so rob me at last of my hardly-earned victory. No such heart-breaking disaster awaits me. Ole, creeping and crouching like a deer-stalker, extends the fatal gaff, buries it deep in the broad side, and drags him, for he is, in very sooth, too heavy to lift, unwilling and gasping to the shore, where, crushing flat the long grass, he flops and flounders till a merciful thwack on the head from the miniature policeman's staff, which I always carry for this purpose, renders him alike oblivious and insensible to past suffering or present indignity. And now I may calmly survey his vast proportions and speculate on the possibility of his proving too much for my weighing machine, which only gives information up to 50 pounds. To a reasonable-sized fish I can always assign an approximate weight, but this one takes me out of the bounds of my calculation, and being as sanguine as Ole is the reverse, I anxiously watch the deflection of the index as Ole, by exercising his utmost strength, raises him by a hook through his under jaw from the ground, with a wild sort of hope still possessing me (foolish though I

A 42-pound salmon caught on the Namsen at Torrisdal in 1919
on a British import, the Jock Scott.

inwardly feel it to be) that the machine won't weigh him.

Forty-five anyhow he *must* be! Yes, he is! no, he ain't! Alas! after a few oscillations it settles finally at 43 pounds, with which decision I must rest content, and I *am* content. I give way to senseless manifestations of extravagant joy, and even Ole relaxes. Early as it is, it is not too early for a Norwegian to drink spirits, and I serve him out a stiff dram of whisky on the spot, which he tosses down raw without winking, while I dilute mine from the river, for this ceremony, on such occasions, must never be neglected. "Now, Ole, shoulder the prey as you best can, and home to breakfast"; for now, behold, from behind the giant shoulder of the Horn bursts forth the mighty sun himself! illuminating the very depths of the river, sucking up the moisture from the glittering grass, and drying the tears of the blue bells and the dog violets, and calling into life the myriads whose threescore years and ten are to be compressed into the next twelve hours. Yet how they rejoice! Their songs of praise and enjoyment positively din in my ears as I walk home, rejoicing, too, after my Anglo-Saxon manner, at having killed something, fighting the battle over again in extravagantly bad Norse to Ole, who patiently toils on under the double burden of the big fish and my illiterate garrulity. In short I am thoroughly happy – self-satisfied and

"AND NOW I MAY CALMLY SURVEY HIS VAST PROPORTIONS AND SPECULATE ON THE POSSIBILITY OF HIS PROVING TOO MUCH FOR MY WEIGHING MACHINE, WHICH ONLY GIVES INFORMATION UP TO 50 POUNDS."

at peace with all mankind. I have succeeded, and success usually brings happiness; everything looks bright around me, and I thankfully compare my lot with that of certain pallid, flaccid beings, whom my mind's eye presents to me stewing in London, and gasping in midsummer torment in the House of Commons. A breakfast of Homeric proportions (my friend and I once ate a seven-pound grilse and left nothing even for a dog) follows this morning performance. Will my reader be content to rest after it, smoke a pipe, bask in the sun (he won't stand that long, for the Norway sun is like the kitchen fire of the gods), and possibly after Norwegian custom, take a midday nap?

Five o'clock pm – we have eaten the best portion of a Norwegian sheep, not much bigger than a good hare, for our dinner, and the lower water awaits us. Here the valley is wider, the pools larger and less violent. It is here that I have always wished to hook the real monster of the river – the 60- or 70-pounder of tradition – as I can follow him to the sea if he don't yield sooner, which from the upper water I can't, because impossible rapids divide my upper and lower water; and if I had not killed this morning's fish where I did I should have lost him, as it was the last pool above the rapids. We take ship again in the Nedre Fiva, a splendid pool, about a mile from my house,

73

subject only to the objection which old Sir Hyde Parker, one of the early inventors of Norway fishing, used to bring against a whole country: "Too much water and too few fish!" I have great faith in myself today, and feel that great things are still in store for me. I recommence operations, and with some success, for I land a 12- and a 16-pounder in a very short space of time; after which towards the tail of this great pool, I hook something very heavy and strong, which runs out my line in one rush almost to the last turn of the reel before Ole can get way on the boat to follow him, and then springs out of the water a full yard high; this feat being performed some 120 yards off me, and the fish looking even at that distance enormous. I have no doubt that I have at last got fast of my ideal monster – the 70-pounder of my dreams. Even the apathetic Ole grunts loudly his "*Gud bevarr!*" of astonishment. I will spare the reader all the details of the struggle which ensues, and take him at once to the final scene, some two miles down below where I hooked him, and which has taken me about three hours to reach – a still back-water, into which I have with extraordinary luck contrived to guide him, dead-beat. No question now about his size. We see him plainly close to us, a very porpoise. I can see that Ole is demoralised and unnerved at the sight of him. He had twice told me, during our long fight with him, that the 43-pounder of this morning was "like a small piece of this one" – the largest salmon he had ever seen in his 50 years' experience; and to my horror I see him, after utterly neglecting one or two splendid chances, making hurried and feeble pokes at him with the gaff – with the only effect of frightening him by splashing the water about his nose. In a fever of agony I bring him once again within easy reach of the gaff, and regard him as my own. He is mine now! he *must* be! "Now's your time, Ole – can't miss him! – now – now!" He docs though! and in one instant a deadly

> "THE HUGE FINS BEGIN TO MOVE GENTLY, LIKE A STEAMER'S FIRST MOTION OF HER PADDLES, AND HE DISAPPEARS SLOWLY INTO THE DEEP!"

sickness comes over me as the rod springs straight again, and the fly dangles useless in the air. The hold has broken! Still the fish is so beat that he lies there yet on his side. He knows not he is free! "Quick, gaff him as he lies. Quick! Do you hear? You can have him still!" Oh, for a Scotch gillie! Alas for the Norwegian immovable nature! Ole looks up at me with lacklustre eyes, turns an enormous quid in his cheek, and does nothing. I cast down the useless rod, and dashing at him wrest the gaff from his hand, but it is too late. The huge fins begin to move gently, like a steamer's first motion of her paddles, and he disappears slowly into the deep! Yes – yes, he is gone! For a moment I glare at Ole with a bitter hatred. I should like to slay him where he stands, but have no weapon handy, and also doubt how far Norwegian law would justify the proceeding, great as is the provocation. But the fit passes, and a sorrow too deep for words gains possession of me, and I throw away the gaff and sit down, gazing in blank despair at the water. Is it possible? Is it not a hideous nightmare? But two minutes ago blessed beyond the lot of angling man – on the topmost pinnacle of angling fame! The practical possessor of the largest salmon ever taken with a rod! And now, deeper than ever plummet sounded, in the depths of dejection! Tears might relieve me; but my sorrow is too great, and I am doubtful how Ole might take it. I look at him again. The same utterly blank face, save a projection of unusual size in his cheek, which makes me conjecture that an additional quid has been secretly thrust in to supplement the one already in possession. He has said not a word since the catastrophe, but abundant expectoration testifies to the deep and tumultuous workings of his soul. I bear in mind that I am a man and a Christian, and I mutely offer him my flask. But, no; with a delicacy which does him honour, and touches me to the heart, he declines it; and with a deep sigh and in scarcely audi-

Graceful silver on canvas: "Leaping Salmon" an oil painting by Roger McPhail.

ble accents repeating "The largest salmon I ever saw in my life!", picks up my rod and prepares to depart. Why am I not a Stoic, and treat this incident with contempt? Yes; but why am I human? Do what I will, the vision is still before my eyes. "I hear the 'never, never'" can the chance recur again! Shut my eyes, stop my ears as I will, it is the same. If I had only known his actual weight! Had he but consented to be weighed and returned into the stream! How gladly would I now make that bargain with him! But the opportunity of even that compromise is past. It's intolerable. I don't believe the Stoics ever existed; if they did they must have suffered more than even I do in bottling up their miseries. They *did* feel; they *must* have felt – why pretend they didn't? Zeno was a humbug! Anyhow, none of the sect ever lost a salmon like that! What! "A small sorrow? Only a fish!" Ah, try it yourself! An old lady, inconsolable for the loss of her dog, was once referred for example of resignation to a mother who had lost her child, and she replied, "Oh, yes! But *children are not dogs!*" And I, in some sort, understand her. So, in silent gloom I follow Ole homewards.

Not darkness, nor twilight, but the solemn yellow hues of the northern midnight gather over the scene; black and forbidding frown the precipices on either side, save where on the top of the awful Horn – inaccessible as happiness – far, far beyond the reach of mortal footstep, still glows, like sacred fire, the sleepless sun! Hoarser murmurs seem to arise from the depths of the foss – like the groans of imprisoned demons – to which a slight but increasing wind stealing up the valley from the sea adds its melancholy note. My mind, already deeply depressed, yields helplessly to the influence of the hour and sinks to zero at once; and despondency – the hated spirit – descends from her "foggy cloud" and is my inseparable companion all the way home.

75

The Night of the Gytefisk

Ernest Schwiebert, 1976

Skree-jah! The terns screamed. *Skree-jah!*

THE SUN WAS STILL LOW on the northern horizon, and strangely bright at two in the morning. The ghillies finally decided to break for lunch along the river. No one fishes except in the 10-hour twilight of the midnight sun. The boatmen expertly worked their slender Karasjok riverboat ashore, and its graceful Viking prow crunched on the gravel. It was cool for midsummer, and a light wind riffled the huge pool at Steinfossnakken. The two boatmen built a fire on the beach while I watched the midnight sun on the waterfalls that spill Yosemite-like from the Sautso escarpment, a thousand feet above the river. The cooking smells of bouillon and hot coffee drifted on the wind, and we listened to the thundering Gabofoss rapids upstream.

Skree-jah! screamed the noisy terns.

The birds were catching mayflies, hovering and fluttering on the wind, and then dropping, like an osprey to catch a hatching dun, with a rapier-quick thrust of their beaks. Dark red-finned grayling were working softly to the hatch in the shallows. The grayling averaged two pounds, but we were after bigger game. My three salmon lay gleaming in the boat, placed cross-wise to ballast its slender hull. The best fish had been taken at Mostajokka, bright with sea-lice and a muscular 33 pounds. The smallest of the three went 21, less than average for the river, and when it cartwheeled awkwardly at the end of its first long run, the old riverkeeper laughed and contemptu-

ously called it a grilse.

The sandwiches and hot soup warmed our bodies, and we finished our coffee, watching the river. Two river Lapps went past in the mail boat on their way to the Sautso Camp. We were in no particular hurry now, with three fine salmon in the boat, even though we would fish another two hours before returning to the middle camp at Sandia.

The original Sandia camp was built for the Duke of Roxburghe in 1873. It was burnt by withdrawing German troops late in the Second World War, and was restored in 1946. I had one night at Sandia before the mailboat ferried me up to Sautso.

Skree-jah! the terns screamed.

The river begins in the snow-melt plateaus and escarpments of the Finnmarksvidda, two hundred miles above the Polar Circle in arctic Norway. The granite outcroppings bear the wounds and grinding scars of the ice-age glaciers that shaped them, leaving a great treeless wilderness pockmarked with dark tea-colored lakes.

The source of the river gathers in a series of potholes in the tundra barrens below Kautokeino, the village that is considered the capital of Lapland. Its surrounding highlands shelter a number of Lapp encampments, with their pyramidal log roofs and conical turf-cabins and storehouses on slender stilts. These are the permanent settlements where the Lapp herdsmen winter with their reindeer flocks and migrate with them in spring, carrying their

A traditional 24-foot Karasjok longboat at the end of an Alta fishing day.

deerskin pole-shelters along on the trek. There is both humor and sadness in their coppery faces, wrinkled deeply with the fierce weather of those latitudes – it is a vanishing tribal way of life, like the world of the Iniupiat and Inuit in its terrible arctic isolation.

The river rises in caribou-moss seepages in the treeless plateau, finally gathering in its deeply eroded valley about 50 miles north of Kautokeino. Its first 20 miles are locked in impenetrable defiles, filled with the lacework of countless waterfalls. There are salmon there too, spawning in a wilderness of impassable cliffs and rapids, but below these headwater canyons its character changes.

Its watercourse is a symphony in three movements: below the first tumbling chutes where the river escapes the gorge, its moods are almost pastoral, flowing into the mile-long mirror of smooth water below the Sautso Camp. Such *pianissimo* passages end in the wild cacophony of the Gabofoss rapids, where the river drops almost 80 feet in a quarter mile. Downstream from the portage, the river gathers in the amphitheater-sized Steinfossnakken, where its Sandia beats begin. These middle pools are a series of stairsteps, flowing swift and smooth into a brief rapids, and then swelling and spreading into another pool. The Sandia mileage ends in the moss-walled gorge above Battagorski, where the current fights its way through cabin-sized ledges and boulders – here are the clamor of brass and the thundering rhythms of kettledrums and cymbals. The river has claimed many lives in these rapids.

Its forests are denser now, thriving in the sheltered valley below the Battagorski water. There is a magnificent salmon pool there, deep and silken-smooth above great boulders in its chocolate depths, still flecked with foam from the rapids. It marks the top of the classic Jøraholmen beats, which wind in a sweeping series of pools – passages for strings and French horns and woodwinds – as they reach the farmstead clearings and villages near the sea.

The estuary is unimpressive, its currents shallow and spreading in a labyrinth of sandbar channels until they reach the fjord itself, a hundred miles below Hammarfest and the North Cape. Bossekop is a brightly painted fishing village at its mouth, its cheerful houses scattered on the hillsides. It was not always peaceful, because the fjord sheltered German pocket-battleships 30-odd years ago, during the bitter convoy battles that took place between Reykjavik and Murmansk.

The river has been fished and loved since the sixth Duke of Roxburghe visited the fjord on his yacht in 1859, and discovered it was filled with huge salmon eager for his flies. Roxburghe and the Duke of Westminster, famed for both fishing and his liaisons with the late Coco Chanel, shared its fishing in the half-century before the Second World War. Roxburghe built the middle and upper camps in Victorian times, but in those first years they made their headquarters on the yacht moored at Bossekop. During the peak of the salmon run, parties poled and portaged upriver to the Sautso beats – fishing back to the luxury of the yacht at the pace of the current, and stopping in several rough camps enroute.

It has been fished in modern times by a whole parade of celebrated anglers. The Duke of Windsor and his imperious equerry, the Earl of Dudley, were regulars a half-century ago. Death-duties and other shifts in the spectrum of British privilege led to an American interregnum on the river at mid-century and anglers like Joseph Pulitzer, Admiral Edward MacDonald, Robert Pabst, Ralph Strauss, James Graham, Warrington Gillet, Herbert Pulitzer, Seward Johnson, Anderson Fowler, Ted Benzinger, Roger Gailliard, Sampson Field, Peter Pleydell-Bouverie, Clare de Bergh, Thomas Lenk, Peter Kriendler, Cornelius Ryan, Edward Litchfield, Robert Goelet, Charles Ritz, and Admiral William Read – who successfully flew the NC-4 across the Atlantic long before Lindbergh – all became regulars over the past 25 years.

The eighth Duke and Duchess of Roxburghe still fish the river together each summer, and although its sport has declined seriously with deep-water drift netting of the salmon of northern Europe, it still remains the finest Atlantic salmon river on earth.

Its fishing history is unique. Twice in the past century, it surrendered more than 30 salmon to a single angler in a single night. Both Roxburghe and Westminster accomplished that feat, taking fish that averaged 26 pounds. Sampson Field holds the modern record with 17 fish in a single night from the storied Gargia, all taken with flies and averaging just under 30 pounds.

The river is the legendary Alta.

Charles Ritz records its fame in his classic *A Flyfisher's Life*, and has been heard singing its praises from the storied Cambon bar of his equally famous hotel in the Place Vendôme in Paris, to the quiet colonial-paneled quarters of the Anglers' Club of New York below Wall Street.

"It is simply unique!" Ritz insists with gestures and staccato speeches. "There are no mountains except the Himalaya, no oceans like the Pacific, no fish like the Atlantic salmon – and only one Alta!"

Charles Ritz is right. Like the alpinist who remains untested without attempting Everest and Dhaulagiri and Annapurna in Nepal, and the big-game hunter who has not stalked the Serengeti in Africa, the salmon fisherman dreams of fishing the Alta. Although its fishing on the Jøraholmen water had surrendered a half-dozen fish over 20 pounds in my two brief visits to the river, its sense of history and a brace of 40-pound salmon killed by the Duchess of Roxburghe and Peter Pleydell-Bouverie, had continued to haunt me for years.

It was the river that quite literally filled my dreams. "Valhalla!" Ritz insists. "It's Valhalla and once you have tasted it, nothing is ever quite the same!"

My first night at Sandia came about by accident. There was a fisherman who became ill there and had been taken downriver. Because I had arrived a day early from some poor fishing on the Reisa, the river-

The powerful currents of the River Alta are equaled only by the river's giant salmon.

keeper sent me upriver on the mail boat to fish out the sick man's last night. It was not so much a night of fishing for me, as half the salmon I might catch belonged to the farmers who own the fishing rights, and were worth considerable money. Although I felt a little like a trawler with my slender Garrison, we contributed ten salmon averaging 23 pounds to the river owners that night of fishing at Sandia.

The boatmen arrived after lunch to carry me upstream with the mail to Sautso, and we traveled through the Ronga and Mostajokka to the foot of the portage in the sprawling Steinfossnakken. We changed boats there, and the boatmen carried my heavy duffle on a pole to the lip of the Gabofoss upstream while I carried my tackle and another duffle of clothes and fly-tying gear over the boulder-strewn trail. The Alta thundered through the Gabofoss rapids' rocky course, blotting out all thought and other sound, until finally we reached the immense tail shallows of the Sautso flowage.

We spooked a huge salmon lying just off our second boat-mooring, and its bow-wave disturbed the ledgerock shallows of the lake. The boatman stared at the last scraps of the sun on the cliffs.

"Sautso is a paradise!" he said in Norwegian.

Finally, they loaded my gear in a second Karasjok boat and we started upriver toward the Sautso camp, crossing the smooth water of the river between Gabofoss and Sirpinakken.

The cabin at Sautso is simple and rough. It was built by the sixth Duke of Roxburghe not long after the American Civil War. There is a simple sitting room with log walls, two bedrooms with rudimentary baths, the kitchen and quarters for a cook and a serving girl. The ghillies sleep in a turf-cabin near the river. The sitting-room wall had the pale pencil tracing of a 59-pound salmon killed by Admiral Read at the Steinfossnakken on a huge hairwing Red Abbey.

79

There was talk of painting the walls, which would have covered the badly fading outline of the great fish, and I reverently retraced its muscular outlines on the wainscoting with a brush dipped in Chinese ink. Anglers with a reverence for tradition owe something to posterity.

The afternoon sun was still bright when the cook informed me solemnly that dinner was scheduled for seven o'clock. Fishing would begin at eight. The black curtains shut out most of the afternoon light, but I slept fitfully, dreaming of the Sautso beat and its giant salmon. It was a setting worthy of my moment of truth, and sleep was difficult.

The dice-cup used to start the week awarded me the upper river from the Toppen, where the Alta escapes its impenetrable gorge, to the famous Dormenin, one of the few bank-fishing pools on the Alta.

We traveled upriver just after supper, portaging the Karasjok boat around the Svartfossen rapids and the wild chutes at Bolvero and Jagorski. Toppen was above, flowing smooth and still in the last reaches of the gorge. The ghillies worked the boat cautiously up the smooth surface, and stopped for a pipeful of tobacco in the cliff-walled narrows below the trail.

"We must rest the fish," they explained in Norwegian. "Give the salmon time to forget our passage upstream."

Finally we began fishing.

It was a roll-casting place, with a sheer basalt wall behind the boat, and I had to loop the fly about 35 feet against the opposite rocks. The old boatman rowed patiently with the smooth current, letting his skiff drop about two feet downstream for each succeeding cast. His was precise work, requiring discipline and strength and a knowledge of the river.

I worked ten casts along the rocks, locking the line under my index finger with the rod-tip low, following the swing when the line came around toward the stern. I lifted the rod to raise it over the ghillie there, and then let it hang a few seconds downstream to the left of the boat. Sometimes a fish following the fly will take when the fly stops. Sometimes one will take as it starts moving again. It will sometimes follow the fly across the current and hang under it, circling its position, and take when the fisherman begins a short, upstream retrieve toward the boat.

Salmon fishing is discipline and patience on a big river like the Alta. One must cover its half-mile riffles with a series of concentric fly swings. The mind can drift and daydream with the rhythm of the oarlocks and the casting: and suddenly there was an immense swirl behind the swinging fly.

"*Laks!*" said the boatman.

The fish had come after the fly-swing without taking it, and we quickly repeated the cast.

"He's coming again!" the ghillie whispered.

There was literally a bow-wave, bulging under the smooth current. Sometimes you can force a take by varying the swing, and this time I slowed the teasing rhythm of the rod-tip, and stripped about six inches of line toward the bellying fly. It slowed the swing, forcing the following salmon to make a choice: soon overrun the teasing fly and turn back, or finally take it.

This one hesitated a millisecond and took. The rod snapped down as the bellying line signalled its weight, and there was a wild tail-splash as it rolled head-down and sounded.

Several times it threatened to leave Toppen, working deep into the shallows at the tail, but each time we forced it back into the deep water in the throat of the gorge. Finally, the boatman slipped out of the main currents, and I pumped the salmon close; the ghillie reached deftly with the gaff, wrestling a fat 30-pound

> "THIS ONE HESITATED A MILLISECOND AND TOOK. THE ROD SNAPPED DOWN AS THE BELLYING LINE SIGNALLED ITS WEIGHT, AND THERE WAS A WILD TAIL-SPLASH AS IT ROLLED HEAD-DOWN AND SOUNDED."

henfish over the gunwale. He dispatched it with a sharp rap of the priest behind the ears and laid it gleaming across the thwarts of the boat.

"*Det var findt!*" He grinned.

We rested the pool again for a half hour and took a second big salmon right at the lip of the rapids. Below the broken quarter-mile downstream is the Jagotku chute, where the late Joe Brooks took a 40-pounder, and I killed a lively 20-pound fish there wading, as the boatmen wrestled our skiff down the whitewater of the other channel.

Svartfossnakken was next, the sprawling pool where the river turned sharply and gathered speed in a dark, ink-colored slick at its tail. The Svartfoss rapids lay below, tumbling through a long, sickle-shaped curve at the base of the mountain. The boatmen hold their skiff expertly here in the gathering currents, stroking evenly and well, while the fisherman casts a lengthening line over the swift, foam-flecked shallows. We hooked a heavy fish there almost immediately, and the ghillies fought to maintain position while I forced the salmon. It did not work, and the fly came out. The ghillies saw that I was not unhappy,

and we laughed together, resting the pool. We had three fish in the boat, and that was par.

We took a second fish from Svartfoss, and I walked downriver to Dormenin while the ghillies lowered the boat on the anchor line through the rapids. Dormenin is perhaps the best greased-line pool on the Sautso beat, and I changed reels to use a floating line. Twice I moved a fish at the head, but it refused to come again. Another rolled sullenly at the tail, where Dormenin eddies and slides into the Harstrommen stretch. It proved unproductive too, and we traveled downriver, having reached the bottom of our first night's beat.

"*Fire fisker!*" The ghillie beamed.

It had been a four-fish night, and we were ahead of the three-fish par on this beat, so the boatmen were pleased. The morning was dark and overcast, and when we reached the camp at the Jotkajavrre tributary, the smooth expanse of Sautso was patterned with the misting rain.

"Stormy tomorrow night," said the boatmen gloomily. "Tomorrow we fish Gabo and Velleniva."

"They're both good pools?" I asked.

The fight is on! An angler prudently stays low to maintain his balance.

"Very good!" they said.

It was raining hard at four in the morning, the drops drumming on the roof-shingles, and it was getting lighter under the heavily overcast skies. The maids brought us our supper (the days and nights being upside down on the Alta) and at six, after dressing several fresh Orange Blossoms on size-3/0 doubles, I finally drew the black, bedroom curtains against the gathering daylight and fell asleep, listening to the rain.

It was afternoon when the young maid awakened me, but it was still gloomy and dark. The overcast had lowered between the ragged escarpments that enclosed the valley, until it hung like an immense shroud a few hundred feet above the river. My breakfast of fried eggs and goat cheese and brislings was ready, and the ghillies waited unhappily in the kitchen.

It did not feel like a fishing night. "The barometer must have drained right through the bottom of the glass," I said.

"*Ja,*" the boatmen agreed sourly.

We traveled upstream to the gravel-bar island at Dormenin and began fishing upper Harstrommen. The overcast was even lower, until scraps of mist drifted through the trees, and it was raining again. We shouldered into our ponchos, studying the sullen current unhappily. Its tea-color had turned milky, and the river was rising. The ghillie selected a fresh Orange Blossom, the pattern that had killed well the night before, and painstakingly knotted it to the nylon. Then we worked across the current and fished the 60-yard pool carefully in spite of the rain and mist.

"Nothing!" I said when we had fished through the entire pool. "It's too gloomy tonight."

"Perhaps it will prove a Gytefisk night," they said.

"Gytefisk night?" I asked.

"There are nights when we catch nothing, even on the Alta," the ghillie in the stern explained. "But our name for a giant cockfish that has spawned before and come back again is a Gytefisk."

"Some nights you catch these Gytefisk?"

"*Ja,*" said the boatman, "and they usually come on nights when nothing else seems to take the fly!"

"Let's pray for a Gytefisk night."

"*Ja,*" they smiled.

The current seemed even more discolored. It called for a pale fly the fish could easily see, and I studied my boxes. There was a bright yellow-hackled Torrish that Clare de Burgh had given me at lunch with Charles Woodman in Oslo. They had been fishing a week earlier with Seward Johnson, Anderson Fowler, and Carter Nicholas on the Jøraholmen beat at Alta, and Clare had been high rod with 37 salmon.

A spectral fog – the perfect setting for an encounter with the Gytefisk.

She had killed a cockfish of 57 pounds.

"Every bloody one on the Torrish!" she laughed. "You take my last one and try it!" The fly lay glittering on the tablecloth.

"I'll enshrine it and make copies!" I said.

It looked rather enticing in the box. There had been no time to copy it, but its bright canary hackles and glittering tinsel seemed perfect. The ghillie seemed skeptical, but he took the Torrish and carefully knotted it to the tippet. It looked good working in the current beside the boat.

It was raining harder when we reached the lower Harstrommen. It is a strong hundred-yard reach of water named for its heavy currents. The boatman expertly maneuvered our long boat into position at the head of the pool, and we began fishing through methodically.

"Good place?" I asked them in Norwegian. "*Gud plass?*"

"*Ja,*" they shook their heads. "We do not catch many salmon here – but they're usually big ones."

"Good place for a Gytefisk?" I suggested.

"Perhaps," they smiled.

It was almost prophetic. The line worked out into the gathering darkness and dropped the fly 65 feet across the current tongue. I lowered the rod and let the fly settle deep into its bellying swing; suddenly there was a sullen pull that stopped its teasing rhythm. The line throbbed with both the fish and the current, and I sat down to fight it. The salmon seemed unusually strong, but it was still much too early to tell, feeling its weight and power alone in such currents.

Gytefisk? I asked.

The boatmen said nothing, working the oars and watching the throbbing, increasingly sullen movements of the rod. They seemed unusually concerned at the tenor of the fight, and suddenly I understood why. The river exploded slightly above the boat, and an immense, sow-sized cockfish cartwheeled awkwardly, landing with a gargantuan splash.

"My God!" I thought wildly.

The fish burst halfway out of the river a minute

later, broaching like a whale and falling heavily.

"Thirty kilos!" guessed the ghillie.

"*Ja!*" the boatman agreed.

Both men were talking excitedly, more excited than I had seen them on the night before, and we settled into the grim business of fighting such a fish in heavy water on a single-handed split-cane rod. It would prove hard work.

The salmon simply hung there for several minutes, and then turned majestically downstream, gathering speed in the tumbling currents below the boat. Its strength seemed to ignore any rod pressure we could exert, and it stripped a hundred yards of backing with almost ridiculous ease. Then it stopped ponderously. The boatmen used those precious minutes to maneuver for better position, and we crossed the Harstrommen to get our longboat into the backwater shallows a little below the fish. It shook its head sourly at midstream.

I had just begun to pump-and-reel saltwater style, holding the rod in a modified tarpon lock, when the salmon started slowly out of the pool. There was nothing we could do, and it simply shouldered us aside, gathering speed as it reached the swift rapids.

But 30 kilos is over 65 pounds, I was thinking wildly. Over 65 pounds!

The backing had dwindled dangerously on the spool, and the boatmen worked desperately to follow, rowing and sometimes poling to keep both the line and the longboat free of the rocks. It was a wild, half-mile trip with little control of the salmon.

It easily fought us through several pools, forcing us another mile through Battanielo and Banas, into the smooth, swelling currents of Sirpinakken. More white water lay below, but it was less tumbling and broken, and we came through easily with the fish still hooked. The fight went better in the lake-sized shallows just above the Sautso Camp.

The huge salmon porpoised weakly, circling about

"It's the best pool ... we should move something there, even on a night like this"

50 yards out. It seemed beaten, and now the rod-pressure could parry its attempted runs. Finally, it surrendered to my saltwater lock, and came grudgingly out of the heavy currents into the pondlike backwater at Jotka.

The fly-line was back on the reel now, its dark green turns covering the pale, Dacron backing. We forced the huge salmon closer and closer until the leader was showing above the water. The big salmon rolled almost under the boat, and we gasped at its size.

"Thirty kilos," the ghillies whispered. The cook and the serving girl were watching now.

The salmon bolted weakly downstream, stripping out 15 yards of line, but I turned it slowly back toward the boat. The ghillie moved the gaff soundlessly into position, waiting like a heron. The fish floundered and surfaced, rolling weakly and working its gills, and it was almost in reach of the gaff when it yawned wide, and the fly came free.

"Damn!" I shouted unhappily.

The ghillie cursed and threw the gaff angrily into the shallows. The boatman hung on his oars and stared as the great fish gathered its strength and turned into deeper water, pushing a bow-wave like a half-submerged submarine. Alta ghillies are usually so taciturn that such an emotional performance startled me, and I recovered line trying not to smile.

Later, the riverkeeper explained that the modern Alta record is a 60-pound cockfish killed by the Earl of Dudley during the time he served as equerry to the late Duke of Windsor. Dudley was so unpopular for his treatment of the ghillies that he is the only foreign angler who ever fell into the Alta, having bellyflopped over a gunwale into the Kirkaplassen shallows. The riverkeeper and his boatman only smile when asked about the story that Dudley's baptism was a planned retribution, executed with a deft shift of balance in the Karasjok longboat.

"The Earl of Dudley was a difficult man," said the

riverkeeper. "We have watched dukes and princes and kings all our lives – and we knew that an equerry is only a ghillie in the world of palaces."

He explained that my boatmen had both wanted to share in a new record for the Alta, and to displace the Earl of Dudley as its holder. Both ghillies had been certain our huge cockfish was over 60 pounds.

The salmon had carried us down several pools, through a good two miles of river, and the unsuccessful fight had gone an hour and 40 minutes. We gathered ourselves with great disappointment, knowing we had failed the chance of a lifetime. It started to rain again, and the gloomy overcast hung 50 feet off the river. The night still held little promise.

"Let's try another place," I sighed.

Goddanienii lies just below the camp, where the foamy current works two hundred yards along the steep toe-faces of the Steinfjedet mountain. It eddies past a rockfall into the similar current called Goddanielo. We fished through both places twice because they had been extremely productive the week before, but there was only a two-pound breakfast grayling that took a salmon fly.

The Sautso water is filled with big grayling here, but even they were not dimpling for the tiny *Anisomera* midges that night. It is discouraging when even the grayling are dour.

"The river seems dead," I shook my head unhappily. "Not even a rise of grayling."

"Let's fish Velliniva," suggested the ghillie.

"Good pool?" I asked.

"It's the best pool at Sautso," he smiled. "We should move something there, even on a gloomy night like this."

"Let's go," I said.

Velliniva is a beautiful hourglass-shaped narrows in the Sautso beat. It was strangely still that night, and the overcast had lifted slightly. There are truck-sized boulders deep in the river, and a ledge crosses it in a series of shallows at the tail of the pool. It is the last place before the gathering currents above the Gabofoss rapids, the impassable reach of water that divides the Sandia and Sautso beats. Gabofoss is a holding-lie I never liked, as it seemed dangerous to row steadily only a cast-length away from a watery death. The ghillies often row simultaneously at the

End game: the final struggle of an Alta salmon.

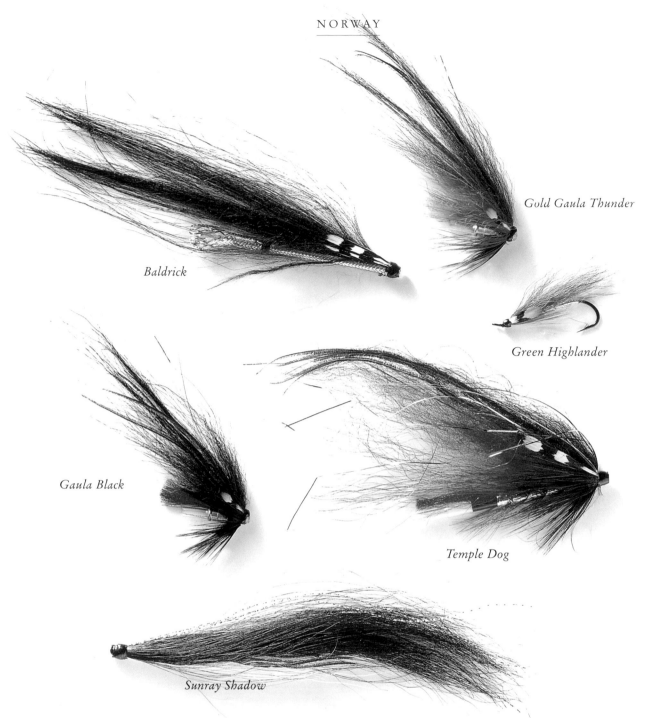

Baldrick

Gold Gaula Thunder

Green Highlander

Gaula Black

Temple Dog

Sunray Shadow

Gabo, watching the lip of the rapids warily to judge their remaining margin of safety.

We fished through both places without moving a salmon. It was getting lighter now and my watch read three o'clock. We started slowly upriver, discouraged with both the weather and our luck, and as our wake marred its still currents its mood seemed imperceptibly changed.

"Let's try Velliniva again," I suggested.

The boatman smiled. "We always try Velliniva on the way home," he explained. "And it's usually worth a serious try."

It was perfectly still, and the night turned strangely warm. Flies were hatching now, and the arctic terns appeared, capturing their fluttering prey in midflight. The smooth current seemed strangely alive while we rested Velliniva, and let its giant salmon forget the passage of the boat.

Twenty minutes passed. "Let's fish."

The fly-swing stopped on the third cast, and the still current bulged with another giant fish. "It's not like the Gytefisk we lost," I said, "but it's big!"

"Twenty kilos," said the ghillie.

The fight went well. I held the fish away from the boulders deep in the pool, and patiently worked it out of the main holding-lie. It did not jump again, and wasted its strength running upriver against the bellying line. The boatman gaffed it cleanly in less than 40 minutes.

"Just under twenty kilos," he said.

It was a fine cockfish, just beginning to lose its polished, sea-armored coloring with the first bronze-washed sheen of spawning. It did weigh just under 20 kilos, pulling my chatillon to the 43-pound mark. The ghillies bled the fish and laid it across the boat. It seemed like a perfect ending, and I started to take down my gear.

"*Nei*!" the ghillie shook his head. "We must fish the pool again after taking such a Gytefisk."

"Think there might be more?"

"*Ja*," they said.

Fifty yards below the holding-lie where the first salmon had taken, the silken currents are perceptibly swift, and the boatman increased his rhythms to lower us more slowly down the current. It made us cover the water with more closely spaced casts, and I realized they considered it the best place in the entire pool. The terns were still working the surface of the river, and the morning sun turned the overcast pink as it burned through the gloom.

Six casts fished out before there was an immense swirl, showing a guillotine-sized tail and a silvery flank that caught the morning light. The line tightened with a wrenching strain, and then the big salmon cartwheeled high, the bright-yellow Torrish clearly visible in its jaws.

"Good lord!" I shouted. "It's huge!"

It was another immense cockfish, pin-wheeling full length from the river and landing with a shattering splash that disturbed the entire pool.

Skree-jah! screamed the terns.

The fish jumped again, falling belly down like a giant marlin, and stripped a hundred yards of backing in a sullen run up the lake. We followed it grudgingly to recover line and hold our angle on the fish, but it turned with sudden, explosive power and bulldogged angrily past the boat. The reel shrieked and protested as the salmon gathered speed, and the pale backing blurred through the guides.

We turned the boat to follow, hoping the line would not foul in the boulders and ledges deep in the belly of the pool. The fish did not sound there, and our luck held. It threshed powerfully in the gathering tail-currents and was over the chutes into the big still-water downstream.

The fish had traveled a current-tongue too risky for our long boat, and we followed down another channel. While we negotiated it safely, the fish achieved a few moments of slack. The backing fouled on a shoal of stones. Its strength was largely spent, and unlike the monster salmon at the beginning of the night, our luck still held. The boatman worked carefully around the shoal while the ghillie in the stern plunged his boat-pole deep in the river, working until my fouled line came free.

The huge salmon was still hooked. It rolled weakly in the still currents now, and I pumped it close until the gaff went home. Its muscled bulk came threshing in over the side, and when a blow with the priest stilled its struggling, we saw it was even bigger than the fish that lay gleaming in the boat. It scaled almost 47 pounds, and I stood looking at the brace in disbelief. When we took a third fish of 39 pounds it seemed a strange anticlimax. After the last salmon was boated, the ghillie reverently examined the Torrish.

Its canary hackles were matted and worn, its hair-wing ragged and thinning. Two long spirals of loose tinsel had wound free of the body, and the frayed working silk revealed the hook. The ghillie cut it from the leader, held it high like a pagan offering and threw it far across the pool.

"It belongs to the river now," he said.

ENGLAND

"OFF HE GOES FOR THE OTHER SIDE OF THE RIVER, AND WE
WILL TAKE THIS OPPORTUNITY OF PULLING HIM DOWN-
STREAM PAST THAT GREAT MASS OF SNAGS AT THE NEXT POINT,
SO THAT WE MAY LAND HIM ON THE SANDY SPIT WHERE THE
DEVIL'S WATER COMES INTO THE MAIN STREAM. AGAIN AND
AGAIN HE REFUSES TO COME DOWN, AND FIGHTS HIS WAY UP
PAST THE SNAGS AND BROKEN WEIRING, BUT AT LAST HE IS GOT
PAST THE POINT AND IS SOON LANDED ON THE SAND, A COCK-
FISH WITH MANY SEA-LICE, BUT ALREADY SHOWING A FAINT
REDDISH AUTUMN COLOUR, AND WEIGHING 13 POUNDS."

From "One of Our Best Days" by A.H. Chaytor, 1908

ONE OF OUR BEST DAYS

by A.H. Chaytor, 1908

MY DEAR BOYS, – Now away with all this teaching: come with me to the fishing, and let us go again over one of our very best days. And so that the details may be fresh, we will take a day that is not only one of our best, but is also, at this present moment, only two days old.

Yesterday, September 6th, 1908, a flood stopped all fishing. This morning the river is very high, and is black as ink with the stained water coming off the peat that lies away up on the moorlands 40 miles away. It is still above fishing height, although it has already fallen many feet.

There is a good deal of dirt in the water, but we hope that it will run down into good order before evening. It is of no use to make an early start, but there may be a chance during the morning with a big minnow.

About ten o'clock Godfrey and I go up to the fishing hut. When we get there a drizzling rain is falling, the wind is from the southeast, and everything looks miserable. We each begin to fish with a

big five-inch phantom minnow well stuffed with bits of lead wire to make it sink as deeply as possible. We each fish the quietest water that we can find, going in opposite ways, and you two shall come with me.

For a long time we see nothing. Then suddenly in an eddy, just as the minnow is being lifted out, there is a slight swirl and a little flicking splash, and some fish has got the minnow and has bolted out into the current. Only a bull-trout, I expect. No! a good fish it is; look at that determined, vicious tugging and at the short, steel-centred rod doubling up, yet without bringing the fish to the surface even in that strong water.

Off he goes for the other side of the river, and we will take this opportunity of pulling him downstream past that great mass of snags at the next point, so that we may land him on the sandy spit where the Devil's Water comes into the main stream. Again and again he refuses to come down, and fights his way up past the snags and broken weiring, but at last he is got past the point and is soon landed on the sand, a cock-

"A cockfish, as bright as new-minted silver."

fish with many sea-lice, but already showing a faint reddish autumn colour, and weighing 13 pounds.

That eddy is a find. We will try it again. At the very tail of it, close under the bank, "jug" goes the rod and we are fast in another fish. This fellow makes no trouble whatever about going down past the snags to reach a landing-place. He, like the famous wife of Jack Spratt, prefers exactly the opposite course to his fellow, and he straightway bolts downstream and keeps on tearing off the line in repeated rushes as we run down the high, rough bank and scramble over a fence. Soon he has reached and passed the Devil's Water foot and is nearing the rapids which are some 70 yards below it. He means going through these rapids into the next pool, but today we cannot cross the Devil's Water anywhere near its mouth, and so at all costs he must not go down. Already he has taken more than 60 yards of line, and is out beyond some formidable stakes just above the rapids. The fish must break rather than be allowed to go any farther, so the line is seized and held fast. A fierce

splashing struggle in the glassy water above the rapid ends in favour of steel wire and sound tackle, and slowly the fish comes up and out of danger. His one great run has finished him, and within little more than five minutes of the hooking he is gaffed and weighed – 14 pounds – a cockfish, and as bright as new-minted silver.

We now put on long waders and go up the Devil's Water to cross it and fish the pool below. The river is very broad, and the Devil's Water, although high, is clear, so it looks as if the fish might see a fly below the junction. We go over the pool with a huge fly – a Jock Scott – and then with a great flaring yellow turkey. When that has proved vain we return to the spinning rod. The very first cast yields a most beautifully shaped cockfish of 24 pounds, which must have been lying in only a foot or two of water at the throat of the rush. There he grabs the minnow when it has been wound up to within ten feet of the rod point. Did you see me strike hard and firmly, keeping the rod low, and then raise the rod, letting the line fly off

"PRESENTLY HE TURNS DOWN AGAIN, WE FEEL THE LINE GRATE AND CATCH, THEN WE SEE THE FISH SPLASH, AND THE LINE COMES BACK LOOSE WITH THE TWISTED GUT OF THE CAST BROKEN ABOUT EIGHT INCHES FROM THE REEL LINE."

the reel almost unchecked? When a big fish takes on a very short line like this you must keep cool and strike firmly, and then instantly and freely let him have line, even at the risk of the reel overrunning, or of the line being slack for a second or two. If you try to hold the fish on this short line you will almost certainly lose him, and you will probably damage your rod as well.

A few casts lower down the pool a fish of 14 pounds seizes the minnow and is landed, and then after a long trial at the very tail of the pool a fish snatches the bait and goes off on a tremendous expedition. First he dashes madly round the pool, just breaking the surface with his tail, then he sets his face for the sea and hustles us downstream, at a run, for just short of half a mile, gradually getting near the opposite bank a hundred yards away, but all the time, or nearly so, keeping close to the surface in a most unusual way. He simply must be foul hooked. Finally he stops running, and after a long, wearisome jiggering is brought to shore and gaffed. He has the tail triangle in the corner of his mouth, but the other triangle is firmly fixed in his right pectoral fin, taking the whole pull of the line, and that seems to explain his activity and the power that he had in the strong stream, although he was by no means a large fish, weighing only 12 pounds.

It is now two o'clock, the rain is still falling and wet through we get back to the fishing hut to find that Godfrey, although using a precisely similar minnow, has been so unlucky as to have had no fish, not even a run from any fish.

We are both sick of minnowing, and we have kept the quietest and best pool till the afternoon in order to fish it with the fly. But this wind, now nearly due east, and the cold rain are disheartening, and it is past three o'clock when we begin again. Godfrey goes first with a very big Dusty Miller, and we follow with

Working a wet fly down and across on the River Coquet in Northumberland, England. The Coquet rises in the Cheviot Hills, and is a fine salmon river.

Nowadays instead of writing (as in the story) you'll probably 'phone to brag about a red-letter day to your children.

a small Jock Scott. In a moment a fish snatches the Dusty Miller, but the hook – badly tempered or perhaps lodging on a bone – opens out and lets him go. A big Popham is put on. Five minutes later a fish grabs it, and this time takes both the Popham and also half Godfrey's cast. Standing out in the stream with hands trembling with excitement, he ties on another Popham at the end of his remaining two feet of single gut, and, resolving not to strike again in such a stream, he begins anew, and after another 20 casts, hooks a good fish. This time all goes well, and in due season we gaff this fish, a real beauty of 18 pounds, and the biggest that he has caught so far. But better is to come for him. Again he begins the pool – a very strong dub – at the deepest part, and almost immediately hooks and presently lands a clinking good fish, weighing 20 pounds. Meanwhile, fishing with a small fly, we have not had even one rise, but on making an extra long cast to a shallow ledge in midstream, there is a big boiling rise, and the fly is snatched almost as it touches the water. The fish – of 17 or 18 pounds –

immediately begins flinging himself about – out of the water and head over heels in all directions. After a few minutes he changes his tactics and bores across the river, over many great boulders which, in a lower water, stand clear out, until he finds himself right under the willows that fringe the bank. Once he is safely got back into the stream, but he repeats the move, and this time he works his way for eight or ten yards upstream under the fringe of willows, his tail breaking the surface as he goes. Although the 18-foot rod is being held high, indeed with the reel overhead, yet there is a great length of line out, 70 or 80 yards, and a good deal is sagging in the water behind the fish. Presently he turns down again, we feel the line grate and catch, then we see the fish splash, and the line comes back loose with the twisted gut of the cast broken about eight inches from the reel line.

He is gone, and I really think we do not much grudge him his freedom; he has been such a gallant fighter. At least we say so on the spot, and try to think that we mean it.

Godfrey, who had come down to ply the gaff for us, goes back and instantly hooks and lands a grilse of seven pounds. This is reversing the fortunes of the morning with a vengeance. Since luncheon he has got three fish and lost two, and we have not landed one. So up goes a big Jock Scott in place of the lost small one, and in a very few minutes a heavy pull under water announces that the change has worked. Godfrey comes down and presently gaffs for us a good fish of 20 pounds. Then he himself begins to fish, and no sooner is his line out than a fish quite close inshore snatches his last Popham and breaks it off. Immediately he puts on the nearest fly that he has to the lost one, and at once gets hold of an exceedingly lively 14-pounder at the very same spot, and we hurry up the gravel bed to watch the fun and to gaff the fish for him, anxiously expecting to find the lost Popham in his jaws. He is landed right enough, but the other fly is not to be found, although we both feel perfectly certain that it is the same fish that took the first fly. We then return and begin casting again at the spot where we had taken the last fish, and 20 yards lower down there comes a slight touch. The cast is repeated and the touch becomes a violent pull, and we are fast in another good fish. He flings himself out once – twice – thrice, and then bolts down the long rapids into the next pool. There he wastes much precious time in a backwater, refusing either to fight hard or to come near the gaff. However, Godfrey, seeing the fight so long, comes down in time to gaff him for me. He proves to be just over 20 pounds, and he has taken quite 25 minutes to land. When we begin again the darkness is fast coming on, and we both fish down our big pool without a rise. Then, as a last chance, we rush off to try the tail of a pool higher up. Precious time is wasted in getting there, but the

The River Dart, a noted salmon stream which rises on Dartmoor in Devon, England.

94

chance turns out trumps, and we hook and safely land a nice fish of 18 pounds. It is now past seven o'clock and almost pitch dark, although the rain, which we hardly noticed in the keenness of our fishing, has stopped. The dogcart was to meet us at the crossroads at a quarter to seven, and it is hopeless to think of taking all these fish so far, so we must be content to get them to the fishing hut and leave them there for the night. But here are eight fish averaging about 16 pounds apiece, and we are half a mile above the hut. Well, Godfrey carries down the rods and baskets and I tie a stout cord through the jaw of one fish, then string the other seven upon the cord and simply wade down the half-mile of water, towing the fish behind me. The night is

" ... THE TOUCH BECOMES A VIOLENT PULL, AND WE ARE FAST IN ANOTHER GOOD FISH. HE FLINGS HIMSELF OUT ONCE – TWICE – THRICE, AND THEN BOLTS DOWN THE LONG RAPIDS INTO THE NEXT POOL. "

very dark, and as one wades down, most of the time waist deep in the dark river under the wooded banks, it is difficult to believe that these eight big fish are still upon the string. In the water they weigh, of course, absolutely nothing, although out of it they weigh together a good deal more than a hundredweight. Time and again one pulls them to the surface to convince oneself that they are really there, and yet in a few minutes the same curious conviction returns upon you that most of them must have slipped off by some means. It makes one realise a little better the folly of holding up a tired salmon – as one so often sees people do – in such a way that his head and shoulders are practically lifted out of the water. Many a fish, and

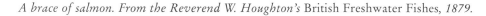

A brace of salmon. From the Reverend W. Houghton's British Freshwater Fishes, *1879.*

more especially many a grilse and small salmon, have we lost in this way. To you, my boys, I would say, never hold the head of any salmon or large fish out of the water, however tired he may be. When reeled up short, if the fish is on the surface, don't hold the rod point above him, but hold it sideways or downstream, so that it does not lift him upwards. If the rod is lifting any part of the fish's weight – that can only be so if some part of the fish is being held above water – then every kick that the fish gives, makes, as he falls back, a very sudden twanging jerk on the line and on the rod top; and if the hold is at all weakened by the fight it will almost certainly give way. After the first few struggles that follow the taking of the fly there is no stage of the fight at which so many fish are lost as that in which the tired fish is resisting the final efforts to bring him to shore, and the cause of loss is almost always a plain and preventible want of care. One forgets that on a very short line the jerks are ten times more sudden and more severe than they are when there is a fair length of line out and the rod is not doubled up like half a hoop.

Well, to return to our catch. Here we are at the fishing hut. Candle-ends are lighted, the fish are laid out on the floor, waders are taken off and rods taken down, and we hasten off to the dogcart and so home to mulled claret and hot baths, and a dinner that we are almost too tired to eat.

It has rained and blown all day, and next morning a flood in the river greets our earliest waking eyes. So the fish are sent for and brought home and are carefully weighed, and there being nothing to do at the

river we pass the time away by laying out the whole catch upon a grassy bank and taking a photograph of them.

We have rather blessed that flood since then, as without it we should not have had the photograph by which to remember that day. You may see it next this page. Godfrey's fish weighed 20, 18, 14, and seven pounds; ours 24, 20, 20, 18, 16, 14, 14, 13, and 12 pounds. His four weighed 59 pounds; our nine 151 pounds, an average of just upon 17 pounds apiece.

Before this we had once taken nine salmon and two bull-trout in a day, but the salmon were not such good fish as these, and the bull-trout hardly count. These fish were all beauties. Just look at them! I think that fish of 24 pounds, which you see near the middle of the picture, is as well-shaped and as hog-backed as you could wish any salmon, and so are the three 20-pounders on the right of him.

For real joy of success I do not think that this day could compare at all with my best spring day with five salmon landed on the fly and two more fish lost, or even with four fish taken on a day in March or April, but still it was a great day, and there was one glorious hour in it, for I have never known fish take the fly more madly than these did during a part of that miserably cold afternoon, although most of the rises did not come my way. The rain pelted steadily, and the wind, veering from southeast to east and then to northeast, blew more or less in our faces all day; the river was, as we usually think, too high for the fly, yet the fish that afternoon would not be denied. It was a glorious piece of luck,

"The River Test at Broadlands" by William Garfit. The River Test, in Hampshire, is one of England's finest chalk-stream salmon rivers, renowned for its large fish.

and all the more so because it was wholly unexpected. I hope that you may both be lucky enough to find such days, but they will not be many, so fish hard, and put on a good big fly after a flood. One other thing I have to say, don't be discouraged by rain or by an east wind – why, perhaps the very best day's salmon fishing of which we have any record was the 9th April, 1795, when the tenth Lord Home, fishing on the Dee, took 38 salmon, of weights ranging from six to 36 pounds, on his own 15-foot rod. One has read of catching grilse on the Grimersta, like troutlets, by the score, but Lord Home's day, even allowing for a large number of kelts, which were all lawful fish in those days, is, to my mind, a far greater performance. And that 9th April, of the year 1795 was a rainy day, with an east wind blowing. I wonder what salmon fisher's mind fails to bridge that hundred years. Can't you see the rain pattering on the grey water, ruffled by a cold wind, and a stout-hearted angler, long ago crumbled into dust, yet still, with his short rod and his thick hair line, fishing envied of us all? I think that it is the matter-of-fact description of ill weather on that long-past day that brings it so vividly to the eye.

A selection of traditional 19th-century gut-eyed salmon flies, tied on large single hooks, in a leather fly-wallet.

97

OCTOBER SALMON

by Ted Hughes, 1980

He's lying in poor water, a yard or so depth of poor safety,
Maybe only two feet under the no-protection of an outleaning small oak,
Half-under a tangle of brambles.

After his two thousand miles, he rests
Breathing in that lap of easy current
In his graveyard pool.
About six pounds weight,
Four years old at most, and hardly a winter at sea –
But already a veteran,
Already a death-patched hero. So quickly it's over!

So briefly he roamed the gallery of marvels!
Such sweet months, so richly embroidered into earth's beauty dress,
Her life-robe –
Now worn out with her tirelessness, her insatiable quest,
Hangs in the flow, a frayed scarf –

An autumnal pod of his flower,
The mere hull of his prime, shrunk at shoulder and flank,

With the sea-going Aurora Borealis of his April power –
The primrose and violet of that first uplifting in the estuary –
Ripened to muddy dregs,
The river reclaiming his sea-metals.

In the October light
He hangs there, patched with leper-cloths.

Death has already dressed him
In her clownish regimentals, her badges and decorations,
Mapping the completion of his service,
His face a ghoul-mask, a dinosaur of senility, and his whole body
A fungoid anemone of canker –

Can the caress of the water ease him?
The flow will not let up for a minute.

What a change! from that covenant of Polar Light
To his shroud in a gutter!
What a death-in-life – to be his own spectre!
His living body become death's puppet,
Dolled by death in her crude paints and drapes
He haunts his own staring vigil
And suffers the subjection, and the dumbness,
And the humiliation of the role!
And that is how it is,
That's what is going on there, under the scrubby oak tree, hour after hour,
That is what the splendour of the sea has come down to,
And the eye of ravenous joy – king of infinite liberty
In the flashing expanse, the bloom of sea-life,

On the surge-ride of energy, weightless,
Body simply the armature of energy
In that earliest sea-freedom, the savage amazement of life,
The salt mouthful of actual existence
With a strength like light –

Yet this was always with him. This was inscribed in his egg.
This chamber of horrors is also home.
He was probably hatched in this very pool.

And this was the only mother he ever had, this uneasy channel of minnows
Under the mill-wall, with the bicycle wheels, car-tyres, bottles
And sunk sheets of corrugated iron.
People walking their dogs trail their evening shadows across him.
If boys see him they will try to kill him.

All this, too, is stitched into the torn richness,
This epic poise
That holds him so steady in his wounds, so loyal to his doom, so patient
In the machinery of heaven.

WALES

"FISHING DEMANDS FAITH. FAITH LIKE ST PETER'S WHEN THE LORD BADE HIM CAST HIS HOOK INTO THE WATER AND CATCH A FISH FOR MONEY TO PAY TRIBUTE TO CAESAR. TO CATCH A FISH YOU HAVE GOT TO HAVE FAITH THAT THE WATER YOU ARE FISHING IN HAS GOT FISH IN IT, AND THAT YOU ARE GOING TO CATCH ONE OF THEM. YOU STILL MAY NOT CATCH ANYTHING; BUT YOU CERTAINLY WON'T IF YOU DON'T FISH YOUR BEST, AND YOU WON'T DO THIS WITHOUT FAITH TO INSPIRE YOU TO DO IT. YOU WON'T APPROACH THE WATER CAREFULLY. YOU WON'T STUDY THE WATER CAREFULLY. YOU WON'T CAST CAREFULLY. YOU WON'T FISH OUT YOUR CAST; TO DO THIS, PATIENCE IS REQUIRED, AND PATIENCE IS GROUNDED ON FAITH."

From The Spawning Run *by William Humphrey, 1970*

THE RIVER GOD

by Roland Pertwee, 1928

WHEN I WAS A LITTLE BOY I had a friend who was a colonel. He was not the kind of colonel you meet nowadays, who manages a motor showroom in the West End of London and wears crocodile shoes and a small moustache and who calls you "old man" and slaps your back, independent of the fact that you may have been no more than a private in the war. My colonel was of the older order that takes a third of a century and a lot of Indian sun and Madras curry in the making. A veteran of the Mutiny he was, and wore side whiskers to prove it. Once he came upon a number of sepoys conspiring mischief in a byre with a barrel of gunpowder. So he put the butt of his cheroot into the barrel and presently they all went to hell. That was the kind of man he was in the way of business.

In the way of pleasure he was very different. In the way of pleasure he wore an old Norfolk coat that smelt of heather and brine, and which had no elbows to speak of. And he wore a Sherlock Holmesy kind of cap with a swarm of salmon flies upon it, that to my boyish fancy was more splendid than a crown. I cannot remember his legs, because they were nearly always under water, hidden in great canvas waders. But once he sent me a photograph of himself riding on a tricycle, so I expect he had some knickerbockers, too, which would have been that tight kind, with box cloth under the knees. Boys don't take much stock of clothes. His head occupied my imagination. A big, brave, white-haired head with cherry-red rugose cheeks and honest, laughing, puckered eyes, with gunpowder marks in their corners.

People at the little Welsh fishing inn where we met said he was a bore; but I knew him to be a god and shall prove it.

I was ten years old and his best friend.

He was 70-something and my hero.

Properly I should not have mentioned my hero so soon in this narrative. He belongs to a later epoch, but sometimes it is forgivable to start with a boast, and now that I have committed myself I lack the courage to call upon my colonel to fall back two paces to the rear, quick march, and wait until he is wanted.

The real beginning takes place, as I remember, somewhere in Hampshire on the Grayshott Road, among sandy banks, sentinel firs and plum-coloured wastes of heather. Summer holiday time it was, and I was among folks whose names have since vanished like lizards under the stones of forgetfulness. Perhaps it was a picnic walk; perhaps I carried a basket and was told not to swing it for fear of bursting its cargo of ginger beer. In those days ginger beer had big bulgy corks held down with string. In a hot sun or under stress of too much agitation the string would break and the corks fly. Then there would be a merry foaming fountain and someone would get reproached.

One of our company had a fishing rod. He was a young man who, one day, was to be an uncle of mine. But that didn't concern me. What concerned me was the fishing rod and presently – perhaps because he felt he must keep in with the family – he let me carry it. To the fisherman born there is nothing so provoking of curiosity as a fishing rod in a case.

A salmon leap on the Ogwen River helps to improve this stream's run of autumn salmon.

Surreptitiously I opened the flap, which contained a small grass spear in a wee pocket, and, pulling down the case a little, I admired the beauties of the cork butt, with its gun-metal ferrule and reel rings and the exquisite frail slenderness of the two top joints.

"It's got two top joints – two!" I exclaimed ecstatically.

"Of course," said he. "All good trout rods have two."

I marvelled in silence at what seemed to me then a combination of extravagance and excellent precaution.

There must have been something inherently understanding and noble about that young man who would one day be my uncle, for, taking me by the arm, he sat me down on a tuft of heather and took the pieces of rod from the case and fitted them together. The rest of the company moved on and left me in Paradise.

It is 35 years ago since that moment and not one detail is forgotten. There sounds in my ears today as clearly as then, the faint, clear pop made by the little cork stoppers with their boxwood tops as they were withdrawn. I remember how, before fitting the pieces together, he rubbed the ferrules against the side of his nose to prevent them sticking. I remember looking up the length of it through a tunnel of sneck rings to the eyelet at the end. Not until he had fixed a reel and passed a line through the rings did he put the lovely thing into my hand. So light it was, so firm, so persuasive; such a thing alive – a sceptre. I could do no more than say "Oo!" and again, "Oo!"

"A thrill, ain't it?" said he.

I had no need to answer that. In my new-found rapture was only one sorrow – the knowledge that such happiness would not endure and that, all too soon, a blank and rodless future awaited me.

"They must be awfully – awfully 'spensive," I said.

"Couple of guineas," he replied offhandedly.

A couple of guineas! And we were poor folk and the future was more rodless than ever.

"Then I shall save and save and save," I said.

And my imagination started to add up twopence a week into guineas. Two hundred and forty pennies to the pound, multiplied by two – 480 – and then another 24 pennies – 504. Why, it would take a lifetime, and no sweets, no elastic for catapults, no penny novelty boxes or air-gun bullets or ices or anything. Tragedy must have been writ large upon my face, for he said suddenly, "When's your birthday?"

I was almost ashamed to tell him how soon it was. Perhaps he, too, was a little taken aback by its proximity, for that future uncle of mine was not so rich as uncles should be.

"We must see about it."

"But it wouldn't – it couldn't be one like that," I said.

I must have touched his pride, for he answered loftily, "Certainly it will."

In the fortnight that followed I walked on air and told everybody I had as good as got a couple-of-guineas rod.

No one can deceive a child, save the child himself, and when my birthday came and with it a long brown paper parcel, I knew, even before I had removed the wrappers, that this two-guinea rod was not worth the money. There was a brown linen case, it is true, but it was not a case with a neat compartment for each joint, nor was there a spear in the flap. There was only one top instead of two, and there were no popping little stoppers to protect the ferrules from dust and injury. The lower joint boasted no elegant cork handpiece, but was a tapered affair coarsely made, and rudely varnished. When I fitted the pieces together, what I balanced in my hand was tough and stodgy, rather than limber. The reel, which had come in a different parcel, was of wood. It had neither check nor brake, the line overran and backwound itself with distressing frequency.

I had not read and re-read Gamage's price list without knowing something of rods, and I did not need to look long at this rod before realizing that it was no match to the one I had handled on the Grayshott Road.

I believe at first a great sadness possessed me, but very presently imagination came to the rescue. For I told myself that I had only to think that this was the

The stately River Usk in front of the Gliffaes Hotel near Crickhowell, Powys, Wales.

The famous Salmon Pool on the Gliffaes water of the River Usk, as painted by William Garfit.

rod of all rods that I desired most and it would be so. And it was so.

Furthermore, I told myself that, in this great wide ignorant world, but few people existed with such expert knowledge of rods as I possessed. That I had but to say, "Here is the final word in good rods," and they would accept it as such.

Very confidently I tried the experiment on my mother, with inevitable success. From the depths of her affection and her ignorance on all such matters, she produced:

"It's a magnificent rod."

I went my way, knowing full well that she knew not what she said, but that she was kind.

With rather less confidence I approached my father, saying "Look, father! It cost two guineas. It's absolutely the best sort you can get."

And he, after waggling it a few moments in silence, quoted cryptically:

"There is nothing either good or bad but thinking makes it so."

Young as I was, I had some curiosity about words, and on any other occasion I would have called on him to explain. But this I did not do, but left hurriedly, for fear that he should explain.

In the two years that followed I fished every day in the slip of a back garden of our tiny London house. And, having regard to the fact that this rod was never fashioned to throw a fly, I acquired a pretty knack in the fullness of time and performed some glib casting at the nasturtiums and marigolds that flourished by the back wall.

My parent's fortunes must have been in the ascendant, I suppose, for I call to mind an unforgettable breakfast when my mother told me that father had decided that we should spend our summer holiday at a Welsh hotel on the River Lledr. The great place was called Pont-y-pant, and she showed me a picture of the hotel with a great knock-me-down river creaming past the front of it.

Although in my dreams I had heard fast water often enough, I had never seen it, and the knowledge that in a month's time I should wake with the music of a cataract in my ears was almost more than patience could endure.

In that exquisite, intolerable period of suspense I suffered as only childish longing and enthusiasm can suffer. Even the hank of gut that I bought and bent into innumerable casts failed to alleviate that suffering. I would walk for miles for a moment's delight captured in gluing my nose to the windows of tackleists' shops in the West End. I learned from my grandmother – a wise and calm old lady – how to make nets and, having mastered the art, I made myself a landing net. This I set up on a frame fashioned from a penny schoolmaster's cane bound to an old walking stick. It would have been pleasant to record that this was a good and serviceable net, but it was not. It flopped over in a very distressing fashion when called upon to lift the lightest weight. I had to confess to myself that I had more enthusiasm than skill in the manufacture of such articles.

At school there was a boy who had a fishing creel, which he swapped with me for a Swedish knife, a copy of *Rogues of the Fiery Cross*, and an Easter egg which I had kept on account of its rare beauty. He had forced a hard bargain and was sure he had the best of it, but I knew otherwise.

At last the great day dawned, and after infinite travel by train we reached our destination as the glow of sunset was greying into dark. The river was in spate, and as we crossed a tall stone bridge on our way to the hotel I heard it below me, barking and grumbling among great rocks. I was pretty far gone in tiredness, for I remember little else that night but a rod rack in the hall – a dozen rods of different sorts and sizes, with gaudy salmon flies, some nets, a gaff and an oak coffer upon which lay a freshly caught

> " AT THE THICK END OF AN IMMENSE SALMON ROD THERE STRODE OUT INTO THE SUNLIGHT THE NOBLEST FIGURE I HAD EVER SEEN. "

salmon on a blue ashet. Then supper by candlelight, bed, a glitter of stars through the open window, and the ceaseless drumming of water.

By six o'clock next morning I was on the river bank, fitting my rod together and watching in awe the great brown ribbon of water go fleetly by.

Among my most treasured possessions were half a dozen flies, and two of these I attached to the cast with exquisite care. While so engaged, a shadow fell on the grass beside me and, looking up, I beheld a lank, shabby individual with a walrus moustache and an unhealthy face who, the night before, had helped with our luggage at the station.

"Water's too heavy for flies," said he, with an uptilting inflection. "This evening, yes; now, no – none whateffer. Better try with a woorum in the burrun."

He pointed at a busy little brook which tumbled down the steep hillside and joined the main stream at the garden end.

"C-couldn't I fish with a fly in the – the burrun?" I asked, for although I wanted to catch a fish very badly, for honour's sake I would fain take it on a fly.

"Indeed, no," he replied, slanting the tone of his voice skyward. "You cootn't. Neffer. And that isn't a fly rod whateffer."

"It is," I replied hotly. "Yes, it is."

But he only shook his head and repeated, "No," and took the rod from my hand and illustrated its awkwardness and handed it back with a wretched laugh.

If he had pitched me into the river I should have been happier.

"It is a fly rod and it cost two guineas," I said, and my lower lip trembled.

"Neffer," he repeated. "Five shillings would be too much."

Even a small boy is entitled to some dignity.

Picking up my basket, I turned without another

word and made for the hotel. Perhaps my eyes were blinded with tears, for I was about to plunge into the dark hall when a great, rough, kindly voice arrested me with:

"Easy does it."

At the thick end of an immense salmon rod there strode out into the sunlight the noblest figure I had ever seen.

There is no real need to describe my colonel again – I have done so already – but the temptation is too great. Standing in the doorway, the 16-foot rod in hand, the

deer-stalker hat, besprent with flies, crowning his shaggy head, the waders, like seven-league boots, braced up to his armpits, the creel across his shoulder, a gaff across his back, he looked what he was – a god. His eyes met mine with that kind of smile one good man keeps for another.

"An early start," he said. "Any luck, old fellar?"

I told him I hadn't started – not yet.

"Wise chap," said he. "Water's a bit heavy for trouting. It'll soon run down, though. Let's vet those flies of yours."

He took my rod and whipped it expertly.

"A nice piece – new, eh?"

"N-not quite," I stammered; "but I haven't used it yet, sir, in water."

That god read men's minds.

"I know – garden practice; capital; nothing like it."

Releasing my cast, he frowned critically over the flies – a Blue Dun and a March Brown.

"Think so?" he queried. "You don't think it's a shade late in the season for these fancies?" I said I thought perhaps it was. "Yes, I think you're right," said he. "I believe in this big water you'd do better with a livelier pattern. Teal and Red, Cock-y-bundy, Greenwell's Glory."

I said nothing, but nodded gravely at these brave names.

Once more he read my thoughts and saw through the wicker sides of my creel a great emptiness.

"I expect you've fished most in southern rivers. These Welsh trout have a fancy for a spot of colour."

He rummaged in the pocket of his Norfolk jacket and produced a round tin which once had held saddle soap.

"Collar on to that," said he; "there's a proper pickle of flies and casts in that tin that, as a keen fisherman, you won't mind sorting out. Still they may come in useful."

Action awaits this traditional tube fly tied to a treble hook.

"But, I say, you don't mean –" I began.

"Yes, go in; stick to it. All fishermen are members of the same club and I'm giving the trout a rest for a bit." His eyes ranged the hills and trees opposite. "I must be getting on with it before the sun's too high."

Waving his free hand, he strode away and presently was lost to view at a bend in the road.

I think my mother was a little piqued by my abstraction during breakfast. My eyes never, for an instant, deserted the round tin box which lay open beside my plate. Within it were a paradise and a hundred miracles all tangled together in the pleasantest disorder. My mother said something about a lovely walk over the hills, but I had other plans, which included a very glorious hour which should be spent untangling and wrapping up in neat squares of paper my new treasures.

"I suppose he knows best what he wants to do," she said.

So it came about that I was left alone and betook myself to a sheltered spot behind a rock where all the delicious disorder was remedied and I could take stock of what was mine.

I am sure there were at least six casts all set up with flies, and ever so many loose flies and one great stout, tapered cast, with a salmon fly upon it, that was so rich in splendour that I doubted if my benefactor could really have known that it was there.

I felt almost guilty at owning so much, and not until I had done full justice to everything did I fasten a new cast to my line and go a-fishing.

There is a lot said and written about beginners' luck, but none of it came my way. Indeed, I spent most of the morning extricating my line from the most fearsome tangles. I had no skill in throwing a cast with two droppers upon it and I found it was an art not to be learned in a minute. Then, from over eagerness, I was too snappy with my back cast, whereby, before many minutes had gone, I heard that warning crack behind me that betokens the loss of a tail fly. I must have spent half an hour searching the meadow for that lost fly and finding it not. Which is not strange, for I wonder has any fisherman ever found that lost fly. The reeds, buttercups, and the little people with many legs who run in the wet grass conspire together to keep the secret of its hiding place. I gave up at last, and with a feeling of shame that was only proper, I invested a new fly on the point of my cast and set to work again, but more warily.

In that hard racing water a good strain was put upon my rod, and before the morning was out it was creaking at the joints in a way that kept my heart continually in my mouth. It is the duty of a rod to work in a single smooth action and by no means to divide its performance into three sections of activity. It is a hard task for any angler to persuade his line austerely if his rod behaves thus.

When, at last, my father strolled up the river bank, walking, to his shame, much nearer the water than a good fisherman should, my nerves were jumpy from apprehension.

"Come along. Food's ready. Done any good?" said he.

Again it was to his discredit that he put his food before sport, but I told him I had had a wonderful morning, and he was glad.

"What do you want to do this afternoon, old man?" he asked.

"Fish," I said.

"But you can't always fish," he said.

I told him I could, and I was right and have proved it for 30 years and more.

"Well, well," he said, "please yourself, but isn't it dull not catching anything?"

And I said, as I've said a thousand times since, "As if it could be."

So that afternoon I went downstream instead of up, and found myself in difficult country where the river boiled between the narrows of two hills. Stunted oaks overhung the water and great boulders opposed its flow. Presently I came to a sort of natural flight of steps – a pool and a cascade three times repeated – and there, watching the maniac fury of the waters in awe and wonderment, I saw the most stirring sight in my young life. I saw a silver salmon leap superbly from the cauldron below into the pool above. And I saw another and another salmon do likewise. And I wonder the eyes of me did not fall out of my head.

I cannot say how long I stayed watching that gallant pageant of leaping fish – in ecstasy there is no measure of time – but at last it came upon me that all the salmon in the sea were careering past me and that if I were to realise my soul's desire I must hasten to the pool below before the last of them had gone by.

It was a mad adventure, for until I had discovered that stout cast, with the gaudy fly attached in the tin box, I had given no thought to such noble quarry. My recent possessions had put ideas into my head above my station and beyond my powers. Failure, however, means little to the young and, walking fast, yet gingerly, for fear of breaking my rod top against a tree, I followed the path downstream until I came to a great basin of water into which, through a narrow throat, the river thundered like a storm.

At the head of the pool was a plate of rock scored by the nails of fishermen's boots, and here I sat me down to wait while the salmon cast, removed from its wrapper, was allowed to soak and soften in a puddle left by the rain.

And while I waited a salmon rolled not ten yards from where I sat. Head and tail, up and down he went, a great monster of a fish, sporting and deriding me.

With that performance so near at hand, I have often wondered how I was able to control my fingers well enough to tie a figure-eight knot between the line and the cast. But I did, and I'm proud to be able to record it. Your true-born angler does not go blindly to work until he has first satisfied his conscience. There is a pride, in knots, of which the laity knows

> "I WONDER HAS ANY FISHERMAN EVER FOUND THAT LOST FLY. THE REEDS, BUTTERCUPS, AND THE LITTLE PEOPLE WITH MANY LEGS WHO RUN IN THE WET GRASS CONSPIRE TO KEEP THE SECRET OF ITS HIDING PLACE."

nothing, and if, through neglect to tie them rightly, failure and loss should result, pride may not be restored nor conscience salved by the plea of eagerness. With my trembling fingers I bent the knot and, with a pummelling heart, launched the line into the broken water at the throat of the pool.

At first the mere tug of the water against that large fly was so thrilling to me that it was hard to believe that I had not hooked a whale. The trembling line swung round in a wide arc into a calm eddy below where I stood. Before casting afresh I shot a glance over my shoulder to assure myself there was no limb of a tree behind me to foul the fly. And this was a gallant cast, true and straight, with a couple of yards more length than its predecessor, and a wider radius. Instinctively I knew, as if the surface had been marked with an X where the salmon had risen, that my fly must pass right over the spot. As it swung by, my nerves were strained like piano wires. I think I knew something tremendous, impossible, terrifying, was going to happen. The sense, the certitude was so strong in me that I half opened my mouth to shout a warning to the monster, not to.

I must have felt very, very young in that moment. I, who that same day had been talked to as a man by a man among men. The years were stripped from me and I was what I was – ten years old and appalled. And then, with the suddenness of a rocket, it happened. The water was cut into a swathe. I remember a silver loop bearing downward – a bright, shining, vanishing thing like the bobbin of my mother's sewing machine – and a tug. I shall never forget the viciousness of that tug. I had my fingers tight upon the line, so I got the full force of it. To counteract a tendency to go headfirst into the spinning water below, I threw myself backward and sat down on the hard rock with a jar that shut my teeth on my tongue – like the jaws of a trap.

Luckily I had let the rod go out straight with the line, else it must have snapped in the first frenzy of the downstream rush. Little ass that I was, I tried to check the speeding line with my forefinger, with the result that it cut and burnt me to the bone. There wasn't above 20 yards of line in the reel, and the wretched contrivance was trying to be rid of the line even faster than the fish was wrenching it out. Heaven knows why it didn't snarl, for great loops and whorls were whirling, like Catherine wheels, under my wrist. An instant's glance revealed the terrifying fact that there was not more than half a dozen yards left on the reel and the fish showed no sign of abating his rush. With the realisation of impending and inevitable catastrophe upon me, I launched a yell for help, which, rising above the roar of the waters, went echoing down the gorge.

And then, to add to my terrors, the salmon leaped – a winging leap like a silver arch appearing and instantly disappearing upon the broken surface. So mighty, so all-powerful he seemed in that sublime moment that I lost all sense of reason and raised the rod, with a sudden jerk, above my head.

Hair-Wing Silver Doctor

Usk Grub

Stoat Tail

I have often wondered, had the rod actually been the two-guinea rod my imagination claimed for it, whether it could have withstood the strain thus violently and unreasonably imposed upon it. The wretched thing that I held so grimly never even put up a fight. It snapped at the ferrule of the lower joint and plunged like a toboggan down the slanting line, to vanish into the black depths of the water.

My horror at this calamity was so profound that I was lost even to the consciousness that the last of my line had run out. A couple of vicious tugs advised me of this awful truth. Then, snap! The line parted at the reel, flickered out through the rings and was gone. I was left with nothing but the butt of a broken rod in my hand and an agony of mind that even now I cannot recall without emotion.

I am not ashamed to confess that I cried. I lay down on the rock, with my cheek in the puddle where I had soaked the cast, and plenished it with my tears. For what had the future left for me but a cut and burning finger, a badly bumped behind, the single joint of a broken rod and no faith in uncles? How long I lay there weeping I do not know. Ages, perhaps, or minutes, or seconds.

I was roused by a rough hand on my shoulder and a kindly voice demanding, "Hurt yourself, Ike Walton?"

Blinking away my tears, I pointed at my broken rod with a bleeding forefinger.

"Come! This is bad luck," said my colonel, his face grave as a stone. "How did it happen?"

"I c-caught a s-salmon."

"You what?" said he.

"I d-did," I said.

He looked at me long and earnestly; then, taking my injured hand, he looked at that and nodded.

"The poor groundlings who can find no better use for a river than something to put a bridge over think all fishermen are liars," said he. "But we know better, eh? By the bumps and breaks and cuts I'd say you made a plucky fight against heavy odds. Let's hear all about it."

So, with his arm round my shoulders and his great shaggy head near to mine, I told him all about it.

At the end he gave me a mighty and comforting squeeze, and he said, "The loss of one's first big fish is the heaviest loss I know. One feels, whatever happens, onc'll never –" He stopped and pointed dramatically.

The Pont Aberglaslyn in northern Wales, from Reverend W. Houghton's British Freshwater Fishes, *1879.*

"There it goes – see! Down there at the tail of the pool!"

In the broken water where the pool emptied itself into the shallows beyond, I saw the top joints of my rod dancing on the surface.

"Come on!" he shouted, and gripping my hand, jerked me to my feet. "Scatter your legs! There's just a chance!"

Dragging me after him, we raced along by the river path to the end of the pool, where, on a narrow promontory of grass, his enormous salmon rod was lying.

"Now," he said, picking it up and making the line whistle to and fro in the air with sublime authority, "keep your eyes skinned on those shallows for another glimpse of it."

A second later I was shouting, "There! There!"

He must have seen the rod point at the same moment, for his line flowed out and the big fly hit the water with a plop not a couple of feet from the spot.

He let it ride on the current, playing it with a sensitive touch like the brushwork of an artist.

"Half a jiffy!" he exclaimed at last. "Wait! Yes, I think so. Cut down to that rock and see if I haven't fished up the line."

I needed no second invitation, and presently was yelling, "Yes – yes, you have!"

"Stretch yourself out then and collar hold of it."

With the most exquisite care he navigated the line to where I lay stretched upon the rock. Then:

"Right you are! Good lad! I'm coming down."

Considering his age, he leaped the rocks like a chamois.

"Now," he said, and took the wet line delicately between his forefinger and thumb. One end trailed limply downstream, but the other end seemed anchored in the big pool where I had had my unequal and disastrous contest.

Looking into his face, I saw a sudden light of excitement dancing in his eyes.

"Odd," he muttered, "but not impossible."

"What isn't?" I asked breathlessly.

"Well, it looks to me as if the joints of that rod of yours have gone downstream."

Gingerly, he pulled up the line, and presently an end with a broken knot appeared.

"The reel knot, eh?" I nodded gloomily. "Then we lose the rod," said he. That wasn't very heartening news. "On the other hand, it's just possible the fish is still on – sulking."

"Oo!" I exclaimed.

"Now, steady does it," he warned, "and give me my rod."

Taking a pair of clippers from his pocket, he cut his own line just above the cast.

"Can you tie a knot?" he asked.

"Yes," I nodded.

"Come on, then; bend your line onto mine. Quick as lightning."

Under his critical eye, I joined the two lines with a blood knot. "I guessed you were a fisherman," he said, nodded approvingly and clipped off the ends.

"And now to know the best or the worst."

I shall never forget the music of that check reel or the suspense with which I watched as, with the butt of the rod bearing against the hollow of his thigh, he steadily wound up the wet slack line. Every instant I expected it to come drifting downstream, but it didn't. Presently it rose in a tight slant from the pool above.

"Snagged, I'm afraid," he said, and worked the rod with an easy straining motion to and fro. "Yes, I'm afraid – no, by Lord Bobs, he's on!"

I think it was only right and proper that I should have launched a yell of triumph as, with the spoken word, the point at which the line cut the water shifted magically from the left side of the pool to the right.

"And a fish too," said he.

In the 15 minutes that followed, I must have experienced every known form of terror and delight.

"Youngster," he said, "you should be doing this, by rights, but I'm afraid the rod's a bit above your weight."

"Oh, go on and catch him," I pleaded.

"And so I will," he promised; "unship the gaff,

young un, and stand by to use it, and if you break the cast we'll never speak to each other again, and that's a bet."

But I didn't break the cast. The noble, courageous, indomitable example of my river god lent me skill and precision beyond my years. When at long last a weary, beaten, silver monster rolled within reach of my arm into a shallow eddy, the steel gaff shot out fair and true, and sank home.

And then I was lying on the grass, with my arms around a salmon that weighed 22 pounds on the scale and contained every sort of happiness known to a boy.

And best of all, my river god shook hands with me and called me "partner".

That evening the salmon was placed upon the blue ashet in the hall, bearing a little card with its weight and my name upon it.

And I am afraid I sat on a chair facing it, for ever so long, so that I could hear what other anglers had to say as they passed by. I was sitting there when my colonel put his head out of his private sitting room and beckoned me to come in.

"A true fisherman lives in the future, not the past, old man," said he; "though, for this once, it 'ud be a shame to reproach you."

I suppose I coloured guiltily – at any rate, I hope so.

"We got the fish," said he, "but we lost the rod, and a future without a rod doesn't bear thinking of. Now" – and he pointed at a long wooden box on the floor, that overflowed with rods of different sorts and sizes – "rummage among those. Take your time and see if you can find anything to suit you."

"But you mean – can I –"

"We're partners, aren't we? And p'r'aps as such you'd rather we went through our stock together."

"Oo, sir," I said.

"Here, quit that," he ordered gruffly. "By Lord Bobs, if a show like this afternoon's don't deserve a medal, what does? Now, here's a handy piece by

*Before and after: a box of flies to catch a salmon
and a "priest" to administer final rites.*

Hardy – a light and useful tool – or if you fancy greenheart in preference to split bamboo –"

I have the rod to this day, and I count it among my dearest treasures. And to this day I have a flick of the wrist that was his legacy. I have, too, some small skill in dressing flies, the elements of which were learned in his company by candlelight after the day's work was over. And I have countless memories of that month-long, month-short friendship – the closest most perfect friendship, perhaps, of all my life.

He came to the station and saw me off. How I vividly remember his shaggy head at the window, with the whiskered cheeks and the gunpowder marks at the corners of his eyes! I didn't cry, although I wanted to awfully. We were partners and shook hands. I never saw him again, although on my birth-

days I would have coloured cards from him, with Irish, Scotch and Norwegian postmarks. Very brief they were: "Water very low." "Took a good fish last Thursday." "Been prawning, but don't like it."

Sometimes at Christmas I had gifts – a reel, a tapered line, a fly book. But I never saw him again.

Came at last no more cards or gifts, but in the *Fishing Gazette*, of which I was a religious reader, was an obituary telling how one of the last of the Mutiny veterans had joined the great majority. It seems he had been fishing half an hour before he died. He had taken his rod down and passed out. They had buried him at Totnes, overlooking the River Dart.

So he was no more – my river god – and what was left of him they had put in a box and buried it in the earth.

But that isn't true; nor is it true that I never saw him again. For I seldom go a-fishing but that I meet him on the river banks.

The banks of a river are frequented by a strange company and are full of mysterious and murmurous sounds – the cluck and laughter of water, the piping of birds, the hum of insects, and the whispering of wind in the willows. What should prevent a man in such a place having a word and speech with another who is not there? So much of fishing lies in imagination, and mine needs little stretching to give my river god a living form.

"With this ripple," says he, "you should do well."

"And what's it to be," say I – "Blue Upright, Red Spinner? What's your fancy, sir?"

Spirits never grow old. He has begun to take an interest in dry-fly methods – that river god of mine, with his seven-league boots, his shaggy head, and the gaff across his back.

FROM
"THE SPAWNING RUN"

by William Humphrey, 1970

June 1st, Wales.

FISHING DEMANDS FAITH. Faith like St Peter's when the Lord bade him cast his hook into the water and catch a fish for money to pay tribute to Caesar. To catch a fish you have got to have faith that the water you are fishing in has got fish in it, and that you are going to catch one of them. You still may not catch anything; but you certainly won't if you don't fish your best, and you won't do this without faith to inspire you to do it. You won't approach the water carefully. You won't study the water carefully. You won't cast carefully. You won't fish out your cast; to do this, patience is required, and patience is grounded on faith. You won't fish each stretch of the water thoroughly before giving up on it and moving to the next stretch. The satisfactions of a day's fishing are deep; and just as deep on a day when you don't catch a fish; but unless you keep faith that you are going to catch a fish that day, then fishing seems a waste – a waste of time, money, effort, and, most depressing, a waste of spirit. Faith and faith alone can guard the fisherman against a demon of which he is particularly the prey, the demon of self-irony, from acquiescence in the opinion of the ignorant that he is making a fool of himself. Few things can make a man more fully a man than fishing, if he has got faith; nothing can make a man feel more fully a fool if he has not got faith.

After nine days of fishing the Teme without once getting a nibble I had lost my faith. Not my faith that there were fish in the river. They were there, all right. With my own eyes I had seen, and with my own knife and fork had eaten, a miraculous draught of Teme

> "FEW THINGS CAN MAKE A MAN MORE FULLY A MAN THAN FISHING, IF HE HAS GOT FAITH ..."

fishes. The fish were there; I had lost my faith that I was going to catch one of them, and my cup of self-irony ranneth over. I cast and I cast and I cast again with that big heavy rod, I beat those waters until my wrists swelled and stiffened and ached me all night long while the peahen screamed, and I marveled how Holloway could make shift to keep on at this drudgery even as a camouflage to the pleasures that he returns here to possesse (*sic*) himself of.

Then this afternoon, defeated, deflated, and dejected, heedless in my approach, clomping along the bank in my heavy, hobnailed boots and casting my shadow I cared not where – the first shadow I had been able to cast since coming into Wales – I came to a bend in the river where the undercutting of the bank by the current made a pool and into this pool I did not cast my Green Highlander, I dismissed it there, with leave to go where it would on its own; I didn't care if I never saw it again.

The big fly lighted at the head of the pool near the opposite bank and quickly sank. Absently I watched the line swing out into the current. I saw it stop. I was hooked on a snag. In my mood this was all I needed and, lowering my rod I grasped the line to break the fly off, disjoint my rod, and go home. But I was using a heavy leader, one bigger in the tippet than any leader I had ever used in my trout fishing back home was in the butt, and it would not break. I gave another angry yank, whereupon my line began to move. I thought I had dislodged the snag from the riverbed and was still hooked to it, until I reflected that an object dislodged from the riverbed would move downstream with the current, not upstream. I had

Could this be a "taker"? Salmon are frustratingly capricious. Painting by Roger McPhail.

had a strike and had struck back without even know-ing it and had hooked the biggest fish of my life.

I reeled in the slack line and raised my rod. He was still on. His run was short. He had gone to the bottom to sulk and I could not budge him. When I put the butt of the rod to him and saw the rod bow and heard the line tighten and felt his size and strength, a sense of my unworthiness came over me and I was smitten with guilt and contrition.

I didn't deserve to land this fish. Fishing without faith, I had done nothing as it ought to be done. He had hooked himself – I just happened to be holding the other end of the line. I pictured him lying there on the riverbed in all his unseen silvery majesty. How mysterious and marvelous a creature he was! I thought how far he had come to get here and of the obstacles he had braved and bested. While keeping pressure on him with my rod held high, I thought of the towering falls he had leapt, driven by the over-mastering urge to breed and perpetuate his kind. And here was I about to kill him before he could achieve the hard-won consummation of his desire. It was the king of fish I was about to assassinate. I felt like a cur.

How often in books published by the most rep-utable houses, with editors who verify their authors' every assertion, had I read with soul dilated of one of that greathearted breed of dry-fly ascetics who, every time he caught Old Methuselah, the venerable yard-long brown trout of Potts' Pool, put him back – until under cover of darkness one night a clod armed with nightcrawlers and a clothesline unblushingly yanked Old Methuselah out and brained him with a car jack and the magic of Potts' Pool departed for ever. I said to my soul now, I won't gaff him. A fish as noble as this deserved a better end than poached in milk or jellied in aspic and garnished with blobs of mayonnaise. I could see myself already, this evening at the hotel, smiling a wistful smile when my fat and fish-fed fellow guests commiserated with me on my day after penning their entries in the logbook. For when I had fought this fish into submission, when I had mastered his valiant spirit with my own even more valiant one, when he turned over and lay floating belly-up at my

Salmon rest until the smell of fresh rain compels them upriver again. Painting by Roger McPhail.

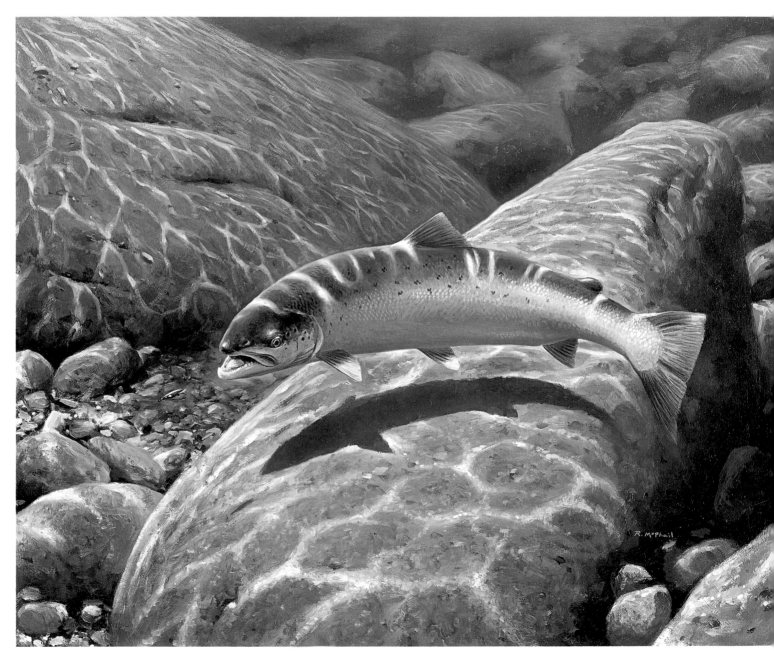

feet, I would carefully extract the hook and hold him right-side-up and facing into the current until he got his breath back, and then I would bid him go, finned friend, go, my brother, and do not slink in shame, go in pride and intact, gallant old warrior, go, and eschew Green Highlanders.

I would like hell. I sometimes return a little fish to the water, but I leave it to those knights of the outdoors who contribute articles to the sporting magazines, and who catch so many more of them than I ever will, to put back big ones.

I raised my rod so high it quivered; still the fish clung stubbornly to his spot. Every once in a while the fish would give a little shake of his head, transmitted to me through the taut line, as if to test whether he still had me hooked. I held on. He would let minutes pass, then would wallow and shake his head as if he were enjoying this. It was like having a bull by the ring in his nose and being afraid to let go of it. At one point, resting one of my wrists by holding the end of the rod between my legs, I had a moment of wild wonder at myself, at the question I had just asked myself: did I really want to catch a fish this big? Heretical thought for a fisherman; yet I could not relate this to fishing as I knew it. I was used to exulting when I netted a 14-inch trout weighing a pound and a quarter. Now my hopes had been overfulfilled. Truth was, I was scared of the sea monster that I had – or that had me – on the line and couldn't get off.

After 15 minutes my fish began to move. The drag on my reel was set to just under the breaking strength of my leader, yet he stripped line from the reel with the speed that made the ratchet buzz like a doorbell. I was not wading but was on the bank; now I began to run along the bank – I should say, I was dragged along it. When he had gone 150 yards upstream – with me giving him precious line at one point so I could negotiate a fence stile, then sprinting, in hobnailed hip boots, to regain it – he braked, shook his head, then turned and sped downstream 150 yards, taking me back over the fence stile. I still had not seen him, and the slant of my line in the water told me I was not going to see him for some time to come. He was deep, hugging the river bottom.

For 45 minutes he kept this up – I clambered over that fence stile six times from both directions – growing an inch longer and a pound heavier in my mind – my wrists, too – each minute. When he quit it was not gradually, it was all at once, as if he had fought with every ounce of his strength and all his determination up to the very end. I stepped into the shallow water at the edge, and, gaining line, began reeling him toward me. Even his unresisting weight strained my big rod. Ten feet from where I stood his dorsal fin broke water. It was three feet back from where my line entered the water, three feet back from it the tip of his tail broke the surface. My mouth was dry with desire. I gaffed him. Or rather, I made a pass at him with the gaff, nicked him, he turned, lunged, and was gone. The line snapped back and wound itself around the rod like a vine. My leader had parted at one of the blood knots I had so tightly tied. There was something detestable in the very shape – curly, coiled, kinky – of the end I was left holding. Imagine a pig the size of a penny and he would have a tail just like that.

IRELAND

"The doctor's audience was now where he wanted it, the one half-skeptical, yet curious, the other brimming with anticipation and willing to believe. He lit a cigarette and leaned back in his chair. 'First, I must warn you,' he said, 'that things can happen in Ireland which could not occur in England or the United States. Just why this is I do not know, nor would I hazard a guess. Some people claim that it is atmospheric, that it has to do with the juxtaposition of the Gulf Stream and the Arctic winds. Others believe that it is an ancient hyperphysical inheritance from the earliest Celtic tribes.'"

From "The Rajah's Rock" by Paul Hyde Bonner, 1954

THE RAJAH'S ROCK

by Paul Hyde Bonner, 1954

THE FINAL BEAT OF THE OWENMORE before it flows into the tidewater is as delightfully varied as a fisherman's dream. It starts with a pool so broad and calm and edged with reeds and lily pads that one might call it a small lake, or lough, as they spell it in Ireland. Salmon do not lie there as a rule, although cruising ones that show occasionally on the edge of the reeds often tempt a fisherman to take a boat out and try for them, without success, as fish on the move are rarely, if ever, interested in a fly or a spinner. The shores of this lake are rough, heathery hillocks, devoid of trees or shrubs and inhabited by scraggy blackface highland sheep. Two streams flow out of this large pool, forming an island in the river, a fat, egg-shaped island of about five acres which is remarkable for three features: it is an oasis of verdant grass and shrubs and stunted oak and beech in a landscape of rocks and heather; it has on its near shore one solitary boulder, round, smooth, about ten feet high, and looking like the egg of some giant prehistoric bird; and it is inhabited throughout the summer by a lone donkey. This great boulder, like a bastion, surveys the left-hand (looking downstream) branch of the river and is known locally

as the Rajah's Rock. Just why it is so called you will learn in due time. It is enough for the moment to remark that this portion of the left-hand branch which rounds the island is a favorite holding ground for salmon. Here they are apt to lie in numbers, not in company front as they do in some pools, but in file along the deep, narrow channel between the waving rows of weed.

Below the island, from the point where the two streams meet until one reaches the long rapid that descends to tidewater, the whole character of the water and the landscape changes. Instead of the gentle flow and the peaceful upland country, there is a noisy, foam-lashed torrent that dashes over rocks, forms black, slick pools in a wild and jagged canyon from which the fair landscape of Connemara is hidden. But it is no place for a fisherman who is not sure-footed, with a steady head and an ability to Spey or loop cast. One has to have the agility of a mountain goat and an expert's control of the line to stand on a slippery rock at the base of the canyon cliff and get a fly over a fish in such a way that he might be tempted.

It was certainly nothing for Mrs Evans, and she

Irish flies against stone: an Irish gillie will encourage you to try something bright, bushy, and small.

knew it and so did her husband and Tom Walsh, the ghillie. When they had parked the car and walked down the hill to the little stone bridge by the luncheon hut, which is at the dividing line between the gentle and wild halves of the beat, Mrs Evans had said, after one glance, "If you expect me to fish down there you're mistaken."

"'Twould be better that you fished the Rajah's Rock, madam," Tom Walsh said.

"Where is that?" Jim Evans asked.

It was their first day on the Owenmore and everything was a little strange and unreal. Only two days before Jim and Gertrude Evans had left their home in Greenwich, Connecticut, and, via Idlewild and Gander, had reached Shannon Airport where a drive-yourself car had met them and they had motored the hundred miles north to the Cashel Hotel in Connemara. For years they had fished together in New Brunswick and Nova Scotia, but this was different. There were no deep forests, no cabins in a birch grove, no red-shirted, leather-booted guides, no long boats in which to be paddled or rowed to a pool. It seemed unlikely to them that the same variety of Atlantic salmon which they had stalked and fought for years in sombre, woodland rivers could inhabit this picture-book stream in an open, rolling country with neat white cottages behind towering hedges of fuchsia. The layout was quaint, but improbable. They had thought so, although neither had expressed the thought, when they had entered the hotel on the previous evening and found it comfortable to the point of luxury with its broad lounge full of deep chairs and couches, its billiard-room bar, its bright dining room with a bouquet of flowers on each table and the water running piping hot in their own bathroom. Then there had been the park about the hotel with its great old beeches and its garden bordered with rhododendron and the river flowing quietly at the foot of a flower-bordered terrace. The sole encouragement had been the long rack in the stair hall, half filled with salmon rods, not little ten-foot rods like their own, but great two-handed poles, 12 to 16 feet in length. Surely, they had thought, guests would not bring those cumbersome weapons here unless there were salmon to be caught. Then, before dinner, when they had gone to the billiard-room bar for a cocktail, they had seen the evidence. On a marble-top table against the oak panelling of the wall lay seven fine salmon, each one with a card placed on its broad side on which was written the name of the fisherman, the beat where it was killed, and the variety of lure used.

Tom Walsh unlocked the door of the hut and put the picnic basket on the table inside. When he came out again, he pointed upstream in the direction of the island. "It'll be up there a piece," he said. "No more'n a short walk."

"Do you wish us to start there?" Jim Evans asked. He believed in following a guide's advice on water with which he was unfamiliar.

"You can do as you're a mind," the ghillie said. He was a tall, lanky man in a threadbare jacket of Connemara tweed and patched trousers that were stuck into a pair of short waders which were covered with vulcanized patches of red rubber. "There's plenty of fish from the bridge down, but the goin' will be rough for the lady."

"Now, Tom," Evans said to the ghillie pleasantly but firmly. "We are going to put ourselves in your hands. We've never fished this river and we know nothing about it. You're the guide on this reach and you tell us what to do." Jim Evans was a lawyer with a precise, orderly mind. He liked things planned, and once the plans were laid, he liked to stick to them.

Tom Walsh eyed him skeptically. "Is it that you'll both be wanting to fish at the same time?" he asked.

"That's up to you," Jim said firmly. "You tell us who is to fish where and when."

"What fly have you on?" the ghillie asked, looking at Gertrude Evans.

"I have a Mar Lodge," Mrs Evans answered. Most fishermen have superstitions about patterns and

Gertrude Evans was no exception. Ever since she had killed an 18-pound salmon on the Miramichi with a Mar Lodge, she was convinced that it was a fly of deadly virtuosity.

"A good fly it is – at times," Tom Walsh said, picking up her rod which was leaning against the side of the hut and examining the fly. "I'm thinkin' that with the brightness the way it is, mebbe they'll fancy a bit of blue. Have you your flybox, sir?"

Jim Evans fished in the sack that was hanging from his shoulder and brought out an aluminum box which he handed to the ghillie. Tom fingered them over thoughtfully, then picked out a low-water Teal and Silver and, without saying a word, took out a pair of scissors, nipped off the Mar Lodge and bent on the new fly. He had barely finished tying the knot when the air was shattered by a hoarse, panting scream.

Gertrude Evans jumped. "Good God! What's that?" she exclaimed.

"Joe, the donkey, it is," Tom Walsh said, a faint smile wrinkling the corners of his beady blue eyes. He gave the fly a strong tug against the nylon leader to make sure that the knot was strong. "Come, madam," he said, putting the barb of the fly into the cork of the handle and picking up his gaff. "We might be risin' a fish at the Rajah's Rock."

"A donkey?" Gertrude said, incredulous. "Can a donkey make a noise like that?"

Jim Evans laughed. "You gave yourself away that time, you little city urchin," he said to his wife. "Have you never heard a donkey bray?"

"Never. I've only read about it," Gertrude said, starting after the ghillie.

"Am I to fish here, or go with you?" Jim called to Tom who was walking rapidly on up the path.

Tom turned his head without slowing his pace. "Better you be comin' with us," he said. "There's likely a fish for the two of ye."

When they had gone about two hundred yards, the path brought them to the rise of a hillock from which they could see the island. It came suddenly into view without warning, a luxuriant oasis, framed by the two streams, and on its edge, like the stone of a ring, the great round rock.

Gertrude stopped to admire. "Oh, Jim, isn't it lovely? But look, there's someone there ahead of us."

Jim had already seen the figure standing on the top of the round boulder. It took him a few seconds to make out that it was a puce-colored donkey, faced directly toward them so that its body and hindquarters were hidden by its thick neck and chest. Then its

ears, which had been attentively, inquisitively erect, started to flap back and forth.

"Whoever it is, he's waving to us," Gertrude said.

Jim laughed. "You need glasses, honey. That's the donkey."

His wife shaded her eyes from the glare as she looked again carefully. She laughed, too. "Of course it is. How funny. It looked just like a little man in tweeds standing there."

"Dr Melrose," Jim said, laughing. "Wait till I tell him you mistook him for a donkey." Dr Melrose was a short, stocky Englishman they had met in the bar the evening before. He had come in from fishing wearing tan corduroys and a Harris-tweed jacket.

They hurried up the path now to catch up with Tom who was almost at the stream by the rock. Jim was carrying his own rod and the canvas sack with his flies and leaders and the other bits of equipment which a practiced fisherman always has with him. He was a pleasant, clean-cut looking man of 55, getting a little round in the belly, as sedentary American businessmen are apt to. The skin of his smooth-shaven face was still the opaque of the commuting lawyer. It would be a week before the wind and the sun would give it a pink tone, but it would never achieve that ruddy glow which the sportsmen of the British Isles seem to maintain the year round, even though their holidays were no more protracted than his. His clothes, too, tagged him unquestionably. The canvas jacket, the red flannel lumberman's shirt, the khaki breeches with elastic knitted cuffs which he wore inside his laced rubber boots, and his tight-fitting cap with its stiff, outsize peak were clearly out of the northeast woodlands and the catalogue of Mr L.L. Bean. They were as strange to County Galway as the *dhoti* of a Hindu.

With Gertrude dressed identically in every detail – they always bought their fishing clothes at the same time and to match – they looked like twins, or rather

The irrepressible waters of the Delphi in Connemara, Ireland.

like members of the same outing club, for Gertrude, who was only 48, was thin and wiry, with a parchment-like, outdoor complexion that came from constant and passionate gardening. They had wondered why everyone in the dining room that morning at breakfast had stared at them so intently, and they had put it down to new faces, and not to their oufits, as they should have.

When they caught up with Tom Walsh, he was standing by the bank at the point where the left-hand stream flows out of the little lake. The great round rock was opposite them a bit downstream, with the donkey still standing on its pinnacle, switching his scrawny tail against the flies and watching them intently, his ears forward stiffly, emphasizing his concentration.

"Why, the donkey is on the island!" Gertrude said, suddenly realizing that the rock was not accessible to their shore except by boat.

"Does he swim across?" Jim Evans asked the ghillie.

"No, sir, he don't," Tom replied.

"Then how did he get there?" Jim asked.

"I ferry him across in the boat," Tom answered.

"And just leave him there?" Gertrude exclaimed, shocked by the poor beast's enforced exile.

"That I do, for the summer indeed," Tom said. "He's plenty of grass to feed on over there, and he don't be gettin' into any mischief."

"He's your donkey?" Jim asked.

"That he is," Tom answered. "And a sinful one at that." He handed Gertrude her rod. "Now, madam, will you be fishin' that bit of water right out there. You mark where the waves is heaviest from the wind.

Juner Shrimp

Hairy Mary

Irish General Practitioner

Connemara Black

Wilkinson Shrimp

That'll be the channel down the middle where the fish lie. 'Twould be best to put your fly on the far side of it and let the current be takin' it down. And mind the weeds when it swings too near this bank."

Tom watched her appraisingly as she stripped line from her reel and false cast until her fly could reach the center of the stream. He could see at once that she knew what she was doing, and he was pleased. The costumes of the couple and the little, ten-foot rods had filled him with misgivings. He had a deepseated distrust of tyros, even though they be Americans, for he had a special sympathy for the United States what with so many of the family there.

"Another foot or two will do it," he said to Mrs Evans, eager to assist now that he saw that she could drift a salmon fly on a greased line.

Gertrude stripped more line and cast again. As the fly hit the water the donkey let out another ear-splitting bray. The noise was so great, with the donkey not more than a hundred yards from them, and so unexpected that Gertrude almost dropped her rod. "Good God!" she said, her hand shaking so that the rod tip quivered. "He frightened me to death. I could feel my heart stop."

"He be tellin' us that the salmon is further downstream," Tom said. "Keep fishing along – one step to each cast."

Gertrude Evans laughed as she cast again. "That's wonderful! Did you hear that, Jim? Tom says that the donkey was trying to tell us that the salmon are further down."

Jim, who was sitting on a hummock of heather below them, grinned. "He's right, too. I saw one roll right out here in front of me. Only I wish he'd whis-

The River Blackwater, Ireland: its water runs dark, but the fish are bright.

per his messages instead of splitting my eardrums. Tom, I didn't know that your Irish leprechauns were that noisy."

"They told you, did they, sir?" Tom said, not taking his eyes from the fly and the water.

"Told me what?" Jim asked.

"That Joe was a leprechaun," Tom replied, pronouncing it "leprehawn." "That he is, as sure as he's standin' there watchin' the fish."

The donkey uttered a couple of short, tentative grunts as if he were getting up steam for another bray.

"Easy now, madam," Tom cautioned. "You be over a fish as will be takin'."

"Did you see him?" Gertrude asked, casting again skillfully, gently over the same spot.

"I did not, but Joe did, " Tom said almost in a whisper.

A salmon boiled at the fly, erupting the surface of the stream, and Gertrude, reacting too quickly, as one is apt to do on the first day out each season, jerked her rod tip and the fly swung high in the air and landed in the heather behind her.

"What a pity!" Jim called. "That was a nice fish."

"Did you prick him, madam?" Tom asked.

Gertrude was about to answer when she saw the donkey stamping his right front foot on the rock as if he were thoroughly disgusted with her. She shook her rod at the beast angrily. "No comments from you, please," she yelled, then started to reel in her line. "No, I didn't prick him," she said to Tom with a sigh of disappointment. "I never gave him a chance to get it in his mouth. I jerked it right away from him."

"We'll give him a bit of a rest," Tom said consolingly. "Like as not he'll be comin' again."

Gertrude sat down on the grass and lit a cigarette. "You come up here and have a try at him," she called to her husband.

"Nothing doing," Jim said. "He's your fish. He likes your fly."

"Is that what they call the Rajah's Rock?"

Taking time as the fly slows, and a salmon makes up its mind. Painting by Roger McPhail.

Gertrude asked the ghillie, pointing to the great boulder on which the donkey stood.

"It is," Tom replied.

"How did it get that name?"

Tom Walsh's beady eyes that were watching the water crinkled into a smile. "An old story it is. I was only a bit of a lad at the time and me father was then the ghillie on this beat. One of them Indian princes let the river for a season. The Rajah of Baypoor they

used to call him. A heathen he was, but not a bad man. One day he was fishin' right where you raised your salmon – there, facin' the big rock – when he gets his fly into a giant of a big spring fish. He was an impatient sort of a man, likin' to do things in a hurry. When he'd seen what he had on his line, he started bearin' hard on the fish to keep him from headin' into the lough. Oh, many's the time I've heard me father tell the story. How he kept sayin' to the Rajah, 'Easy now, your Highness. Be lettin' him have line, your Excellency. Keep his head outa the weeds, sir. Don't be pullin' him so strong! Ach, you've lost him, you bastard!'"

Gertrude laughed heartily. "What a marvelous story! So the rock is a monument to the Rajah's lost fish. I think that's wonderful. He was a really big salmon, was he?"

"Thirty-seven pounds four ounces when he was sold in the market at Clifden," Tom said.

"But you said the Rajah lost him."

"That he did, but me uncle, Joe Walsh – may his soul rest in peace – caught him the following night."

The donkey started again to grunt the preliminary bars of his song.

"Come on, madam," Tom said. "Joe says that salmon is ready to have another go at your Teal and Silver."

Gertrude threw away her cigarette and stood up. She picked up her rod and started casting upstream, as far away as possible from the spot where she had had the rise, until she had out the right amount of line. Then precisely, holding her rod at the top of the swing long enough to let the line change its arc behind her, she cast so that her fly would travel the same route as before. When the salmon came, she was prepared. She let him take it and turn before she came up with a smart twitch of the rod tip.

The battle was a good one, although she could have done with slightly less advice. Tom Walsh confined his brief remarks to warnings about weed and the danger of letting him get into the lake where he might take all of the line and backing. Her husband, whose steady, thoughtful character had a way of changing, of becoming emotional and excited whenever she had a salmon on, dashed up to stand near her, telling her to reel in, to hold her rod tip up, to let the fish go, to mind her footing, in a voice so loud anyone might have thought she was deaf. And Joe, the donkey, made his own comments with sighs, grunts and violent flapping of his ears.

In the end Tom Walsh stepped down into the shallow edge of the stream and gaffed the salmon skilfully, swinging its wriggling body over on to the grass of the bank where he held it securely while he gave the *coup de grâce* with the blackthorn handle of the gaff. It was a well-formed henfish with a good depth in the belly and weighed, on Jim's hand scales, just under nine pounds.

"My first Irish salmon," Gertrude said proudly as the three of them stood looking down at the beautiful silver fish which lay at their feet in the grass.

Jim Evans was about to remark that the sea lice were still on it when he was interrupted by another rending bray from Joe.

"Is he congratulating me?" Gertrude asked the ghillie when the horrifying noise had subsided into a series of short, squeaking gasps.

"Might be he is," Tom said, glancing at the donkey on the opposite shore. "He's an eye for the ladies." The donkey shifted his position, pricking up his ears and looking at a spot downstream of them. "'Tis likely, too, that he sees another takin' fish."

Jim walked back into the heather and picked up his rod. He tried to move calmly, with measured tread, but the anticipation forced him to hurry. "Damn it, Tom," he said, annoyed with himself for succumbing to the excitement, which a sober lawyer should never do, that is, not where he can be observed by other eyes, "you've got me believing that Joe is really trying to give us a tip. Where does he want me to fish?"

Tom Walsh smiled. "Pity he ain't a man. He'd be a powerful poacher. As it is I have to be putting him on the island all summer to keep him from stealin'."

"Can't you tie him up?" Gertrude asked, still feeling sorry for the exile.

"There ain't a knot known to man he can't untie with the teeth of him," the ghillie answered. "And once he's loose he'll be stealin' corn and sugar and apples and pears from every byre and cottage within a mile of Cushatrower. Oh, a wicked, cute beast he is."

"What do you do with him in winter?" Gertrude asked.

The donkey brayed again, ruling out talk.

"I had better get going," Jim Evans said, believing now that the donkey was urging him, although cross with himself for believing.

"Pay no mind to him, sir," Tom said. "Like all thieves, 'tis impatient he is. 'Twill do no harm to let the pool quiet down a bit after the last fish." He turned to Gertrude. "In winter, madam, he's plenty of work to do, haulin' turf and takin' the car to Roundstone. He's kept tight in a box in me byre, which no man can get out of from the inside, let alone a schemin' donkey."

"Can't you keep him there in summer, too?" Gertrude asked.

"And let him be eatin' his head off of corn and turnips? No, madam, only a rich man, like Mr Evans now, or me brother Paddy who owns a pub in New York, could afford that. He's fine where he is, with plenty of grass to eat and the salmon to watch."

"Okay. Let's go. Where do I start fishing?" Jim said impatiently.

"You might be startin' right there where the missus left off," Tom said. "Fish it along as she did, sir, a step to each cast."

It was a repetition of the first performance. When Jim had progressed about four yards downstream, covering the water expertly, Joe had uttered his three or four grunting coughs and on the next cast Jim was fast to a salmon. He fought it well, although he had a tendency to horse it. Gertrude noted this and worried that the leader might part at the hook, but she said nothing. She was a wise woman who realized that husbands dislike wifely advice in the heat of a contest, or in the presence of others. He brought it to gaff finally, after 15 minutes of struggle. It was not as big a fish as Gertrude's, weighing only about seven and a half pounds, but it had been a strong, dashing fighter and Jim was proud and happy as he surveyed it on the grass.

Dr Melrose was in the billiard-room bar when they came in at six that evening, followed by Tom and the two salmon. They had not touched a fish after Jim had killed his before lunch. The wind had dropped entirely and the sun had made the still water too bright. But they were happy with their brace, and not ashamed to have them placed on the official scales and ticketed by Tom as he laid them on the marble slab. They read the legends with pride – "The Island Beat. 8 lbs 14 oz. Teal & Silver. Mrs James Evans." and "The Island Beat. 7 lbs 6 oz. Silver Doctor. Mr James Evans."

"Jolly good!" Dr Melrose said, peering between them at the salmon. "Where were they taken, Tom?" he asked the ghillie.

"At the Rajah's Rock, sir," Tom replied.

"Ah! Fine spot that when the water's right," the doctor said. "Needs a breeze of wind, though."

"We had it, sir, for the morning only," Tom said, then touched his forelock to Jim and Gertrude. "Well, sir, goodnight, sir. Goodnight, madam. It'll be time for me to be pedallin' home."

"Can't I buy you a drink, Tom?" Jim asked.

"Thank you, sir, but I'd best be on my way. 'Tis a good ride I have on my bicycle back to the Island Beat."

"Do you live there?" Gertrude asked.

"I do. Over the hill and beyond the hut."

Jim took two pound notes out of his pocket and folded them up. "Thanks for a splendid day, Tom," he said, shaking hands with the ghillie and giving him the money at the same time.

"And thank Joe for me, Tom," Gertrude said. "The next time we fish your beat, which will be a week from Friday, I'm going to bring him some sugar and a carrot."

Tom shook his head. "Mind you don't be too good to him. He's easy spoilt, that rogue of a Joe is."

When Tom had left, Jim rang for the barman and asked Dr Melrose to join them in a drink. The three of them drew up chairs around a little table in the corner of the room.

Jim started laughing softly to himself.

"What's so funny?" Gertrude asked.

"That story of Tom's about the donkey," Jim answered. "Of all the Irish malarky I ever heard that beats anything. And to think that I fell for it, believed that Joe was actually telling me where the salmon were lying."

"So Joe performed for you, did he?" the doctor said. "Jolly lucky you are. He won't do it for everyone."

"It's a good show, anyway," Jim said, still laughing. "The trick is, of course, that the keen fisherman is usually tensed with excitement when he's on the river. This tends to give him an emotional lift which clouds his ability to reason. The donkey brays, a salmon takes his fly, and he is in a frame of euphoria to believe that the beast has supernatural powers."

"I don't care what you say, Jim," his wife stated firmly, "that donkey guided me to my salmon. Do you remember when he brayed while I was fishing up at the top? Remember that Tom said to me, 'He's saying the fish is further down, so walk along, a cast at each step'?"

"Sure. It was Tom who knew where the fish was," Jim said. "He'd probably seen a flash with those keen eyes of his. The donkey on the rock is just part of the act, the leprechaun touch to give the visiting fishermen a taste of Irish folklore, and to get a bigger tip for Tom Walsh."

"How about those little snorts he gave just before my salmon rose?" Gertrude persisted. "He did it again before you hooked yours."

Jim winked at the doctor, as if to say, we hardheaded males are not taken in by such fairy tales. "Tom probably waved his gaff, gave him some sort of a signal to sound off." He turned to Dr Melrose. "Has Tom ever put on this show for you?"

"Oh yes, two or three times in past years," the doctor replied. "But, you know, I should hardly call it Tom's show, unless, of course, you mean that Tom puts Joe on the island to help him make a good job of the fishing."

"Just as I say – for added interest, to keep the customers happy," Jim said.

"No, I don't mean that," Dr Melrose said quietly, weighing his words. "I mean that he uses Joe as an actual aid, as an indicator of fish in the Rajah's Rock pool."

The barman brought the drinks, a gin-and-tonic for Gertrude and whisky-and-sodas for the men.

The doctor lifted his glass to the two Americans. "Congratulations!" he said.

"And thanks to Joe," Gertrude said.

"You don't mean to tell me, Doctor, that you think Joe actually sees the fish and notifies Tom," Jim said, finding it hard to believe that any sober physician could be taken in by a ghillie's little joke.

Dr Melrose sipped his drink and put it down on the table before answering. "Oh, I'm convinced that he does. But that is not all of it, for as you have seen and I have experienced, he does not indicate just any salmon lying in the channel, and, with the water as it is now, there might well be twenty three. By some means which I will not attempt to explain he gives notice only when a salmon is ready and eager to take. It may be that a taking fish is more restless than the others and flashes about way down there where Joe from his high perch can see him. That is one theory, but I do not altogether fancy it. It has been my experience over many years of fishing that the restless fish is the least inclined to take. If that is true, then one must assume that Joe can detect the inner impulse of a given salmon by some supersensory perception. That animals have such gifts, far beyond anything of which man is capable, is well known to science."

"Granted," Jim Evans said, "but why should a donkey have any instincts related to fish? He doesn't eat them. He doesn't fear them. They live in a water world totally unrelated to his life and habits."

"Righto," Dr Melrose said with a smile. "As you say, the whole performance is so illogical as to appear to a practical American to be a hoax. And that brings us to another realm, a realm that is uniquely Irish. I might even say, uniquely Connemara. Tell me, just what did Tom tell you about Joe and the Rajah's Rock?"

"He told us ... " Jim began.

"He told me," Gertrude interrupted. "I don't think you heard it all, Jim. He told me that Joe was a thief who had to be exiled to the island during the summer to keep him from stealing from other people's barns and cottages. He said that Joe could untie with his teeth any knot one could put on his halter rope."

"Did he tell you how the rock got its name?" the doctor asked her.

Gertrude laughed. "Indeed he did. The story about the Indian prince and the big salmon he lost. Very funny, I thought. 'You've lost him, you bastard!'"

Dr Melrose chuckled. "Yes, it is a good story, although it loses somewhat from repetition. It is the most popular anecdote in this part of the country. They never seem to tire of telling it. Naturally old Mike Walsh, Tom's father, never said those words, but I'm quite prepared to believe that he thought them and much worse ones. Did he tell you how the salmon was finally caught?"

"I believe he said his uncle caught it the next night," Gertrude answered. "It seems it weighed over thirty seven pounds."

"And did he tell you the sequel?" Melrose asked.

"What sequel?"

"What happened to the late Joe Walsh as a result of that bit of poaching," the doctor replied.

"No, he didn't tell me that."

Dr Melrose took a long drink, then put his glass down on the table while his hazel-brown eyes behind his spectacles flicked back and forth from Jim to Gertrude.

"Aren't we getting away from the donkey?" Jim asked, believing that the doctor had got himself out on

> "AND AS THE STORY SPREAD, IT WAS NATURAL THAT THE SIZE OF THE FISH GREW UNTIL IT BECAME AS BIG AS ANYTHING EVER SEEN IN NORWAY. WELL, THIS WAS TOO MUCH FOR THE ARTFUL JOE."

an untenable limb and was trying to lead them off on a new branch.

"Quite the contrary," Melrose said, his eyes twinkling, sensing Jim's suspicion. "The fate of Joe Walsh is the nub of the story. It explains everything, even that brace of fine, fresh-run salmon on the marble over there."

"Oh, do tell us. I'm fascinated," Gertrude exclaimed impatiently.

The doctor's audience was now where he wanted it, the one half-skeptical, yet curious, the other brimming with anticipation and willing to believe. He lit a cigarette and leaned back in his chair. "First, I must warn you," he said, "that things can happen in Ireland which could not occur in England or the United States. Just why this is I do not know, nor would I hazard a guess. Some people claim that it is atmospheric, that it has to do with the juxtaposition of the Gulf Stream and the Arctic winds. Others believe that it is an ancient hyperphysical inheritance from the earliest Celtic tribes. Be that as it may, we doctors know that belief can produce fact. A psychosomatic illness, for example, can be as real and as fatal as any strictly pathological one. You are Americans. In America, as your Miss Gertrude Stein has said, a rose is a rose is a rose. Donkeys and fish do not communicate there except through the medium of Mr Walt Disney. You told me last evening that this was your first visit to Ireland. If you will pardon my saying so, you are both still wrapped in sterilized cellophane. In a matter of hours you were whisked from New York to the highlands of Connemara. Then, in a few more hours you were subjected to an occurrence which, as seen through your American insulation, seems improbable and fantastic. So I must suggest to you that you rip off the cellophane and listen to this story through Irish ears.

"In 1923 this hotel, which was then a country house, and the river belonged to Lord Balater. As he was then in India on a special mission for the Viceroy, he let this place for the summer to the Maharajah of Baipur, a keen sportsman and, from all accounts, a very genial, attractive chap. I believe it was more or less of a swap – Baipur was to have the Owenmore fishing and Cashel House, and Balater was to have one of the Prince's minor palaces, together with the tiger and sandgrouse shooting. At that time Michael Walsh of storied fame was the ghillie on the Island Beat, as his son, Tom, is today. Mike was a good and faithful ghillie who bore on his shoulders a very heavy burden. He was the brother of Joseph Walsh who was known from Clifden to Galway as the greatest and most cunning poacher in Connemara. To say that Mike disapproved of his brother's profession would be an understatement. It shocked and horrified him

that any man, let alone his brother, would stoop to thieving salmon from private water. Curse him and berate him he did, but he could hardly call the constable against his own flesh and blood. However, it was well understood between them that the Island Beat was strictly off limits for Joe's pursuits. Mike had made it quite clear that if he ever caught Joe on his territory, he would turn him in to the police.

"Of course the story of Baipur's lost fish was all over the countryside within an hour. Even those famous injunctions which Mike is supposed to have given to the Maharajah were thought up by some wit in the Cushatrower pub that very day. And as the story spread, it was natural that the size of the fish grew until it became as big as anything ever seen in Norway. Well, this was too much for the artful Joe. When he heard the stories of a salmon that weighed in the neighborhood of fifty or sixty pounds, he quickly

Heading for home after a long day on Connemara's Lough Mask.

calculated that at six shillings a pound a veritable fortune was lying in wait in the cool waters off the island. Yes, it was the very size of the fish that did him in. Had it been of normal size for these waters, say even twenty pounds, he might well have got away with it. As it was, the minute he showed the fish to the fishmonger in Clifden the jig was up. Like lightning, word came back to Cushatrower that Joe had snagged Baipur's salmon. When Mike heard it, he boiled over. Without saying a word to his wife or his children he got on his bike and pedaled to the house of Father O'Malley, the parish priest of Balinafad. With a face so drawn with anger that it would have frightened the Pope, he called upon the good priest to accompany him to Cushatrower pub, where he knew his brother would be standing drinks to all on the proceeds of his sale. Father O'Malley wanted to know what the trouble was, thinking it might be a drunken brawl, which was more rightly a matter for the constable. When Mike said that it had to do with his brother Joe, the priest guessed at once that it was an affair of poaching.

A last cast into the sunset on an Irish lough. Many of Ireland's massive stillwaters hold salmon.

"You see, good old Mike, in spite of his threats, could still not bring himself to put his brother into the hands of the law. He first had to try the Church, and then the salmon's owner. What he really wanted, I feel sure, was Father O'Malley's moral support while he denounced his brother to the Maharajah. Well, they found Joe right enough, and the two of them took him,

much against his wish as you may surmise, straight here to Cashel House.

"The scene that took place here has been described many times. One has to make allowances for the native proclivities of Irish storytellers to embellish and ornament. From a distillation of the various versions, the facts would appear to be more or less as follows:

"Baipur, quite alone and not encumbered by secretaries and retailers as Indian princes are apt to be, brought the three Irishmen into this billiard room and bade them sit down – probably right here where we are sitting this minute. Mike, who still was boiling with anger, at once accused his brother of having poached the very salmon which Baipur had lost on the previous day. He gave the weight of the fish and said that it had been sold to Mr Joyce, the fishmonger in Clifden, who could confirm the weight and the fact that a small, number-ten Silver Doctor had been found embedded in the fish's lower jaw. The Prince then asked Joe if the accusation was true. Had Father O'Malley not been there, the chances are that Joe would have hotly denied it. The presence of the priest was too much for him. He knew that he would have to confess his guilt anyway the coming Sunday, so the words of denial stuck in his throat. He merely lowered his head and said nothing.

"Baipur then assumed his most princely manner and proceeded to pronounce judgment. It was true, he said, that he had hooked an exceptionally large salmon in the pool beneath the rock on a small Silver Doctor, and that the fish had broken the cast. It had been a noble salmon worthy of a fine sportsman, a better one than he, who in his eagerness had put too great a strain on the tackle. It made him sad, he said, to think of that splendid fish being wrenched from the stream in the night by a miserable poacher and sold in the market for anyone to eat. Such things were against the laws of God and man, and the thief would receive his just punishment.

"Here he turned to Father O'Malley and said, 'You are a Christian, Father, whereas I am a Hindu, or to be exact, a Brahmin. You teach, I believe, that the soul of man, when it passes from this earth, goes to a purgatory where it is purified or punished in accordance with its mortal behavior, and thence to an eventual Heaven or Hell. The Vedic abode of temporary sojourn is indeed similar to your purgatory. There, also, the departed spirit is blessed or punished. But from this point our beliefs take different roads – yours to Heaven and Hell, and mine to another chance on earth to atone and struggle up the long road to Brahma. Our teachings tell us that the soul of a poacher would be directed by Yama into the body of an humble beast, probably a poor beast of burden, and as such he would have to atone for the sin of stealing the fish of others.

"'But this is a matter for the all-powerful Deity,' he went on as Father O'Malley crossed himself against any heathen taint. 'I may do no more,' he said, 'than pronounce an earthly punishment for one who has illegally taken my salmon. So, Joseph Walsh, I order you to give to Father O'Malley, for the use of his Church, all the money which you received from the sale of that fish, and to obtain from Mr Joyce, the fishmonger, that Silver Doctor, and to wear it in your hat as long as you shall live.'

"With that, he arose and walked with dignity out of the room, looking every inch the potentate in his well-cut Harris tweeds and his turban of baby blue silk."

Dr Melrose reached for his glass and poured the last of the whisky down his throat.

"Did Joe Walsh do as he was told?" Gertrude asked.

"Indeed he did," the doctor replied. "Father O'Malley saw to that. But the damage to his pride was too much for him. The taunts and jibes that were piled on him when he went to the Cushatrower pub with that fly in his cap were more than he could take. He soon ceased to be seen about, staying at home in his cottage and never appearing beyond his hedge before he had made sure there was no one on the road. Then the chagrin made him sickly and rheumatic, and the next winter he caught pneumonia and died in the night before Father O'Malley could reach his bedside for a final absolution."

Dr Melrose stopped to light a fresh cigarette, but it was clear from the smile on his face that he had not finished.

"It was on his way home from the funeral and wake that Mike heard strange noises in his barn and went in to investigate," he went on. "He found that his jenny had given birth to a fine male foal. Being very full of whisky and sentiment at the time, he named the little donkey Joe."

"The same Joe we met today?" Gertrude asked.

"The very same," the doctor answered. "Though now he is a middle-aged fellow of twenty nine, who is working his way back to grace by aiding you in your sport."

Gertrude raised her glass. "God rest his soul!" she murmured before drinking.

Jim Evans motioned to the barman. "Another round. Make them doubles." He turned to Dr Melrose. "Maybe that's the way to imbibe the spirit of this country," he said.

"As good a way as any," the doctor answered, grinning.

ICELAND

"It was flat calm when I arrived there that after-noon, but I decided to make no change in the method of the morning, except for keeping low and keeping my distance. Two fish followed the fly and surged at it near the head of the pool, but I felt neither. Then near the tail, I hooked a fish that went completely wild. He jumped and ran and jumped and ran again through every foot of the pool, no matter how I tried to calm him. Fish boiled and twisted away from him in every direction and one even jumped clear out of the water. He wouldn't leave the pool and I couldn't lead him up away from it toward the lake. When I got him under control I had landed him just below the tail."

From "Salmon of the Vatnsdalsa" by Roderick Haig-Brown, 1969

SALMON OF THE VATNSDALSA

by Roderick Haig-Brown, 1969

A WIDE, FLAT GREEN VALLEY with red-roofed farm buildings and a bright, clean river; steep green slopes on either side climbing quickly to black rock outcrops and snow-filled gullies; low clouds along the mountain tops, shifting valley winds, break of blue sky and sunlight; handsome, pale gold people of great antiquity; arctic terns, golden plover, and black-backed gulls; wild flowers blooming in profuse succession. All these things make up northern Iceland in mid-July – all these and the salmon.

When my friend Bill Gregory called from Minneapolis in May, I had only an uncertain impression of all this, but I thought immediately: Atlantic salmon, small but lots of them, attractive streams, country something like the Canadian Arctic. "It's a small stream," Bill said. "Only twenty miles long, limited to four rods. Fly only and all wading, no boats. I have it for mid-July and we're a rod short. Can you come?"

I knew I was going, of course, but even in this age of easy travel, a journey across a continent and half an ocean takes a moment or two of thought.

I found myself in Iceland only one day later than I had expected, checking into the Saga Hotel in Reykjavik in broad daylight at 2 a.m. The lovely city was silent, not a car or a person moving in its streets, the elegant buildings unlighted, even the flags quiet on their masts. I drew the heavy curtains firmly against the daylight and then slept gratefully in the silence.

The river we were to fish is the Vatnsdalsa, one of several flowing into Hunafloi, the great fjord that cuts widely back into the northwest coast of Iceland. It is a six-hour drive, north and east of Reykjavik, by a gravel road that skirts the edges of two west coast fjords, climbs over a low divide, and then drops down across three or four valleys and their rivers to come to Flodvangur, the comfortable lodge in the Vatnsdalur, the valley of the Vatnsdalsa. It was a fine introduction to the country. We passed green farms in the valleys with good herds of dairy cattle; on the unfenced tundra were the beautifully formed small

The Vatnsdalsa is only 20 miles long, but its reputation flows much further.

Native horses graze near the Vatnsdalsa, where, in the words of Roderick Haig-Brown, there is
"green everywhere with a richness of short grasses."

native horses, and native sheep with long, silky fleeces that rippled in the wind. Wild swans were paired, nesting in the potholes; eider ducks, terns, and black-backed gulls rested along the shorelines; and in places the polar ice was piled in formidable blue and white drifts for miles.

We had come to Flodvangur without seeing the river itself. The lodge overlooks a small shallow lake (Flod) through which the river flows. Below the lake are two highly productive pools, Landslide and the Peat Pool, just above tidewater. Immediately above the lake the stream is slow and flat, meandering through peat-bog meadows and around bright green islands for three or four miles to the tiny church that serves the valley. Salmon do not hold anywhere in this stretch, which is known as the Trout Water and is full of Icelandic char and brown trout.

Above the Church Pool is another 12 to 14 miles of river, divided into three beats, each with several fine pools, each with its own special character.

All this was quite vague in my mind on that first evening, compounded of talk and maps and a list of the names of the pools – Dalfoss, Green Banks, Grettis, Char, Grimstunga, Junction, Red Braes, President's, and Corner Pool, were a few of them. The fish were late, we were told, nearly two weeks late because of the cold late spring and the ice floes we had seen piled along the beaches. They were beginning to show quite well in the Peat Pool and Landslide, below the lake, but very few had yet passed through to the upper beats. In front of the lodge the little lake was flat calm under the gray daylight of midnight; low clouds hung along the dark faces of the mountains across the valley, golden plover called from the rough land nearby. It was enough to go to sleep on – a new country, a new river, new birds, unfamiliar fish, a thousand questions that the next week or ten days might answer.

The river was far more beautiful than I had expected. Between the pools one could wade easily almost anywhere, yet the pools themselves were large enough to call for a good long cast and plenty of searching. The valley is practically treeless – a few dwarf birches fenced off from the sheep, here and there sad little plantations of ailing pines less than ten feet high, a few thrifty rowans in the churchyard – but it was green everywhere with a richness of short grasses and sedges and mosses; in amongst the green and even on the gravel bars, was a profusion of wild flowers, little arctic creatures making the most of the short northern summer. On both sides of the river were handsome white farm buildings with red roofs – the oldest farm in the valley, we were told, had been there for over a thousand years. The valley's first quarrel, one which ended in murder and which is recorded in the sagas, was over salmon rights.

Above the Trout Water the valley continues flat and wide and green but the river is faster, with alternating pools and rapids over a gravel bed that clearly shifts and changes in the winter floods. Just below the Grimstunga Bridge is the Junction Pool, where the little Alka River comes in from the west. Junction is considered one of the best pools on the river and had produced two or three fish the week before we arrived.

It is a simple, straightforward pool, with a fast run at the head, good depth, a nice spread toward the tail. It was the first pool we fished and someone fished it at least once every day we were there, but it did not yield another fish until the very last day.

Above Grimstunga Bridge the valley narrows and the hills crowd steadily closer until the river is flowing through a gentle canyon, still with steep green

When delicacy is reqiuired Icelandic salmon flies can be distinctly small.

banks between the rock outcrops. At the head of the canyon is a fine fall, about 12 feet high, and below it a boil of turbulent water between high rock walls that spreads into a deep pool with a wide tail and a good shallow glide under the far bank. I saw one salmon jump at these falls, but it was a frail attempt that did not carry him more than half their height. It is possible, though, that salmon do pass them under high water conditions, in which case they would reach another three-quarter mile of fast, rocky water before coming to a much higher fall.

This pool is known as Stekkjar Foss, or Dalfoss, and always holds fish, some of which drop back to lie in the glide at the tail. The first time I saw the pool Jesse Oppenheimer of Texas was fishing it and had been for an hour or more. I saw him first from a

distance, but even so it was evident that there were fish in the tail of the pool and he was approaching the limits of frustration. His fly box was open on a rock on the near side of the pool. After every half dozen casts he would return to it and change his pattern. By this time, I had come up to the pool and could see four good fish lying almost abreast between two big rocks on the far side, in three or four feet of water. Jesse came to his final change and put up a dry Gray Wulff as a gesture of desperation. His first cast was short. I forget about the second. The third was just right and a fish took it perfectly. It ran around the pool for a few minutes, then went out through 200 yards of white water chutes to where we landed it in the next pool down.

I felt at that point that life was going to prove

Close to the Atlantic salmon's marine feeding grounds, Iceland could not be better placed.

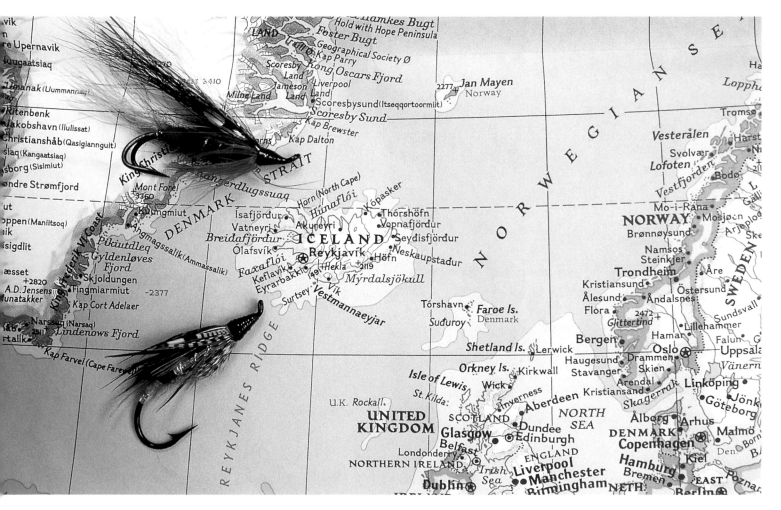

pretty simple. A nice hair-wing floater would take fish without any trouble. A day or two later I watched another fisherman attempt the same thing, with the fish in much the same position. They showed interest all right. But it took well over a hundred casts and several changes of fly to bring one up – this time to a fly with bushy white wings and a black body, known as a Pass Lake. When the pool had settled down and one or two fish had moved back into position, I tried it. There was little interest until I put on a wet Blue Charm that dragged over them at enormous speed. A fish chased the second cast ten or 15 feet downstream with half his side out of water. He didn't catch it, so I threw back. He chased again, in exactly the same spectacular way, but this time he had it securely and in due course was landed.

Fishing the upper beats in this way was a delight. I was only some ten days out of the hospital and not feeling too strong, so I did more watching than fishing. But there was always a fish or two to be found

" ... IT WAS BITTERLY COLD – THE ONLY REALLY COLD DAY OF THE TRIP – WITH A WIND BLOWING 25 OR 30 MILES AN HOUR STRAIGHT DOWN FROM THE POLAR ICE. "

somewhere, in Green Banks, Long Pool, Char Pool, Red Braes, or one of the others, and we were never blanked. The weather was uncertain but generally warm and often sunny, nearly always with a changing wind. In the canyon area it could change through all four points of the compass in the duration of a single cast, calling for some pretty sharp adjustments if things were to go smoothly. There were always new flowers to examine, sometimes hanging banks that were a complete garden of grasses, sedges, mosses, and star-like flowers, sometimes violas and harebells and arctic fireweed scattered in a gray gravel. The birds were lively and beautiful: the arctic terns everywhere performing wonders of flight; the magnificent whooper swans sweeping up and down the valley; whimbrels, practically the same bird as the Hudsonian curlew; mallards and goldeneyes and harlequins; snow buntings, redshanks, rock plover, and abundant golden plover.

I could truthfully say that I needed no more to

Stout salmon rods and reels ready for the ever-changing conditions on the treeless tundra found in Iceland.

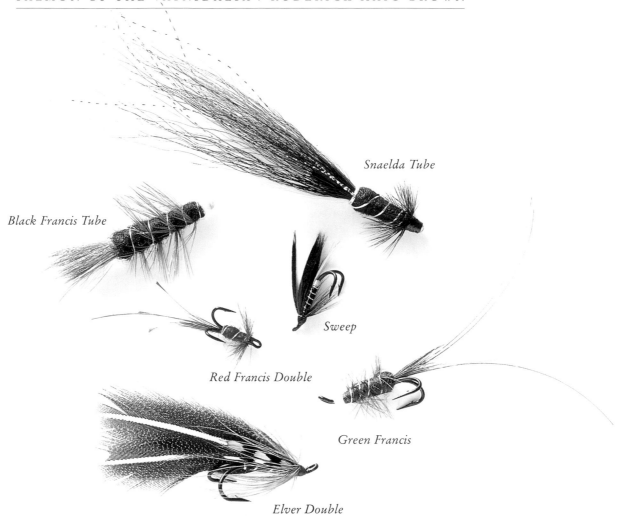

Snaelda Tube

Black Francis Tube

Sweep

Red Francis Double

Green Francis

Elver Double

keep me happy. But it was a slow way to learn about the fishing. When fish are scarce, one experiments endlessly and proves very little. It was in the Peat Pool and Landslide that we learned, when the rotation of beats took us down that way. Fresh fish were moving into the Peat Pool from the sea every day. One would see them passing the long shallow rapids between there and Landslide and even passing above Landslide to disappear into the little lake. It seemed impossible that they were not passing on out at the other end, through the Trout Water and into the upper pools. But they were not.

The first day I fished the Peat Pool and Landslide it was bitterly cold – the only really cold day of the trip – with a wind blowing 25 or 30 miles an hour straight down from the polar ice. I was using an intermediate line, ungreased and therefore sinking, and rather large flies. I think I lost all of the few fish I

hooked and I came away with no clear idea of how the pool should be worked.

Three days later I fished it again for an hour or so on a pleasant morning. By this time I was using a floating line with a size-6 fly and had pretty well settled to the idea that the only pattern needed was a Blue Charm. Thunder and Lightning, Black Doctor, Lady Caroline – any small dark fly would do equally well; what mattered was the size and how the fly was worked. I was casting well across and about 45 degrees downstream, letting the fly come through the current without artificial movement and picking it up quite fast as it came into the slacker water. I hooked a fish almost as soon as I started and lost him at the net ten minutes later. I went back to the head of the pool, hooked another fish almost at once and killed him.

It would be easy to write much more of the Peat Pool, which is both an easy pool and a great pool. I

never saw it without fish and never left it without knowing I could have taken another fish there. And I believe I solved it in the end. One morning I lost four fish in succession, each one right at the net, on a size-6 Blue Charm. Then I had the wits to change to a size-8 and killed the next three fish I raised.

The last time I fished the Peat Pool was a beautiful Icelandic morning, with little wind and a lightly clouded sky. There had been some rain and the river had risen two or three inches during the night. The major dropped me off there on his way up to Landslide. "It looks like a good day," he said. "Don't work too hard. Sit down and rest for a while when you get a fish." I made up my mind to do exactly that.

It was the first time I had had the pool entirely to myself and I did everything deliberately: parked my net at the edge of the eddy, checked my gear carefully, walked slowly up to the head of the pool, talking to the nervous, scolding terns to try and persuade them I had no designs on their downy young. Up at the head I sat on a rock and watched the pool until I had seen two or three fish roll, then slowly crossed the riffle and put out line until I was reaching the cut bank. I was into a fish almost at once and landed him safely – a handsome cockfish of 14 pounds. I admired him, photographed him, and looked at my watch. It was 9.50 a.m.

I walked slowly back to the head of the pool, found a comfortable rock and sat down with my back against it. For 20 minutes I watched the mountains, watched the terns as they chased off some ravens, watched the slow flight of seven swans low across the tundra on a line where I had never seen them before. Then I went back into the pool and in 15 minutes landed another fish.

By 12.30 I had still not passed the upper part of the pool and I had five fish on the bank, all between 12 and 16 pounds, without losing a single one. I

Picture perfect: a handsome salmon on a beautiful Icelandic morning on the Laxa-I-Adaldal.

wanted no more from the pool and sat down to wait for the major to come down from Landslide.

There was time to reflect on the calmness and precision of the whole morning. There had been no fumbling, no wasted effort, and the tiny fly had held firmly even through those final dangerous struggles. Most of it was due to the fish themselves. Every rise had come on the swing, most of them toward mid-current. They were quiet, deliberate rises, plainly visible in a shouldering movement that seemed scarcely to break the surface. I did not strike to the rises, but waited to feel the fish, then set the hook as far as possible from the side.

Landslide in the afternoon adjusted my perspective a little. It is about as different from the Peat Pool as it is possible to be. It lies just below the lake, close under one of a number of little round hills, about 50 feet high, left by volcanic or glacial action. It is a small pool, perhaps 50 feet wide and 200 feet long, no more than six feet deep with a very slow, smooth current. Fish lie well in it and one can see them plainly from the shoulder of the little hill or even, if there is no wind, from the level of the pool itself. With a strong ripple on the water it is easy to take fish there, but in a flat calm it can be quite difficult.

It was flat calm when I arrived there that afternoon, but I decided to make no change in the method of the morning, except for keeping low and keeping my distance. Two fish followed the fly and surged at it near the head of the pool, but I felt neither. Then near the tail, I hooked a fish that went completely wild. He jumped and ran and jumped and ran again through every foot of the pool, no matter how I tried

A "killed" salmon. On many of Iceland's otherwise well-managed rivers, there is no catch-and-release angling.

to calm him. Fish boiled and twisted away from him in every direction and one even jumped clear out of the water. He wouldn't leave the pool and I couldn't lead him up away from it toward the lake. When I got him under control I had landed him just below the tail.

Below Landslide is the long shallow rapids that goes all the way down to the Peat Pool, half a mile away. There are small potholes in the rapids where fish hold briefly and I had seen a fish roll in one of these, by a large tuft of grass about 70 yards below Landslide.

I decide to try for him and was wading out to get in position when I saw a good fish lying in less than a foot of water about 15 feet away. I froze, then cautiously withdrew, moved upstream, and cast the little Blue Charm over him. To my surprise, he took it at once and was firmly hooked.

What happened from then on was totally without precision, deliberation, or any other quality except excitement. The first place he went into was the hole by the tuft of grass, exactly where I didn't want him. Even so, I tried to keep him there and tire him a little, but he went off across the rapids and into a maze of half-submerged rocks hung with trailing green weed. I scrambled back to shore, picked up the net, and went after him. He eased up a little and I steered him back among the rocks somehow. He was far from ready for the net, but I began to wonder just where I could hope to net him. The best chance seemed to be just below Landslide or up in the pool itself, if possible. But my fish thought otherwise. He came back all right, to within 30 or 40 feet of the rod tip and swirled sulkily as I tried to lift him. Then he went off again.

He was past the grass tuft and 40 yards into the backing before I decided to follow. Even then he was still running and the glass rod was singing to the strain – a disconcerting metallic sound I was still not entirely used to. Not far below us was a wide, shallow ford and I didn't like the idea of his flopping around on that at the end of a hundred yards of line. He turned short of it and I managed to bring him back, obviously tiring. Again I looked for a place deep enough to get the net under him, but there was nothing. I dropped the net and decided to beach him.

He was not ready for that. When I tried to lead him in he went off again, half swimming, half flipping and sliding over the shallows. Soon he was onto the ford and I had to ease up and let him find his own way over it. There was a little more water below, but nowhere a shelving place where he could be led unsuspecting to his fate. I tried it four or five times only to have him flip and scramble away. When I finally managed to keep him quiet for a moment it was a good 400 yards downstream from where he had started, and even then I had to tail him and swing him up onto the grassy bank.

The next day was my last day of salmon fishing. Only three of us were on the river – the major, Bill Negley of Texas, and I. The major suggested I try the Peat Pool again, but I wanted to see the upper pools once more; after all, they were the real river, with the spirit and weather moods, the beauty and remoteness of Iceland about them. I knew that Bill Negley, who is an excellent fisherman, had been up there the day before and found only one fish. But there had been a rise of three inches or more in the river, and the fish had to go through sometime.

So Bjarni and I started out in the Land-Rover. Bjarni is a schoolteacher from the great peninsula that swells northward on the west side of the Hunafloi. He knows all the pools and the easiest approaches to them; he is calm and good with the net, and very good, quiet company. "Where are we going?" he asked. "To Dalfoss?"

"No," I said. "We would waste too much time there. We'll try the Junction, then go straight on to Krubba and Green Banks and fish all the way down."

Unwisely we stopped on the bridge over the Alka River and looked down into the pool below the canyon. For the first time in all the times we had looked, there was a fish resting there, and a good one.

The fish was lying in quite shallow water near the tail of the pool; there was only a slight current and

Icelandic pools call for good long casts.

the surface was perfectly smooth. I crept down under the bridge and threw the little Blue Charm to him. Bjarni told me he had moved to it. He moved to the next cast also, then no more. I eased a few feet downstream to change the angle and again he moved twice and no more. I changed to a larger fly. He paid no attention to it until I dropped it behind him, then he turned after it and turned away. I reeled in, crept down past the fish, keeping under the shadow of the high bank, and asked Bjarni for my other rod, the little Pezon-Michel that was ready with a floater.

The fish flickered his fins and moved slightly at the first drift. At the second he made an abrupt, agitated circle, but did not come up. He managed to appear steadily less interested through the next half-dozen casts. I thought of changing the fly, but instead I told Bjarni: "We're wasting as much time here as we would at Dalfoss. Let's go." Bjarni grinned and we went.

Below Dalfoss is the Trout Pool, which does not hold fish very well, then the Non Pool and the Dog Pool, both of which are small. Below these are Krubba and Green Banks, two of the finest pools on the river. Krubba lies under a high rock face on the east bank. The current enters rather narrowly at the head, turns sharply against the rock, slides along it, and spreads to a broad deep pool. The west bank is smooth and grassy, but climbs steeply.

Green Banks starts about a hundred yards below Krubba, with a formidable run-in of white water that swirls and settles among several big boulders. The rock face is on the west side and the current flattens and eases all along it as far down as a big, round, reddish boulder in midstream, which is about the end of the holding water. The west bank slopes

Opposite: A helping hand – a man-made ladder will help salmon negotiate otherwise impassable falls.

very gradually from the water's edge, a rich green garden of grasses and wild flowers with a steeper slope, still green, rising behind it. A place to dream of, to lie in the sun and listen, to make love; far too perfect, certainly, for the needs of a simple fisherman.

I fished Green Banks first and saw a fish roll by the rock at the tail almost as I started. A fish touched my fly near a corner of the rock face, but would not come again. The fish at the tail rolled at my fly but did not touch it. So I went up to Krubba, but I knew I was not finished with Green Banks.

In spite of its looks and reputation, Krubba had not shown me any signs of a fish. I had fished it several times, and watched others fish it, with floating and sinking lines, large and small flies. I had looked into it from the top of the rock bluff and seen nothing. I fished again now, with deep faith, carefully and with my best technique. Nothing moved. Bjarni had gone upstream to look over the Dog Pool, but there was nothing there either, so we had lunch to give Green Banks a longer rest.

It was a pleasant day of clouds and occasional sun and twisting, uncertain winds. I very much wanted a fish from Green Banks and hoped to find one among the big boulders at the head. But the first fish took at the start of the rock face and right against it. He moved quietly into midstream and let go of the fly. Half a dozen casts later a second fish did exactly the same thing and I began to wonder if the little Blue Charm was right after all. I fished on down to the big boulder at the tail, raised my fish there, and hooked him solidly. Bjarni landed him for me and I knew, sadly, that it was time to go on.

The Grettis Pool, Bjarni told me, is so called because it is the place where the Viking killed the ghost. Bjarni reads the sagas as he waits beside the river and says they are very gloomy and tragic; and in that northern valley it was easy to imagine the

> " A PLACE TO DREAM OF, TO LIE IN THE SUN AND LISTEN, TO MAKE LOVE; FAR TOO PERFECT, CERTAINLY, FOR THE NEEDS OF A SIMPLE FISHERMAN. "

sources of old legends and feel them all about you. The valley's first settlers, in that farm of a thousand years ago under the frowning mountain, would have felt the challenge of the unknown hinterland. Sea people, huddled through the long dark winters in the strange land, they would have told stories. And in the long daylight of summer some brawny younger son would have shouldered his spear and gone forth to meet the challenge, bold yet fearful. Certainly he might have met, among other terrors, a ghost by the Grettis Pool.

For the Grettis Pool lies just where the valley begins to open up to farmland, although still a dozen miles above the site of that first farm. A foaming rapids dances briskly into it, strikes hard against a low rock outcrop in the west bank, swirls from there to spread into shelving tail and back eddy. A tiny pool, but deep and good to hold in. The sun was bright as I came to it – too bright, I thought, as a fish rolled

lazily at my fly and missed at the edge of the current just below the outcrop. He missed on the next swing, too, but had the third one firmly. Bjarni landed him 50 yards below the pool and I went back to finish out. There was another fish at the tail, but he missed the fly and would not come again, so I left him.

By this time it was getting late and I had not covered nearly as many pools as I had hoped to, so we ran down toward the other beats. I fished the Junction again and rolled a good fish near the tail, raised and felt a fish in Red Braes, fished Pollarnir without moving anything, and came to President's Pool, under the dark clay bluff, at 9.15 p.m. It was too late to fish the pool properly, but I swung a fly quickly down it and saw one fish clearly against the white clay bottom on the far side. Bjarni waded out to stand beside me, then we saw two more fish in the shallow water right at our feet. Obviously they were moving up.

We had fished until the stroke of 9.30, but were

Pastoral repose: fishing a bend pool on the Midfideral River, Iceland.

Mound Pool near Bustarfell on the River Horsa. Oil painting by William Garfit.

still first back at the lodge. The major and Bill Negley arrived shortly after with 17 fish from the Peat Pool and Landslide. Bill had hooked the last fish of the day, a magnificent 21-pounder which had taken over an hour to land.

When I am asked what I think of the fishing in Iceland, the only sensible answer I can think of is: "I wouldn't want it any better." True, we may have been a little unlucky in the late arrival of the fish. It would have been wonderful to have had fair numbers in the upper pools all through, instead of just on the last day. What else should one want? Larger fish? Perhaps, but I'm not at all sure. Larger fish would mean fewer fish and probably less willing fish. However I assess them, the last three or four days I spent on the Vatnsdalsa were as exciting as any fishing days in my life.

Iceland is a beautiful country and a romantic one. The people, if one must generalize, are friendly, charming, and quite remarkably handsome. The summer climate is as pleasant as a fisherman could want, except when the polar wind blows, and there may even be a little more sun than is good for the fishing. There are no mosquitoes or biting flies, only a blun-

dering creature that looks and acts like a blackfly except for the bite. The wild flowers and grasses are beautiful. The streams are varied and challenging, clean and unlittered.

It would be nice to say that the future is secure. Perhaps it is. The streams are well managed and the government is fully alert to the value of the runs. More intensive management would be possible, but at present there seems little need for it. The salmon disease that is plaguing British and Irish stocks has not yet reached Iceland and one hopes it never will. But Danish fishing in Greenlandic waters and on the high seas may be a more serious threat. No salmon runs can stand up in the face of uncontrolled fishing, and there is no really accurate or effective means of controlling a high-seas salmon fishery. One can only hope that the nations which reap the shortsighted harvest will have some change of heart and conscience. Without seed and seedbed there can be no harvest.

USA

"The Narraguagus was, and is, like so many of Maine's scandalously mis-managed freshwater fisheries, a pretty enough river, located in a somewhat drab locale, which I suspect, however, wasn't nearly so drab before the white man came with the axe and saw and other toys of commerce to mis-manage lots of Maine land no less scandalously than its waters. Most of the river's 60-odd miles from its source in Eagle Lake to where it empties into island-dotted Narraguagus Bay is low-lying, and so the river is much more slitherer than tumbler. Once upon a time, I'm told, its upper reaches could boast terrific brook trout fishing. But this, too, was little better managed in the end than the salmon resource."

From "Rotation" by Art Lee, 2000

ROTATION

by Art Lee, 2000

I HAVE ONLY SEEN one sea-run Atlantic salmon caught within the borders of the United States of America. In fact, I might have caught it had I been a little less generous (or lazy) or perhaps a little more confident, given the scarcity of the fish. It was an eight-pounder, taken by a Cherryfield local who claimed to be late for supper, and so I let him take my place in the ongoing angler rotation down the Cable Pool on Maine's Narraguagus River back in the late Sixties when L.L. Bean was still best known for its gumshoes.

In those days about a thousand fish, or about as many as came into lots of small streams in eastern Canada and Iceland, ascended the Narraguagus annually. But most of us from "down below" who made that Narraguagus expedition, as we chose to think of it, in May each year were very young and decidedly full of piss and vinegar, and I guess our optimism rubbed off on the older folks among us, and so what came to be known by all of us, rather pretentiously it's

easy to recognize now, as "the meeting of the clan" was a sort of pan-generational stream with not catching salmon running through it.

So, in point of fact, had I caught that salmon, I might have spoiled everything.

Actually, I suppose two factors really prompted us to the Narraguagus each year; it was open when other rivers to be visited later weren't, and the Narraguagus was close enough to where most of us lived to represent a painless and relatively inexpensive cure for cabin fever. I'm also inclined to believe that making the trip prompted most of us to think of ourselves as "real salmon fishermen" as opposed to the "transplanted trout fishermen," who opted for keeping "bankers' hours" knee-deep in riffles and rills until the time came for them to lodge on New Brunswick's Miramichi – a small-fish river in those days – during the meat of the salmon season. Or put another way, we derived a certain pride in just being the first North American salmon fishers each year to be munched on by black flies, which had to seem more than a little curious to anglers hailing from Cherryfield and other nearby towns who, it was evident, regarded us with what had to be an essentially charitable synthesis of indulgence and disdain.

The Narraguagus was, and is, like so many of Maine's scandalously mis-managed freshwater fisheries, a pretty enough river, located in a somewhat drab locale, which I suspect, however, wasn't nearly so drab before the white man came with the axe and saw and other toys of commerce to mis-manage lots of Maine land no less scandalously than its waters. Most of the river's 60-odd miles from its source in Eagle

The sun sets over a Maine river.

Lake to where it empties into island-dotted Narraguagus Bay is low-lying, and so the river is much more slitherer than tumbler. Once upon a time, I'm told, its upper reaches could boast terrific brook trout fishing. But this, too, was little better managed in the end than the salmon resource. And even though conservation groups, public and private, would pop up from time to time, especially when a hunk of "pork" was spotted on the horizon, they also seemed inevitably somehow to self-digest like so many shaggy mane mushrooms, leaving in their wakes only the inky-black spots of the status quo.

Twinkle-yarn, jungle-cock eye, purple maribou, copper rib: a blend of old and new makes a killing fly.

Ironically, some of the salmon's woes, which culminated in the November 2000 US government's designation of the wild Atlantic salmon of eight downeast rivers, including the Narraguagus, as an endangered species, may have derived from the extraordinary State of Mainer sense of humor within which it's difficult for an outsider to recognize outrage. How well I remember sitting in the lean-to of cedar post and shake shingle erected at Cable for purposes of sign-up and waiting your turn to fish the rotation a couple of dozen times a day – if only, it came to feel, to keep them honest – and listening to a local tell one of those signature State of Mainer stories just loud enough for you to hear which no doubt went something like this:

"Yah know, this fellah from down bahlow e come tah Maine'ta do some fishin'. Well now, 'e set down 'long soyd'th' bank'uv'a pawnd wuth'is long cane pole an' pro-ceeded'ta baitin'is'ook with'a fat, juicy wuhm. Then don'chah know, 'e cast thaht wuhm out intah th' pawnd an' leaned back on'is elbows'tah wait fer a boite.

"Well ahs yah'd expect, i't'wasn't long be-foah th' black floyes foun'im an' commenced'tah swawhmin' an' bitin'im all ovah. They wuz a'bitin'im on th'neck an'th'eahs an' all ovah 'is clean-shaved face, an' on'is han's 'n'ahms'an' ankles an' heaven-only-knows-whayah-all-alse, if'n'yah know whot'I mean, once't'they foun' they'ah way intah'is down-below clothin'.

"T'weren't no sup-preoyse, then, thet this pooah fellah'd commence-tah wavin' 'is ahms asif'e wuz sign'lin' th'fleet, an' slappin'n' scratchin' in mo-ah places thehn it'd seem any human be-in'd'ave digits'tah git'tah'h'twonce.

"Now, who'dah'yah sup-pose wuz a'sittin' on'th' uthah soyd'ah thet pawnd but ow-ah ol' fren' Vuh'gil Scoffles, an' d'spoite bein'th polites' man in those'r any pa-ahts I'm famil-yah with, 'e jus' couldn't ruh-strain 'imself from slappin' 'is soydes'an' laughin' ow't loud.

"Tah which'th' fellah from down below, when'e finahly seen ol' Vuh'gil, shouted out – an' 'ho c'ld blame 'im – 'You laughin' a't'me, buddy?' O-ah some othah down below way'ah puttin' things they'ah prone'tah usin' when they'ah losin' they'ah tempah with a fellah humin-bein'.

"Well now, this got undah ol' Vuh'gil's skin jus' a mite, don'ch'yah know, an' so 'e commencee'tah callin' back ovah th' wah-tah, 'Yah know, th'las'toime Oy seen black floyes ah'swahmin' like that, they wuz ah'swahmin' 'roun'a hosee's ass.'

"Tah'which'th' fellah from down below 'e reployed. 'Ah you a'callin' me a hosse's ass?'

"Tah'which ol'Vuh-gil 'e called 'crost th' pawnd ahgin in'th' gentl'm'nly way we all know'e poh-sseses, 'I ain't a'callin' you nuthin', straingah, bu't'you cahn't fool them black floys, by Jeezus.'"

Even as the intended brunt, who could help but laugh your ass off? And although, too, the tale and how it was told might have been intended to show us where we stood, put us of our place, we had to roar both at the tale and how it was told, and by thus roaring, somehow this very testimony to the gulf between "them" and "us" served to bring everyone closer together in a strange and lovely way, until finally by week's end each year, segregation no longer existed under the lean-to, and to do something like deferring to a fellow angler to shield him from spousal wrath – the tribute paid by all husbands on occasion for license to live close by flowing water – was probably inevitable. A small price for me to pay, indeed I suppose, even at the likely cost of the only salmon I might have caught within the boundaries of my native land, since it turned out that my gesture would not be forgotten during the decade or so I returned to the Narraguagus, the lean-to at Cable and the same faces. In fact, although I don't recall specifically, I have a hunch that were I to rifle through the reams of paper that clutter every available nook and cranny of my home and office, I'd find a scrap or two with names and 207 area code telephone numbers handed me for purposes pre-departure gen.

But among the things I *do* recall specifically amid otherwise misty memories of those long-ago seasons on the Narraguagus is that among the great charms of the downeaster was that while a certain amount of xenophobia might have existed, it was magnificently cloaked in humor – rare to have found for a guy like me who so often finds himself a stranger.

That notwithstanding, as your horizons expand, it's altogether too convenient to forget where you cut your teeth. And so I have to admit I had seldom thought of those Narraguagus days until I found myself, of all places, on the Castle Grant beats of Scotland's Spey with the Earl of Kimberley who had invited 16 guests, all Brits but me, to help give him a shove into his seventies. While I hasten to add that never in my sporting life have I been treated with greater warmth and good cheer than during this largely fishless week, it should surprise no one to be reminded that the English and Scots, generally speaking, aren't wild about us Yanks, or any "foreigners" for that matter. So, even as my host and his pals went out of their way to make me feel at home, I can't say the same for our Scottish gilly, who didn't seem to like anybody very much and made no downeast-like effort, by way of jest or other means to hide it.

He spared no one, not even Lord Kimberley, and like everybody else, or so it seemed, I was scared shitless of the guy. And so as the week passed, I found myself suddenly reflecting on the Narraguagus experience with a distinct feeling of *ennui*.

No red-and-black jacket and gum rubbers for him, no siree. You had to see him – decked out in tweed from breeks to deer stalker, a walking one-track mind, especially where choice of fly pattern was concerned. It was the Willy Gunn tube or bust, or so it seemed, notwithstanding that bust was clearly going to prevail, even as the river, it appeared to me, was in ideal condition for small conventional flies. But the gilly never wavered from having everyone lob the big weighted tubes, and yours truly, like everyone else, spent endless hours, day after day, flinging these things without seeing a fin.

Then at last one afternoon he informed me in an ominous tone that he had to go to "tune" to conduct some crucial business but that he'd be back "dirrrec'ly." What to do? Did I dare? Questions like these were leaping into my head even as the estate's Land-Rover rounded a corner in a shower of gravel. Then all at once I felt liberated, euphoric, and terrifically brave. For it's astounding, is it not, how easy it becomes to shout "screw you" at the back of an authority figure?

And so, nothing loathe, I cut off the damned Willy Gunn, boxed it unceremoniously, and chose in its stead a lovely little size-8 Mar Lodge double, brilliantly dressed by Galen Mercer, my fishing partner back home. And sure enough, not a half-dozen casts later, a sweet swirl materialized behind the fly, my line tightened, and not long after that a sleek silver salmon writhed on the bank, my first from the Spey, or one more than I'd ever been able to take from the Narraguagus which crossed my mind once again at that moment.

As it turned out, the gilly didn't return to my beat before lunchtime but was standing at the center of a circle of anglers outside the hut when I arrived on foot carrying my rod and salmon. "Well done, well done," cried my fellow fishers in unison, and everything seemed to be aces until one of them, innocently enough I'm certain, posed what I suppose had to be the inevitable question. "What did it take?" and with that my whole life flashed before my eyes. I had two options, untruth or consequences, and when I chose the latter, the gilly stopped on a shilling mid-sentence and proceeded to stride, the circle breaking to make way, to where as we say on this side of "the pond" he was "in my face."

"An' 'ow much wid'ya see y'rrr fish weighs, sirrr?" he asked, folding his arms across his chest and looking me square in the eye.

"Nine pounds," I responded as politely as I could, although matching his stare and fighting back my Irish.

A lone angler fishing a river in Maine, where salmon were once so plentiful that early colonists spread them for fertilizer.

Without even blinking, the gilly unfolded his arms and with one hand reached into the pocket of his tweed jacket to locate a set of those beautiful brass British scales and reaching out the other for my fish. His eyes still fixed, he hung the fish from the hook of the scale, which he raised to eye-level, to take just the quickest of peeks. You could have heard a pin drop as everyone in our party seemed to be holding a collective breath. "Aye, nine pund" conceded the gilly finally, removing the scales and returning them to his pocket, his eyes still fastened to mine.

Then, suddenly, he reached down and, clasping the salmon both fore and aft, he looked down and commenced to studying it carefully. "An' d'ya ken whot this be, sirrr?" He was pointing at a circle about the size of a quarter just behind one of the salmon's gill plates.

"Looks to me like an old lamprey scar, wouldn't you say?" I responded so quickly I can't be certain that his r's weren't still rolling.

"Aye," he said in the wake of a long pause, nodding, and after seeming to be sizing me up in some depth, it appeared that he was turning to walk away when he abruptly reversed himself and stuck out his hand. I took it. And he said, "A rrright bonny bi'ta fishing t'was thot, Misterrr Lee." And then he did turn and walk away, my fish still clasped through the gill, slapping the side of his tweedened leg with each step.

Now, while it is true that I never did get his address or telephone number, the rest of our party was, if possible, even more affable than ever toward me, although as far as I know, all continued to fish with Willy Gunn tubes no less exclusively and fruitlessly for the rest of our stay. So I guess it's fair to presume that no matter who you are and where you fish Atlantic salmon, you must earn or learn your place in the scheme.

Which leads me wonder today, had I been all the places I've been since those days on the Narraguagus and as a consequence known everything I now know about how to catch salmon, would the Narraguagus

have blanked me still. Or had I arrived on the Narraguagus decades earlier than I had, as my first real fishing partner, the late Dave Danzig of Schenectady, New York, did, when there were so many more salmon about, whether I would have been rewarded with plenty of fish, as he was, in part anyway, just for having undergone the ordeal of getting there and back.

Dave was 32 years my senior and was the "real deal" both as man and sportsman in the context of his time. He made his living organizing steel workers with I.W. Abel and was the last guy on earth you wanted to screw with, as four poachers on Quebec's Matane River must have reckoned as they lay scattered around the beach. I remember sitting fascinated as Dave spun yarns about fishing salmon back in the days when just "getting there" was half the battle. He told of it taking more than 24 hours in his Model A Ford to get to the Matane, and how during this first Gaspé trip, Dave, always the "working man" and proud of it, spent at least as much time pounding nails into the roof of a new place that would become the renowned Belle Plage with its creator Raoul Roux as he did fishing, and how from that day until the day Dave died, or Raoul sold the place – I can't recall now which came first – David's money was "no good" there (or a lot of other places) and how his room overlooking the St Lawrence was always ready and awaiting his arrival.

Dave also told of how he would put a pack on his back and take a train to Boston, another from Boston to Bangor, another from Bangor to Hancock where he'd hitch a ride on what was called then the Shoreline Railroad, or "the logging train," as Dave dubbed it, and how the Shoreline engineer would stop the train to drop him off just shy of the railroad bridge that crosses the Narraguagus just below Cable and how he'd fish the river for a few days before being picked up again by the train, to begin his long journey home. Dave's Narraguagus salmon fishing required a lot of hoofing, which he clearly relished after months of smoky mills and walking picket lines, and sometimes he "hit 'em" and sometimes he didn't, but fishing for salmon all day,

*An orange-bodied Rusty Rat hooked to the cork. This fly is a
Canadian import once popular on American rivers.*

then sleeping under the stars was, in Dave's inimitable, if somewhat profane, way of describing everything he touched or that touched him, "a friggin' circus."

But it is also true that by the 1950's, at least a decade before my time on the river, they were already writing of the need to "restore" the salmon runs of the once prolific Narraguagus, until by the year 2000, a couple of decades after my time, it was clear that

Narraguagus salmon, along with those of the Machias, the Dennys, among other streams, had to be tagged endangered by the Feds or be lost forever. And so I should count myself fortunate just to have fished the river when there was still a chance of getting a fish, even if I never succeeded in doing so.

I did raise one, though. It came hard to a size-4 Orange Cosseboom single about a third of the way through the fly swing and half the way through the Cable rotation. The rise surprised me so much, given the thousands and thousands of wayworn casts that had come before, that I jelly-legged. Whether I would likely hook the fish today, I can't say. What I can say, however, is that I worked and worked it as well as I knew how then and that none of the older, more experienced anglers, including several locals who followed when someone finally convinced me that if ten people tell you you're drunk you'd better lie down, caught the fish either.

Since that afternoon I've caught more Atlantic salmon in more places than any angler has a right to, including the largest fish logged in Iceland one year and the biggest ever landed on one Canadian river. Not bad for a paddy whose old man never saw an Atlantic salmon, much less hooked one. The Atlantic salmon has been good to me, and I have always tried to return the favor. But I do still have a "wish list" of rivers I hope to fish, including several with imperial names. Not one on that list, though, is more compelling to me than an opportunity to be able to return to the Narraguagus, although whether or not I ever catch a fish there is immaterial. Rather it is because just to be permitted to wet a line once again would mean that the Narraguagus salmon would no longer be endangered, or put another way, that those of us who live within the boundaries of the United States of America had finally seen the light and gotten it right.

CANADA

"The Slide Pool is in the wildest and most picturesque part of the river, about 35 miles above Metapedia. The stream, flowing swiftly down a stretch of rapids between forest-clad hills, runs straight toward the base of an eminence so precipitous that the trees can hardly find a foothold upon it, and seem to be climbing up in haste on either side of the long slide which leads to the summit. The current, barred by the wall of rock, takes a great sweep to the right, dashing up at first in angry waves, then falling away in oily curves and eddies, until at last it sleeps in a black deep, apparently almost motionless, at the foot of the hill. It was here, on the upper edge of the stream, opposite to the slide, that we brought our floating camp to anchor for some days. What does one do in such a watering-place?"

From "The Ristigouche from a Horse-Yacht" by Henry Van Dyke, 1899

THE RISTIGOUCHE FROM A HORSE-YACHT

by Henry Van Dyke, 1899

THE BOUNDARY LINE between the Province of Quebec and New Brunswick, for a considerable part of its course, resembles the name of the poet Keats; it is "writ in water." But like his fame, it is water that never fails – the limpid current of the river Ristigouche.* The railway crawls over it on a long bridge at Metapedia, and you are dropped in the darkness somewhere between midnight and dawn. When you open your green window-shutters the next morning, you see that the village is a disconsolate hamlet, scattered along the track as if it had been shaken by chance from an open freight-car; it consists of 20 houses, three shops and a discouraged church perched upon a little hillock like a solitary mourner on the anxious seat. The one comfortable and prosperous feature in the countenance of Metapedia is the house of the Ristigouche Salmon Club – an old-fashioned mansion, with broad, white piazza, looking over rich meadow-lands. Here it was that I found my friend Favonius, president of solemn societies, pillar of church and state, ingeniously arrayed in grey knickerbockers, a flannel shirt and a soft hat, waiting to take me on his horse-yacht for a voyage up the river.

Have you ever seen a horse-yacht? Sometimes it is called a scow; but that sounds common. Sometimes it is called a house-boat; but that is

too English. What does it profit a man to have a whole dictionary full of language at his service, unless he can invent a new and suggestive name for his friend's pleasure-craft? The foundation of the horse-yacht – if a thing that floats may be called fundamental – is a flat-bottomed boat, some 50 feet long and ten feet wide, with a draft of about eight inches. The deck is open for 15 feet aft of the place where the bowsprit ought to be; behind that it is completely covered by a house, cabin, cottage or whatever you choose to call it, with straight sides and a peaked roof of a very early Gothic pattern. Looking in at the door you see, first of all, two cots, one on either side of the passage; then an open space with a dining-table, a stove and some chairs; beyond that a pantry with shelves, and a great chest for provisions. A door at the back opens into the kitchen, and from that another door opens into a sleeping room for the boatmen. A huge wooden tiller curves over the stern of the boat, and the helmsman stands upon the kitchen roof. Two canoes are floating behind, holding back, at the end of their long tow-ropes, as if reluctant to follow so clumsy a leader. This is an accurate and duly attested description of the horse-yacht. If necessary it could be sworn to before a notary public. But I am perfectly sure that you might read this through without skipping a word, and if you had never seen the creature with your own

*Ristigouche is the archaic spelling of Restigouche.

The porch at the Ristigouche Salmon Club's "Indian House." The fishing club was founded in
1880, making it one of the oldest of its kind in the world.

eyes, you would have no idea how absurd it looks
and how comfortable it is.

While we were stowing away our trunks and bags
under the cots, and making an equitable division of
the hooks upon the walls, the motive power of the
yacht stood patiently upon the shore, stamping a
hoof, now and then, or shaking a shaggy head in
mild protest against the flies. Three more pessimistic-
looking horses I never saw. They were harnessed
abreast, and fastened by a prodigious tow-rope to a
short post in the middle of the forward deck. Their
driver was a truculent, brigandish, bearded old fellow
in long boots, a blue flannel shirt, and a black som-
brero. He sat upon the middle horse, and some wild
instinct of colour had made him tie a big red handkerchief around his shoulders, so that the eye of the
beholder took delight in him. He posed like a bold,
bad robber-chief. But in point of fact I believe he was
the mildest and most inoffensive of men. We never

heard him say anything except at a distance, to his
horses, and we did not inquire what that was.

Well, as I have said, we were haggling courteously
over those hooks in the cabin, when the boat gave a
lurch. The bow swung out into the stream. There was
a scrambling and clattering of iron horse-shoes on the
rough shingle of the bank; and when we looked out
of doors, our house was moving up the river with the
boat under it.

The Ristigouche is a noble stream, stately and
swift and strong. It rises among the dense forests in
the northern part of New Brunswick – a moist
upland region, of never-failing springs and innumer-
ous lakes – and pours a flood of clear, cold water 150
miles northward and eastward through the hills into
the head of the Bay of Chaleurs. There are no falls in
its course, but rapids everywhere. It is steadfast but
not impetuous, quick but not turbulent, resolute and
eager in its desire to get to the sea, like the life of a

man who has a purpose: "Too great for haste, too high for rivalry."

The wonder is where all the water comes from. But the river is fed by more than 6000 square miles of territory. From both sides the little brooks come dashing in with their supply. At intervals a larger stream, reaching away back among the mountains like a hand with many fingers to gather "The filtered tribute of the rough woodland", delivers its generous offering to the main current. And this also is like a human life, which receives wealth and power from hidden sources in other lives, and is fed abundantly from the past in order that it may feed the future.

The names of the chief tributaries of the Ristigouche are curious. There is the headstrong Metapedia, and the crooked Upsalquitch, and the Patapedia, and the Quatawamkedgwick. These are words at which the tongue balks at first, but you soon grow used to them and learn to take anything of five syllables with a rush, as a hunter takes a five-barred gate, trusting to fortune that you will come down with the accent in the right places.

For six or seven miles above Metapedia, the river has a breadth of about 200 yards, and the valley slopes back rather gently to the mountains on either side. There is a good deal of cultivated land, and scat-

Three anglers on the Restigouche River, flies in their hats, a split cane rod, a net and a priest,
one holding a perfect salmon, fresh from the sea.

tered farmhouses appear. The soil is excellent. But it is like a pearl cast before an obstinate, unfriendly climate. Late frosts prolong the winter. Early frosts curtail the summer. The only safe crops are grass, oats and potatoes. And for half the year all the cattle must be housed and fed to keep them alive. This lends a melancholy aspect to agriculture. Most of the farmers look as if they had never seen better days. With few exceptions they are what a New Englander would call "slack-twisted and shiftless". Their barns are pervious to the weather, and their fences fail to connect. Sleds and ploughs rust together beside the house, and chickens scratch up the front-door yard. In truth, the people have been somewhat demor-alised by the conflicting claims of different occupations; hunting in the fall, lumbering in the winter and spring, and working for the American sportsmen in the brief angling season, are so much more attractive and offer so much larger returns of ready money, that the tedious toil of farming is neglected. But for all that, in the bright days of midsummer, these green fields sloping down to the water, and pastures high up among the trees on the hillsides, look pleasant from a distance, and give an inhabited air to the landscape.

At the mouth of the Upsalquitch we passed the first of the fishing-lodges. It belongs to a sage angler from Albany who saw the beauty of the situation years ago, and built a habitation to match it. Since that time a number of gentlemen have bought land fronting on good pools, and put up little cottages of a less classical style than Charles Cotton's "Fisherman's Retreat" on the banks of the River Dove, but better suited to this wild scenery, and more

"An angler ... regards hospitality as a religious duty. There seems to be something in the craft which inclines the heart to kindness and good-fellowship."

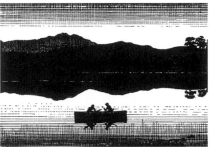

convenient to live in. The prevailing pattern is a very simple one; it consists of a broad piazza with a small house in the middle of it. The house bears about the same proportion to the piazza that the crown of a Gainsborough hat does to the brim. And the cost of the edifice is to the cost of the land, as the first price of a share in a bankrupt railway is to the assessments which follow the reorganisation. All the best points have been sold, and real estate on the Ristigouche has been bid up to an absurd figure. In fact, the river is over-populated and probably over-fished. But we could hardly find it in our hearts to regret this for it made the upward trip a very sociable one. At every lodge that was open, Favonius (who knows every-body) had a friend, and we must slip ashore in a canoe to leave the mail and refresh the inner man.

An angler, like an Arab, regards hospitality as a religious duty. There seems to be some-thing in the craft which inclines the heart to kindness and good-fellowship. Few anglers have I seen who were not pleasant to meet, and ready to do a good turn to a fellow-fisherman with the gift of a killing fly or the loan of a rod. Not their own particular and well-proved favourite, of course, for that is a treasure which no decent man would borrow; but with that exception the best in their store is at the service of an accredited brother. One of the Ristigouche proprietors I remem-ber whose name bespoke him a descendant of Caledonia's patron saint. He was fishing in front of his own door when we came up, with our splashing horses, through the pool; but nothing would do but he must up anchor and have us away with him into the house to taste his good cheer. And there were his daughters with their books and needlework, and the photographs which they had taken pinned up on the wooden walls, among Japanese fans and bits of brightly coloured stuff in which the soul of woman delights, and, in a passive, silent way, the soul of man also. Then, after we had discussed the year's fishing, and the mysteries of thc camera, and the deep question of what makes some negatives too thin and others too thick, we must go out to see the big salmon which one of the ladies had caught a few days before, and the large trout swimming about in their cold spring. It seemed to me, as we went on our way, that there could hardly be a more wholesome and pleasant summer-life for well-bred young women than this, or two amusements more innocent and sensible than photography and fly-fishing.

It must be confessed that the horse-yacht as a vehicle of travel is not remarkable in point of speed. Three miles an hour is not a very rapid rate of motion. But then, if you are not in a hurry, why should you care to make haste?

The wild desire to be forever racing against old father time is one of the kill-joys of modern life. That ancient traveller is sure to beat you in the long run, and as long as you are trying to rival him, he will make your life a burden. But if you will only acknowledge his superiority and profess that you do not approve of racing after all, he will settle down quietly beside you and jog along like the most companionable of creatures. It is a pleasant pilgrimage in which the journey itself is part of the destination.

Below and left: *In the 1930's, getting to good salmon water meant poling upstream and camping on the riverbank.*

A sport, a gillie, and a salmon. "Salmon Fishing," by Currier and Ives, 1872.

As soon as one learns to regard the horse-yacht as a sort of moving home, it appears admirable. There is no dust or smoke, no rumble of wheels, or shriek of whistles. You are gliding along steadily through an ever-green world; skirting the silent hills; passing from one side of the river to the other when the horses have to swim the current to find a good foothold on the bank. You are on the water, but not at its mercy, for your craft is not disturbed by the heaving of rude waves, and the serene inhabitants do not say "I am sick." There is room enough to move without falling overboard. You may sleep, or read, or write in your cabin, or sit upon the floating piazza in an arm-chair and smoke the pipe of peace, while the cool breeze blows in your face and the musical waves go singing down to the sea.

There was one feature about the boat which commended itself very strongly to my mind. It was possible to stand upon the forward deck and do a little trout fishing in motion. By watching your chance,

when the corner of a good pool was within easy reach, you could send out a hasty line and cajole a sea trout from his hiding place. It is true that the tow-ropes and the post made the back cast a little awk-ward; and the wind sometimes blew the flies up on the roof of the cabin; but then, with patience and a short line the thing could be done. I remember a pair of good trout that rose together just as we were going through a boiling rapid; and it tried the strength of my split-bamboo rod to bring those fish to the net against the current and the motion of the boat.

When nightfall approached we let go the anchor (to wit, a rope tied to a large stone on the shore), ate our dinner "with gladness and singleness of heart" like the early Christians, and slept the sleep of the just, lulled by the murmuring of the waters, and defended from the insidious attacks of the mosquito by the breeze blowing down the river and the impregnable curtains over the beds. At daybreak, long before Favonius and I had finished our dreams, we were under way again; and when the trampling of the horses on some rocky shore wakened us, we could see the steep hills gliding past the windows and hear the rapids dashing against the side of the boat, and it seemed as if we were still dreaming.

At the cross point, where the river makes a long loop around a narrow mountain, thin as a saw and crowned on its jagged edge by a rude wooden cross, we stopped for an hour to try the fishing. It was here that I hooked two mysterious creatures, each of which took the fly when it was below the surface, pulled for a few moments in a sullen way and then apparently melted into nothingness. It will always be a source of regret to me that the nature of these animals must remain unknown. While they were on the line it was a general opinion that they were heavy trout; but no sooner had they departed, than I became firmly convinced, in accordance with a psychological law which holds good all over the world, that they were both enormous salmon. Even the Turks have a proverb which says, "Every fish that escapes appears larger than it is." No one can alter that conviction, because no one can logically refute it. Our best blessings, like our largest fish, always depart before we have time to measure them.

The Slide Pool is in the wildest and most picturesque part of the river, about 35 miles above Metapedia. The stream, flowing swiftly down a stretch of rapids between forest-clad hills, runs straight toward the base of an eminence so precipitous that the trees can hardly find a foothold upon it, and seem to be climbing up in haste on either side of the long slide which leads to the summit. The current, barred by the wall of rock, takes a great sweep to the right, dashing up at first in angry waves, then falling away in oily curves and eddies, until at last it sleeps in a black deep, apparently almost motionless, at the foot of the hill. It was here, on the upper edge of the

The skillful hand-tailing of a fresh-run fish on the Grand Cascapedia, Quebec.

stream, opposite to the slide, that we brought our floating camp to anchor for some days. What does one do in such a watering-place?

Let us take a "specimen day". It is early morning, or to be more precise, about eight o'clock, and the white fog is just beginning to curl and drift away from the surface of the river. Sooner than this it would be idle to go out. The preternaturally early bird in his greedy haste may catch the worm; but the fly is never taken until the fog has lifted; and in this

the scientific angler sees, with gratitude, a remarkable adaptation of the laws of nature to the tastes of man. The canoes are waiting at the front door. We step into them and push off, Favonius going up the stream a couple of miles to the mouth of the Patapedia, and I down, a little shorter distance, to the famous Indian House Pool. The slim boat glides easily on the current, with a smooth buoyant motion, quickened by the strokes of the paddles in the bow and the stern. We pass around two curves in the river and find ourselves at the head of the pool. Here the man in the stern drops the anchor, just on the edge of the bar where the rapid breaks over into the deeper water. The long rod is lifted; the fly unhooked from the reel; a few feet of line pulled through the rings, and the fishing begins.

First cast – to the right, straight across the stream, about 20 feet: the current carries the fly down with a semicircular sweep, until it comes in line with the bow of the canoe. Second cast – to the left, straight across the stream, with the same motion: the semi-circle is completed, and the fly hangs quivering for a few seconds at the lowest point of the arc. Three or four feet of line are drawn from the reel. Third cast to the right; fourth cast to the left. Then a little more line. And so, with widening half-circles, the water is covered, gradually and very carefully, until at length the angler has as much line out as his two-handed rod can lift and swing. Then the first "drop" is finished; the man in the stern quietly pulls up the anchor and lets the boat drift down a few yards; the same process is repeated on the second drop; and so on, until the end of the run is reached and the fly has passed over all the good water. This seems like a very regular and somewhat mechanical proceeding as one describes it, but in the performance it is rendered intensely interesting by the knowledge that at any moment it is liable to be interrupted.

> "Now he stops, shakes his head from side to side, and darts away again across the pool, leaping high out of water."

This morning the interruption comes early. At the first cast of the second drop, before the fly has fairly lit, a great flash of silver darts from the waves close by the boat. Usually a salmon takes the fly rather slowly, carrying it under water before he seizes it in his mouth. But this one is in no mood for deliberation. He has hooked himself with a rush, and the line goes whirring madly from the reel as he races down the pool. Keep the point of the rod low; he must have his own way now. Up with the anchor quickly, and send the canoe after him, bowman and sternman paddling with swift strokes. He has reached the deepest water; he stops to think what has happened to him; we have passed around and below him; and now, with the current to help us, we can begin to reel in. Lift the point of the rod, with a strong, steady pull. Put the force of both arms into it. The tough wood will stand the strain. The fish must be moved; he must come to the boat if he is ever to be landed. He gives a little and yields slowly to the pressure. Then suddenly he gives too much, and runs straight toward us. Reel in now as swiftly as possible, or else he will get a slack on the line and escape. Now he stops, shakes his head from side to side, and darts away again across the pool, leaping high out of water. Drop the point of the rod quickly, for if he falls on the leader he will surely break it. Another leap, and another! Truly he is "a merry one", as Sir Humphry Davy says, and it will go hard with us to hold him. But those great leaps have exhausted his strength, and now he follows the line more easily. The men push the boat back to the shallow side of the pool until it touches lightly on the shore. The fish comes slowly in, fighting a little and making a few short runs; he is tired and turns slightly on his side; but even yet he is a heavy weight on the line, and it seems a wonder that so slight a thing as the leader can guide and draw him. Now he is close to the boat. The boatman steps out on a rock with his gaff. Steadily now and slowly, lift the rod, bending it backward. A quick sure stroke of the steel! a great splash! And the salmon is lifted upon the shore. How he flounces about on the stones. Give him the *coup de grace* at once, for his own sake as well as ours. And now look at him, as he lies there on the green leaves. Broad back; small head tapered to a point; clean, shining sides with a few black spots on them: it is a fish fresh-run from the sea, in perfect condition, and that is the reason why he has given such good sport.

We must try for another before we go back. Again fortune favours us, and at eleven o'clock we pole up the river to the camp with two good salmon in the canoe. Hardly have we laid them away in the ice-box, when Favonius comes dropping down from Patapedia with three fish, one of them a 24-pounder. And so the morning's work is done.

In the evening, after dinner, it was our custom to sit out on the deck, watching the moonlight as it fell softly over the black hills and changed the river into a pale flood of rolling gold. The fragrant wreaths of smoke floated lazily away on the faint breeze of night. There was no sound save the rushing of the water and the crackling of the campfire on the shore. We talked of many things in the heavens above, and the earth beneath, and the waters under the earth; touching lightly here and there as the spirit of vagrant converse led us. Favonius has the good sense to talk about himself occasionally and tell his own experience. The man who will not do that must always be a dull companion. Modest egoism is the salt of conversation: you do not want too much of it; but if it is altogether omitted, everything tastes flat. I remember well the evening when he told me the story of the Sheep of the Wilderness.

"I was ill that summer," said he, "and the doctor had ordered me to go into the woods, but on no account to go without plenty of fresh meat, which was essential to my recovery. So we set out into the wild country north of Georgian Bay, taking a live sheep with us in order to be sure that the doctor's prescription might be faithfully followed. It was a young and innocent little beast, curling itself up at my feet in the canoe, and following me about on shore like a dog. I gathered grass every day to feed it, and carried it in my arms over the rough portages. It ate out of my hand and rubbed its woolly head against my leggings. To my dismay, I found that I was beginning to love it for its own sake and without any ulterior motives. The thought of killing and eating it became more and more painful to me, until at length the fatal fascination was complete, and my trip became practically an exercise of devotion to that sheep. I carried it everywhere and ministered fondly to its wants. Not for the world would I have alluded to mutton in its presence. And when we returned to civilisation I parted from the creature with sincere regret and the consciousness that I had humoured my affections at the expense of my digestion. The sheep did not give me so much as a look of farewell, but fell to feeding on the grass beside the farmhouse with an air of placid triumph."

After hearing this touching tale, I was glad that no great intimacy had sprung up between Favonius and the chickens which we carried in a coop on the forecastle head, for there is no telling what restrictions his tender-heartedness might have laid upon our larder. But perhaps a chicken would not have given such an opening for misplaced affection as a sheep. There is a great difference in animals in this respect. I certainly have never heard of any one falling in love with a salmon in such a way as to regard it as a fond companion. And this may be one reason why no sensible person who has tried fishing has ever been able to see any cruelty in it.

Suppose the fish is not caught by an angler, what is his alternative fate? He will either perish miserably in the struggles of the crowded net, or die of old age and starvation like the long, lean stragglers which are sometimes found in the shallow pools, or be devoured by a larger fish, or torn to pieces by a seal or an otter. Compared with any of these miserable deaths, the fate of a salmon who is hooked in a clear stream and after a glorious fight receives the happy dispatch at the moment when he touches the shore, is a sort of euthanasia. And, as the fish was made to be man's food, the angler who brings him to the table of destiny in the cleanest, quickest, kindest way is, in fact, his benefactor.

There were some days, however, when our benevolent intentions toward the salmon were frustrated; mornings when they refused to rise, and evenings when they escaped even the skilful endeavours of Favonius. In vain did he try every fly in his book, from the smallest Silver Doctor to the largest Golden Eagle. The Black Dose would not move them. The Durham Ranger covered the pool in vain. On days like this, if a stray fish rose, it was hard to land him, for he was usually but slightly hooked.

I remember one of these shy creatures which led me a pretty dance at the mouth of Patapedia. He came to the fly just at dusk, rising very softly and quietly, as if he did not really care for it but only wanted to see what it was like. He went down at once into deep water, and began the most dangerous and exasperating of all salmon-tactics, moving around in slow circles and shaking his head from side to side, with sullen pertinacity. This is called "jigging" and unless it can be stopped, the result is fatal.

I could not stop it. That salmon was determined to jig. He knew more than I did.

The canoe followed him down the pool. He jigged away past all three of the inlets of Patapedia,

Early autumn patterns whisper "big fish" on the Miramichi River.

169

The Great Room at the Ristigouche Salmon Club looks the same as it did 120 years ago.

and at last, in the still, deep water below, after we had laboured with him for half an hour, and brought him near enough to see that he was immense, he calmly opened his mouth and the fly came back to me void. That was a sad evening, in which all the consolations of philosophy were needed.

Sunday was a very peaceful day in our camp. In the Dominion of Canada, the question "to fish or not to fish" on the first day of the week is not left to the frailty of the individual conscience. The law on the subject is quite explicit, and says that between six o'clock on Saturday evening and six o'clock on Monday morning all nets shall be taken up and no one shall wet a line. The Ristigouche Salmon Club has its guardians stationed all along the river, and they are quite as inflexible in seeing that their employers keep this law as the famous sentinel was in refusing to let Napoleon pass without the counter-sign. But I do not think that these keen sportsmen regard it is a hardship; they are quite willing that the fish should have "an off day" in every week, and only grumble because some of the net-owners down at the mouth of the river have brought political influence to bear in their favour and obtained exemption from the rule. For our part, we were nothing loath to hang up

our rods, and make the day different from other days.

In the morning we had a service in the cabin of the boat, gathering a little congregation of guardians and boatmen and people from a solitary farmhouse by the river. They came in *pirogues* – long, narrow boats hollowed from the trunk of a tree; the black-eyed, brown-faced girls sitting back to back in the middle of the boat, and the men standing up bending to their poles. It seemed a picturesque way of travelling, although none too safe.

In the afternoon we sat on deck and looked at the water. What a charm there is in watching a swift stream! The eye never wearies of following its curls and eddies, the shadow of the waves dancing over the stones, the strange, crinkling lines of sunlight in the shallows. There is a sort of fascination in it, lulling and soothing the mind into a quietude which is even pleasanter than sleep, and making it almost possible to do that of which we so often speak, but which we never quite accomplish – "think about nothing". Out on the edge of the pool, we could see five or six huge salmon, moving slowly from side to side, or lying motionless like grey shadows. There was nothing to break the silence except the thin clear whistle of the white-throated sparrow far back in the woods. This is almost the only birdsong that one hears on the river, unless you count the metallic "*chr-r-r-r*" of the kingfisher song.

Every now and then one of the salmon in the pool would lazily roll out of water, or spring high into the air and fall back with a heavy splash. What is it that makes salmon leap? Is it pain or pleasure? Do they do it to escape the attack of another fish, or to shake off a parasite that clings to them, or to practise jumping so that they can ascend the falls when they reach them, or simply and solely out of exuberant gladness and joy of living? Any one of these reasons would be enough to account for it on weekdays. On Sunday I am quite sure they do it for the trial of the fisherman's faith.

But how should I tell all the little incidents which made that lazy voyage so delightful? Favonius was the ideal host, for on water, as well as on land, he knows how to provide for the liberty as well as for the wants of his guests. He understands also the fine art of conversation, which consist of silence as well as speech. And when it comes to angling, Izaak Walton himself could not have been a more profitable teacher by precept or example. Indeed, it is a curious thought, and one full of sadness to a well-constituted mind, that on the Ristigouche "I.W." would have been at sea, for the beloved father of all fishermen passed through this world without ever catching a salmon. So ill does fortune match with merit here below.

At last the days of idleness were ended. We could not "Fold our tents like the Arabs, / And as silently steal away;" but we took down the long rods, put away the heavy reels, made the canoes fast to the side of the house, embarked the three horses on the front deck, and then dropped down with the current, swinging along through the rapids, and drifting slowly through the still places, now grounding on a

hidden rock, and now sweeping around a sharp curve, until at length we saw the roofs of Metapedia and the ugly bridge of the railway spanning the river. There we left our floating house, awkward and helpless, like some strange relic of the flood, stranded on the shore. And as we climbed the bank we looked back and wondered whether Noah was sorry when he said goodbye to his ark.

A Rusty Rat sits atop one of Stanley Bogdan's magnificent salmon reels.

Spare the Rod

by John Alden Knight, 1942

In this tale Donald's non-responsive answers remind one of Emily Post's reply to the inquiry "How should an orchid be worn; with the stem up or down?" Mrs Post replied, "It depends on which way you think it looks best."

DONALD ANGUS MACQUEEN is a guide on the salmon rivers of New Brunswick. It will not come as a surprise to learn that he is a Scotsman. Being such, we find ourselves always making allowances for Donald. Not that he expects us to – far from it. Donald is sufficient unto himself. He knows the rivers and the vagaries of the fish that use them each year as passageways to and from the spawning grounds. His 50-odd years have taught him the lore of the white water and he handles a canoe as though it were a part of him and he part of it. He knows his duties as a guide and he performs them faithfully and to the letter. All he asks in return is his just wage – at the going rates and to the last penny – and the proper respect that his years and experience tell him is his due. In other words, Donald is Donald and we can take him as he is or else. Yet, as I say, we always find ourselves making allowances for Donald and his ways.

Being a bachelor and having lived most of his life in solitude – and there is plenty of solitude to be found on the salmon rivers of New Brunswick – Donald is not given to conversation. Perhaps his inherent Scotch thrift prevents him from indulgence in the waste of words. Again, it may be that this form of economy is the way in which he humors the trait of laziness that is common to us all, although in other things Donald is not lazy. Be that as it may, he makes it a point to use the absolute minimum of words in his intercourse with fellow men. I honestly believe that he would spend an entire salmon-fishing trip, be it for days or weeks, in unbroken silence, were such a thing possible. To say that he is laconic would be a gross understatement. "Monosyllabic" might be more accurate.

It so came to pass that my friend, Joel Robinson, when he and a few others leased a tributary of the Restigouche, hired Donald as head guide on his first trip to the river. Conversationally, Joel is the antithesis of Donald. Give him a good listener and plenty of time and Joel is content with the world. He has opinions and he expresses them – at length. He not only views each side of a question; he turns it upside

A guide takes a drop on one of the Restigouche River's long pools.

down and inside out so that when he has done with it there is little left save the bare skeleton. Now and then, just to find out where he stands, he will pause long enough to learn if his listener is or is not in agreement with him. This involves asking a question and, more important, getting an answer to it. It was at this point that Joel was apt to bog down in his talks with or, more correctly, *at* Donald.

During the first half-hour in the canoe, Joel regaled Donald with a blow-by-blow account of his night in what is laughingly referred to as a sleeping car. Winding up with the difficulty of shaving in cold water, he inquired whether or not he, Donald, found it unpleasant to shave without hot water. Donald looked at him for several moments with no change of expression. Then he shifted his tobacco from one cheek to the other. Joel learned later that this maneu-

ver invariably was the forerunner of verbal expression, but he didn't know it then, so he repeated his question.

"Do you like to shave without hot water?" he asked.

Donald regarded him intently for another three minutes. Then he turned and looked at the right-hand bank. Next he faced the left-hand bank and spat – copiously – into the river. Finally the answer came.

"I do – an' I don't."

Wiser men than Joel have made the same mistake that he made then. Not knowing Donald, he attempted to pin him down as to the exact meaning of such a vague reply. Cross-examination, with many "stage waits" on Donald's part, revealed that water was a nuisance to heat sometimes; that cold water might serve for shaving if a man were in a hurry and if his beard were not too stiff; that Donald's beard was of a variable nature – sometimes stiff, sometimes quite pliable, depending, perhaps, upon the weather or the season of the year. As to the exact meaning of Donald's original reply and of Donald's preferences, if any, in the matter of shaving he learned absolutely nothing. Joel had not yet learned to make allowances for Donald.

Being a forthright soul, Joel was a little baffled at such evasiveness. Accordingly, he made inquiry.

"Ain't surprised you had trouble," answered the extra guide. "Donald don't hold with expressin' his ideas. Leps from one side of th' fence to t' other like a cat in a strange alley. Nope – don't never expect no inf'r'mation from Donald. He don't give any. Never has."

Thus began Joel's great experiment. Starting at first as a mild form of diversion while journeying to and from fishing locations, the thing gradually grew until it became almost an obsession. He found himself thinking about it when he went to bed at night and again when he awoke. The result was a fixed determination to get a direct answer out of Donald. It was a large order.

The first day in camp, Joel and Donald went salmon fishing. Having lowered the "killic" to hold the canoe in place while they fished the first drop at the head of Slope-wall Pool, Joel, a seasoned salmon fisherman, feigned ignorance. He handed his fly box to Donald and said, "What fly would you use today?"

Donald reached out his ample paw and took the box from Joel. For at least ten minutes he scrutinized those flies, individually and collectively, before handing the box back to its owner. Then, having completed the ceremony of tobacco shifting and

A bright fish rests in a holding pool of Quebec's Grand Rivière.

Rusty Rat

White Wulff

Night Hawk

Green Bomber

Silver Rat

Royal Wulff

expectoration, he spoke, "They're all right purty."

Undaunted, Joel extracted a Jock Scott from the box and held it up for inspection.

"How about this Jock Scott?"

In due course, Donald answered, "It's a right fair fly."

Conceding defeat, Joel bent on the Jock Scott and went to work. Sure enough, the Jock Scott proved to be "a right fair fly" indeed. He returned to camp at noon with three bright fish, all between 15 and 20 pounds. Although he had tried no less than a dozen patterns that morning, all standard dressings and favorites throughout the Restigouche district, the fish he killed came to the Jock Scott. In addition, Donald had handled the canoe and the gaff to perfection. Joel's estimation of Donald underwent considerable revision. But his determination to get a direct answer from him was in no way altered.

That afternoon, after some thought as to the best wording, he tried again. When the canoe was in position, Joel held up a size-8 Mar Lodge.

"How about this one for this afternoon?" he inquired.

Donald regarded the fly intently for some time. Then he looked at the sky, the sun, the water, and held up a moist finger for wind direction. At last came the reply.

"Some folks likes 'em."

Joel fished the Mar Lodge. With it he duplicated the morning's performance, although he had given that same fly a thorough trial that morning. He returned to camp, well satisfied with Donald as a salmon guide.

The week ended with Donald's record still intact. Joel had learned that it might or might not rain – "depended." A long line often took fish, but so, for that matter, did a short line. The river was not high for that time of year, neither was it low, yet it could be in better condition for fishing, although it might suit some folks as it was. Joel took the train at the tiny station convinced of two things. He had met the best salmon guide in the whole of Canada and, at the

same time, the most contrary of all human beings.

Joel returned to his river the following June. With him were his wife, also a confirmed angler, and a business friend, still in the novice class as a fisherman. Donald met them at the station dressed in his working clothes and his cloak of Scotch reserve. He shook hands all round but his only word of greeting was a softly murmured "Mum" as he touched his battered hat to Mrs Robinson.

Knowing that she would be in safe hands, Joel assigned Mrs Robinson to Donald's canoe for the trip upriver. From time to time, when opportunity to observe them presented itself, he noticed that they seemed to be getting along famously. To be sure, she did all the talking and Donald all the listening. She asked no questions and Donald volunteered no remarks of his own. But it was evident to Joel that the austere Scotch frown was somewhat less severe and the expression on the old, granite features showed a shade more warmth than was customary. Joel couldn't decide whether he was pleased or just surprised. Probably both, he concluded. Eventually, they arrived at camp.

The next morning found Joel and Donald with the canoe in place to fish the first drop at the head of Elbow Pool. Joel looked at the river reflectively.

"Doesn't look so good, Donald," he said. "Hardly enough current to keep a wet fly off the bottom, much less fish it anywhere near the surface. Never saw the water so low in June."

Donald inclined his head slightly in what might have been a nod but said nothing. Drop after drop was fished without success. Reaching the tail of the pool without so much as a short rise, Joel pushed back his hat and scratched his head in thought. Then he turned to Donald.

"Guess I'll switch to dry flies," he said, "and we can work our way up to the head of the pool again."

Opposite: *An angler waits for the right moment to tail an energetic salmon on the Miramichi.*

Donald nodded but offered no comment.

Handing his rod to Donald, Joel stripped the line out through the guides and coiled it on the floor of the canoe. Next he ran the coils through a bandanna handkerchief to dry the line before he gave it a thorough coat of line dressing. Then he removed the wet fly leader and looped on a fresh one, 14 feet in length and tapered to 2x. Preparation complete, he opened the box of dry flies and selected two – a brown Bivisible and a gray Bivisible. These he held up so that Donald could see them.

"Which one, Donald?" he asked.

Donald looked at Joel, then at the flies. Next he looked at the water beside the canoe, the pool above them, the sky, the sun and both banks. His gaze returned to the flies and did not leave them as he slowly turned his head and spat over the side.

"Brown one's – right purty. So's th' gray one."

Joel bent on the "right purty" brown one. He was learning to make allowances.

The lower drop was fished out with the brown fly, but no salmon rose to the offering. Donald backed them up to the next drop and lowered the killic to hold the canoe in place. Once more Joel lengthened line and cast the brown fly up and to the left. The current was so slow that it took minutes for the fly to drift down to the end of its float. The whole prospect of taking fish seemed rather hopeless. There on the placid surface of the pool sat the brown fly, the leader (which refused to sink) and the well-greased line. Joel regarded them thoughtfully. At the end of the float, he picked up the fly and cast it up and to the right. Once again, line, leader, and fly rested on the placid surface.

"Do you suppose," said Joel, "that it would make any difference if I moved the fly some – gave it a little life?"

Donald watched the fly as it made its leisurely way down past the canoe. For a full minute his gaze was unwavering. Then, as though he had timed his reply to meet the instant when "drag" was inevitable, he said, "'T helps – sometimes."

As we have seen, Joel had learned, at least in part, to make allowances for Donald. Accordingly, he raised his rod tip and caused the fly to skip across the surface in short, erratic jumps. As he did so, a dark shape detached itself from the river bottom. Slowly the shape drifted up under the fly. Then, without warning, the big fish struck. The quiet pool was rent asunder by the flashing silver body and the thrashing tail sent a geyser of water into the air as the fish dived for the bottom. Joel tightened and the war was on.

More than an hour later, Donald lifted the big salmon out of the river with the gaff. While he dispatched the fish with his hardwood priest Joel leaned back in the canoe seat and flexed his tired fingers.

"Put him in the boat, Donald," he said, "and let's get back to camp and weigh him before he dries out. Ought to go close to thirty-five pounds."

The day being warm, Joel and Mrs Robinson loafed around camp after lunch. Their guest had gone to fish the upper river, taking with him the extra guide, and he was not expected back until dark. They sat on the screened veranda and read for a while, but Joel soon wearied of his book and tossed it aside. Lighting a cigarette, he paced up and down the enclosure, every now and again stopping to watch Donald and the camp cook as they labored over the installation of some stone steps in a steep place in the path that led down to the Home Pool. Mrs Robinson, who knew her man even better than he knew himself, watched him with the faint suspicion of a smile playing around her attractive mouth.

"That damn Scotchman," said Joel. "I'll get an answer out of him that means something if I have to stay here all summer."

"Why?" said his wife. "What difference does it make what he actually says so long as you know what

he means?"

"Well, why'n time can't say what he means like other people?"

"It's just his way, dear. Given enough provocation or in an emergency and I'm sure Donald would say exactly what he means. You must admit he's efficient. I think he'd speak plainly to save time if time happened to be limited at the moment. Up here, you know, minutes aren't very important."

"They're important to me," said Joel. "I'll bet I lose two hours a day – all good fishing time – waiting for that Scot to make up his mind. It makes me mad every time I think of it."

> " ... A DARK SHAPE DETACHED ITSELF FROM THE RIVER BOTTOM. SLOWLY THE SHAPE DRIFTED UP UNDER THE FLY. THEN, WITHOUT WARNING, THE BIG FISH STRUCK. "

Joel ground out his cigarette in the ashtray, grabbed his pet rod from the rod rack (at some risk to the rod) and carefully backed through the door with it. Then he stamped his way down the path toward the Home Pool, hardly glancing at Donald and the camp cook as he passed them. He had no hope of hooking a salmon under the bright overhead sun, but the call of the river was strong and a little casting practice might serve to ease the tension.

Mrs Robinson's gaze followed her husband riverward. She regarded him thoughtfully until he disappeared around a bend in the path. Then she smiled to herself, shook her head slightly and picked up her book. For perhaps 15 minutes she read before laying aside the book once more. Then she rose and opened the screen door.

When their guest had arrived at camp, Joel learned that he had brought with him, contrary to instructions, what he called his fishing tackle. Joel had told him that there would be plenty of tackle in camp, but that had made no difference. His guest's fishing tackle had come along and, on arrival, was promptly displayed for approval. It was just as promptly relegated to the discard. Briefly, it consisted of three general items. There was a book of wet flies – eights and tens mainly – in the more common patterns and with heavy snells attached. In the book also were some six-foot leaders labelled "finest quality – trout size." Item number two was a nickel-plated, single-action reel equipped with an expensive "enameled" line. Last, but by no means least, came the rod. Having more faith in standard man-made products than in those furnished by nature, rods of wood had been eyed with disfavor when this tackle was purchased. This rod was of tubular steel. It was of the collapsible, self-rusting variety that the beginner buys in the spring and throws away in the fall. The guest,

only partially discouraged by his host's acid comments, had mounted the reel on this rod, strung the line through the guides and had tied on one of the "trout-size" leaders, embellished by three of the snelled flies from his stock. Even his inexperienced hand had showed him the fallacy of his judgment in purchasing such an outfit, once he had cast with one of Joel's first-class rigs. So now the rod stood outside the camp where he had left it, leaning against a bush.

As she walked down the path, Mrs Robinson absent-mindedly picked up this steel atrocity and carried it with her to the river. Passing Donald, she stopped a moment to comment on the stone steps he

Laying a long line down and across a holding pool of the Miramichi.

was building. Then she strolled down to the Home Pool, where she found her spouse standing on top of a boulder, absorbed in a futile attempt to cast a salmon fly to the far bank.

For several minutes she watched Joel. Then, curious to learn if it were actually possible to cast a fly with the outfit she was carrying, she climbed to the top of another boulder, so that her backcast would be clear of the bushes behind her, and stripped some line from the nickel-plated reel. At first the fact that the reel was located above the hand-grasp made casting a bit awkward. In a few minutes, however, she was laying out quite a respectable line across the troubled waters of the rapids at the head of the pool. She had no thought of hooking a salmon; in fact, she wasn't even fishing. She merely wished to see how the rod would handle. After a particularly good cast, the best thus far, the flies had settled well out in the rough water and she was stripping in line to try again – the thing happened. Out of the depths, up through the white water, rose a sizeable salmon that engulfed the tail fly – a size-8 Royal Coachman – and sank again from sight. From force of habit, Mrs Robinson raised the rod tip and tightened.

With the first run of the big fish, the line melted from the reel as though by magic. A salmon reel is equipped with one hundred feet of casting line and several hundred feet of additional line called "backing." This backing is smaller in diameter, consisting either of laid linen or woven silk, and it is on this line

Much of Nova Scotia's salmon water is found on small, gem-like spate rivers such as this one.

that most salmon are fought and killed. The one hundred feet of casting line as a rule are out of sight in the water during the greater part of the fight. In this case, Mrs Robinson had only the comparatively short casting line with which to fight the fish. It looked like an impossible task.

Donald's first intimation that something had gone amiss came when he heard Joel's first frantic bit of advice to his wife.

"Hang on to him," screamed Joel when he saw what had happened – this in spite of the fact that she was hanging on for dear life, the rod bent in a sharp bow and the line burning her fingers. It was then that Donald tossed aside a piece of pulpwood he had been using as a lever, motioned to the cook to follow him and ran toward the river. The fight had reached the point where disaster seemed inevitable. Unmindful of blistered fingers, Mrs Robinson seized the racing line more firmly and applied extra pressure with the rod. The run of the big fish slowed somewhat but only for a second. With renewed vigor the salmon surged against the light leader and she had to give line again to keep the tackle intact. Only a few turns of line remained on the reel drum when Donald's quiet voice came to her over her right shoulder.

"Throw the rod – into the river – Mrs Robinson."

Without hesitation she lowered the rod tip to ease the strain and tossed the entire contraption into the foaming waters beneath her.

Up to this point, Joel had been vocal in the

Early season high water on the queen of Nova Scotia rivers, the Margaree.

extreme. His comments went something like this.

"Keep your rod up!"

"Snub him!"

"Not so tight – he'll break you!"

"Don't let him run – hold him!"

"Lower your rod – he'll break you!"

"Let him run – no, hold him!"

As the rod disappeared into the pool, Joel's shouts died with its going. For once in his life he was at a loss for words. Being so, he stood on top of his boulder and stared first at his wife, then at the spot where the rod sank from sight.

Donald, meanwhile, had been busy. As they reached the bank he had taken the camp cook by the shoulder.

"Get the canoe – into the water. You take the bow."

After throwing away her rod, Mrs Robinson, dubious of the wisdom in such a radical move, stood on her boulder and, like her husband, peered into the water where the rod was last seen. Then she turned to find Donald holding out his hand to help her down from her high perch. He actually smiled.

"Better climb – into th' canoe," he said.

Having deposited her in the angler's seat in the center of the canoe, Donald took his placc in the stern. The camp cook already was in the bow, paddle in hand. Slowly Donald paddled the canoe out to midstream, while he looked over the side into the deep, clear water. Suddenly he spoke to the camp cook.

"Hand me – th' gaff."

Down went the gaff into the crystal depths, then Donald's arm, well above the elbow. When, at last, the gaff was slowly drawn from the water, the cheap enamelled line lay across its curve. Carefully, so that the fish would not be disturbed, Donald took in line hand over hand until the tip of the rod appeared. Grasping the tip, he quietly brought in the rod and reeled in the slack line. Then he handed the rod to Mrs Robinson.

"Better tighten," he said.

As soon as the big fish felt this renewed pull of the line, he made a determined rush diagonally across toward the lower end of the pool. Donald swung the nose of the canoe straight down the stream.

"Paddle," he said to the camp cook.

It was a close race. Mrs Robinson, an able angler, put all the pressure she dared on the tackle as the fish tore line from the reel. The canoe shot over the shallows and almost into the next rapids before Donald turned its nose toward the far shore. Then the fish, feeling the direction of the pull of the line changed so that he was being forced downstream, turned and made his way back into the deeper waters of the Home Pool once more. Donald had at least won the first victory, getting his position below the fighting fish.

Mrs Robinson, however, was having her troubles. The line on the reel was growing thin, showing metal between the coils. Donald watched with interest until the danger point was reached. Then he spoke again.

"Better throw it – over again – Mrs Robinson."

Joel had followed the course of events from shore. Also, he had become the self-appointed cheering section. The valley fairly resounded with the echoes of his shouts of advice, most of it conflicting. Finally Donald leaned forward and spoke over Mrs.Robinson's shoulder.

"Don't pay any attention – to him, Mrs Robinson. Just do – what I tell yuh."

The manner of the killing of that 23-pound salmon is now history in the Restigouche valley. The fight lasted for nearly two hours. Donald, having won his vantage point at the tail of the pool, made sure that it was not lost. Four times the rod went over the side, and four times the big fish rested while Donald retrieved the line with the gaff. Not until the salmon had reached the point of exhaustion and lay without motion on its side did Donald ease the canoe toward shore where the gaff could be used with safety.

Joel was beside himself with joy.

"Good girl, good girl," he kept shouting, while he

Autumn colors on the Miramichi. A Wilson Camp guide gives advice to a sport.

hugged Mrs Robinson.

"Good work, Donald," he bellowed, as he hammered him on the back.

Next he shook hands with the camp cook and then hugged Mrs Robinson again.

"Never lost your head for one minute. Proud of you, honey, proud of you. Finest piece of canoe work I ever saw. Let's hurry and weigh him before he loses a single ounce."

As they walked up the path toward camp, Joel carrying the fish and speculating as to its weight, his wife said to him:

"You see, dear, he does talk when he has to."

"By gosh!" said Joel. "He did, didn't he? Honey, you mark my words. He's going to answer a question before I leave here. I've got one figured out that he won't be able to dodge."

On the afternoon of the last day in camp, Joel and Donald fished the Home Pool. They had killed one fish and, after resting the pool for an hour, were trying for another. As Donald set the canoe in place to fish the next drop before the last, Joel said:

"You know, Donald, if I live to be a hundred, I'll never forget the fight you and Mrs Robinson had with that twenty three-pounder. Right here's where you gaffed up the line the last time. How deep is that water under us?"

Donald regarded Joel for a full minute with his usual dour expression. Then he looked down into the water on the right side of the canoe. Next he looked into the water on the left side. Then he shifted his tobacco to the other cheek and looked over the right side again. That done he expectorated – magnificently – into the river, turned in his seat and looked down over the stern.

"By golly!" thought Joel, "I've *got* him."

Donald shifted his tobacco again, glanced once more over each side, as though to make sure of his estimate, and finally turned his gaze full on Joel.

"'T varies," said Donald.

ROBINSONVILLE, NB

by John Cole, 1989

MY CLUMSINESS ANGERS ME. If I belonged, if I had been properly introduced to the traditions of Atlantic salmon fishing and the manners of its fishermen, I would be less discomfited. But I have been on the Upsalquitch River just once before, and the humiliation of those two days a year ago still ripples my memory's surface. This morning is on its way to becoming a sequel, and I churn at the prospect of further embarrassment. It will, I know, take a salmon to rescue me, and I am certain I will continue to be baffled by the challenge.

This is, I tell myself, a silly way to fish: standing at the center of a 24-foot wooden canoe, fly rod in hand, casting a trifle of feathers, steel, silk, and thread on the curling current of this remote river, hoping to provoke a salmon's strike. The process requires little skill, I tell myself. After all, Mrs Hildreth returned to camp last evening with her guide, and he carried a 14-pounder she had landed. I have seen her cast and know I can do as well.

But with difficulty. This fly rod, this nine-and-a-half-foot, slim reed of fiberglass resins and its basic reel with its small handles and schoolboy look, these are not the fishing tools of my saltwater history. These are alien, and demand unfamiliar techniques. I surrender grudgingly, struggling to maintain decorum, as rattled as an actor who forgets his lines on opening night, looking to the wings for escape from public mortification.

And I have an audience. Bill Murray, with all the cockiness of his 21 years and his lifetime with this river, is my guide. Or, as he would put it, I am his "sport." The advantage is his. He has brought me here to the river's upper reaches, threading shoals, following channels I cannot see, steering this long, thin canoe with its seven-horsepower outboard, or, when he needs to, paddling or poling with the riverman's steel-tipped pole he himself cut from the forest, peeled, planed, and tipped in perfect replication of other poles made by his father, brothers, uncles, and

cousins who share this small, fragile community high in New Brunswick's distant northeast corner.

Two days ago, I drove alone across the 350 miles that separates this forest wilderness from my home in Maine, pondering as I drove the reasons for my return to the site of my prior misery. Pride is one reason. I am certain of that. I think of myself as a fisherman, and a year ago, I left this place with my angling identity woefully unverified.

Joe Sewall, my host, was too gracious to indicate anything but well-mannered concern. "You'll have another chance," he said, after my two clumsy days on the river. "You can try again next year." The farewell of a gentleman, but the words circled ears crimson with my awareness of my shortcomings, and my knowledge that Joe, too, expected I might do better, and was disappointed.

Although we had met once earlier, we got to know each other in Augusta, the state capital, during the 103rd session of the Maine Legislature. Brought together by my work as a journalist and Joe's position as a state senator and chairman of the Appropriations Committee, we learned we shared several friends from earlier days. One of the brightest, most capable, and surely the most charming person then in public office, Senator Sewall was an honest, articulate, and intelligent source of information and insights on the workings of state government, its prospects and its personalities. He could read character in minutes and count House and Senate votes even faster. For a newspaperman like me, just arrived to cover the 103rd, Joe was an invaluable resource who considered it an obligation to keep the public informed. He, his information, and his introductions made my work look good. His friendship and his generosity brightened my life and we became friends.

He kept a fly rod in his office adjoining the Senate chamber, and when I asked him during one lunch hour how anyone could fish with such a long and ungainly stick, he said, "Follow me."

The clear waters of the Upsalquitch hold large and often demanding salmon.

Taking the rod, he went into the deserted Senate, one of the most handsome governmental chambers in New England. Standing in the center aisle, under a soaring domed ceiling trimmed in gilt and Corinthian flourishes, Joe stripped 20 or 30 feet from the reel and gave me an indoor casting demonstration. As he lifted his arm and brought hand and wrist straight up and flipped back the large, strong hand holding the rod, the line arced behind him over the high-backed chair on the rostrum reserved for Ken MacLeod, President of the Maine Senate.

When the rod tipped forward, the line followed it, pulling more of itself through the guides. I could hear it whisper as it slid, then fell, almost precisely in the center of the Senate aisle, straight, true, through the doorway leading to the Senate gallery.

"You try it," Joe said after a few more demonstrations.

By then, a dozen spectators had gathered in the gallery, watching with glee, awe, and amazement as the only senator ever to cast a fly in that august chamber held out the rod to a newspaperman, of all people. Uncertain of whether I should even be seen on the Senate floor, much less as a participant in my first fly-casting lesson, I declined.

In mid-June, a few weeks after the incident that kept the State House buzzing for the rest of the session, I found an invitation in the mail. Beneath a silhouette of a leaping salmon engraved on costly paper, the message read: "You are invited to join us at the Upsalquitch Salmon Club for two days of fishing, June 12 and 13, arriving the evening of June 11 and departing after the morning fishing on June 13. RSVP, Joseph Sewall, Robinsonville, New Brunswick, Canada, EOK 1EO."

It took me a while to locate Robinsonville on the map, and several days to inquire about Joe's place. None of the State House lawmakers had been there, but most had heard of it. Joe had bought the lodge and the water two years before, I was told, and had designed and built a new lodge that was one of the finest in New Brunswick. I decided to make the long drive on unfamiliar roads even though that fly rod I'd watched weaving back and forth through the heavy Senate air was the first I'd ever seen in action.

Seven-and-a-half hours after I left home, I opened

"Fishing in New England" shows a solid hook-up in heavy water. The painting is by Winslow Homer.

the lodge door in Robinsonville and stepped into a friendly, high-ceilinged room discreetly equipped with handsome creature comforts: a fully stocked bar, glasses engraved with fishing scenes, bookshelves filled with rows of fly-fishing essays, the salmon's life history, and popular novels for those guests who might want to read themselves to sleep. Paintings of fishing moments by Winslow Homer and other artists brightened wood-paneled walls, and recent copies of the *Atlantic Salmon Journal* and other angling publications were arranged in an orderly row along one side of an elegant coffee table. This was, I decided, definitely several cuts above any image of a fishing camp I had conjured as I drove. This was

well-planned luxury, and my spirits brightened. I would not, I was relieved to learn, spend my night in a sleeping bag wrestling with mosquitoes and black flies.

Nevertheless, what should have been a gentle rest on a comfortable bed in a private room was disturbed by the swarming of doubts and anxieties that pestered me until dawn. They had begun gathering at supper by the coal stove in the kitchen: a splendid evening meal of thick pea soup, sandwiches on home-baked bread, a lemon-meringue pie with a crust lighter than air. That meal would have sent Hamlet's spirits soaring, but as course followed course, gloom overtook me.

Salmon, I soon learned, and the techniques, times, and places for hooking them, were the only conversational topics that had any chance of survival at that table. The talk was jovial enough, at times boisterous, but it never veered from its focus on the fish that even at that moment, according to Joe, were swimming up the Restigouche and turning the corner at the mouth of the Upsalquitch, on the journey to their upriver spawning grounds that brought them to our doorstep.

For two hours, talk of Rusty Rats, Orange Blossoms, Bogdan reels, Fenwick rods, weight-forward lines, tapered leaders, grilse, taking, not taking, Home Pool, Mouth Pool, Rock Pool, Mill Brook, Bill Murray, Ollie Moores, Glenn Murray, Jim Moores, Murdock, high water, low water, good water, and bad water rattled off the walls in an endless cascade of salmon-fishing shop talk that seemed specifically designed to underscore my ignorance of the very process I had driven all those miles to experience.

When, with borrowed rod in hand, I stepped into a canoe at eight that bright morning, I was relieved to learn that I would fish alone with my guide, Glenn Murray. Neither Joe nor his guests would be within watching distance. Only Glenn, who seemed to me young to be a guide, could witness my inaugural day as a fly-fisherman.

For almost five hours that morning and again in the late afternoon and evening, I fought the fly rod, the line, the wind, and the impossibly small fly tied at the end of a flimsy, all-but-invisible leader with an affinity for knotting and tangling itself as I waved it around through the air, trying mightily to force the line to straighten, extend itself, and alight on the river's surface with the delicacy needed to avoid traumatizing every fish within a hundred feet of the boat.

I might have succeeded once or twice during the entire day. Each of the rest of my scores of attempts at casting evolved into a melange of small disasters that fired my cheeks with the crimson blush of end-

less shame. Glenn's day was equally unproductive, but it was irritation that brought blood rushing to his weathered face and kept his temples throbbing beneath the band of his visored guide's cap.

Bent over my leader, frowning at the maze of knots, he somehow maintained patience, tried his best to keep me fishing, changed leaders, changed flies, and, every now and then, offered quiet advice in response to my repeated question, "What am I doing wrong?" "Everything," would have been the correct response, including showing up in Robinsonville with no understanding of even the most fundamental skills required.

By the time the day ended in the long and tender twilight of a northern summer, I was shattered by the weight of my failures. Hour by hour from dawn till dusk, error after error had been added to the tally, until, as I walked the gravel drive from the boathouse to the lodge, I could not rationalize any purpose to my existence in New Brunswick. All that faced me was yet another evening of salmon talk; my potential for participation would be the same at a dinner given by a Serengeti chieftain for his two witch doctors.

I had been on the water for ten hours, and I had seen not one shred of evidence, not one signal, one scale, one turbulent circle on the surface, nothing to indicate salmon, or any other fish for that matter, can live in this crystal river.

Such sterility in fish-bearing waters is not a part of my history. Ever since my early days at Three Mile Harbor, the sea had testified to the presences beneath it. Tails broke the surface, bait fish hissed the desperation of their flight, and often the quarry itself would leap before me, silver scales flashing their verification of life beneath the surface.

But that first day on the Upsalquitch had passed with no such display. I saw only the endless welter of boulders, rocks, and pebbles left by glaciers along the

Bill Taylor powers out a long cast over the fog-draped Grand Cascapedia on Quebec's Gaspé Peninsula.

river's winding spine 10,000 years before, each one visible in the light-hearted current, each one rounded smooth by the millennial waters washed over it. I believed I could reach through 12 feet of that water and touch a pebble, such was the river's purity. Surely no fish could hide in the midst of that elemental transparency. Yet even though I had known what to look for, even though I had learned not to doubt my fish-watching skills, I had seen nothing. I could have stared at a glass vase filled with tap water and discovered as much.

Three pairs of eyes searched my visage for clues as I entered the living room to sit by the fire, but I revealed nothing. I struggled to hold the entire day's disaster at the core of my being, knowing that if one tendril of frustration escaped, the entire catastrophe would spill and my humiliation would be complete. Not only had I failed to hook a salmon, my fellow fishermen would say, but I had the wretched manners to complain about my misfortune.

A Bogdan reel catches the sun beside Canada's Eagle River.

When I awoke the next dawn to the soft rumble of rain on the roof above my bed, I smiled for the first time since leaving Maine. That's it for the fishing, I announced to myself. I'll get an early start on the drive home. But when I reached the dining room where breakfast was served us by a cheerful and talented cook, Joe said, "Today's the day, isn't it, John? Get the sun off the water, and the fish won't be so sulky. Nothing they like better than a nice, steady rain."

Not only would fishing continue, I soon understood, but it would have to be pursued with zeal, regardless of the wind-driven rain rattling against the windows like thrown sand. Salmon fishermen, it seemed, simply ignored every element of every configuration.

With breakfast quite finished, departure for the boathouse became my only choice. Looking like a Gloucester deck hand magically transported to Indian country, I soon stood in my canoe dressed in the yellow oilskins of saltwater. My back stayed dry, but the chill rain blew against my face, where it gathered, streamed off my nose and chin down past my clavicle, and from there slid to the inner intimacies of my chest, belly, and loins. And all the while I was expected to cast a fly into the sterile waters of the Upsalquitch as if I actually believed a fish existed there.

If young Glenn Murray acknowledged the weather, he did not do so publicly. From his seat in the stern, his butt in a firsthand meeting with rainwater gathered in the canoe's ribbed insides, he tracked every wavering passage of every cast I made, as if each was on its way toward the maw of a trophy salmon. In the face of his inept passenger, the morning's dismal miseries and the river's apparent poverty, I admired his commitment, even as I questioned the reason for it.

So when he said, "Look there! Look there!" I not only had no sense of where, but thought he was commenting on the errant sloppiness of my most recent cast, an effort that had put the fly some 20 feet off our stern.

"There he is again," said Glenn, pointing this time.

I followed his arm's line to a circle of the river's surface that bulged, as if a rock just beneath the current forced rushing water to reveal its curving profile. There was, I knew, no rock there. I had been watching the same stretch of water for the past half hour. When the bulge faded as I looked, I knew it had been caused by a living presence.

"That's a heavy fish," young Murray said, still staring at the place on the surface where the bulge had been. "A heavy fish."

"What kind?" I asked. Of each of the uncounted indignities I had inflicted on my guide, that question was the most painful. For once he took his eyes off the river, turned in the stern to look at me, rainwater dripping from his cap's visor, his blue eyes wide, as if he saw some image of ignorance so awesome that it might, indeed, be dangerous.

"A salmon, of course. That there is a big salmon. Maybe twenty-five pounds."

I had seen nothing but the suspect bulge, yet there was in Glenn's taut voice a tremor, the slight trembling of excited anticipation that often betrays even the most seasoned professionals when, at last, they discover the object of their lifelong training and sacrifice.

Which of these? Finding the right fly on the day can often be more luck than judgment. They all look so good.

"Now," he said deliberately, talking more to himself than to me, "now that fish rose twice, but he didn't take."

"Maybe he don't like that fly."

Turning toward me again, his eyes communicating urgency, he said, "Bring in that line. I'll tie on a different fly. Give the fish a rest."

I turned the handle on the small reel, retrieving the short length of line that had dangled astern. Reaching over the gunwale, Glenn pulled the leader gently through his hands until he reached its end. Putting that in his mouth, he bit through the nylon and picked the unattached fly from the puddle in the canoe's bottom and carefully rested it on the thwart

behind him.

Opening a tin fly box, he bent his head close, studying each bit of feathers perched in small rows of colors, like tiny flowers in an aluminum window box. I found his deliberation excruciating. If, indeed, the bulge we had seen was a 25-pound salmon, then I was convinced haste should be the order of the day. Fish I had known tended toward the mercurial, darting here and there, seldom, if ever, holding to one spot long enough for a fisherman to read several pages of angling instructions.

Glenn, however, was quite unperturbed. His motions were the essence of care as he tied on the fly he had selected after reviewing his feathered troops for at least five long minutes.

"Green Butt," he said, "number six hook. The bigger the fish, the smaller the fly. That's what they say, eh?" He held out a black speck no bigger than a button on a baby's shirt. The notion that any creature weighing more than a pound might be deceived or even tempted by such a minuscule offering seemed unrealistic to me, but then, as the past 24 hours had taught me, I told myself I had a great deal to learn about whatever it was I was doing at the moment.

"Now," he said, his words each a breath apart, painstakingly enunciated in the twangy accents of New Brunswick Scots, piercing wind and rain with no chance I could misunderstand, "now, begin casting the same way you would if this was the beginning of a new drop, eh? Start close to the boat and work back, about two feet on each new cast. And cast to both sides of the boat, first one side, then the other."

I had learned that much. After six or seven hundred casts. I had memorized the process. Strip off just enough line to make casting possible, flick it off one side at about a 60-degree angle and let the river's perpetual current carry the fly downstream until it swung straight behind the stern. The only skill I needed to master after I got the cast off was to swing the rod so it followed the fly, keeping the line straight between my rod tip and the lure. Then repeat the process on the opposite side, and then strip two feet more of line off the reel and try again. "Covering the water," I was told, was what I had been doing.

On my fifth cast of the size-6 Green Butt, as the line straightened behind the stern, a boulder fell from the gray heavens, landed just beside the fly, blowing great gouts of white water into the rainy air.

"Jesus," Glenn said. "He's a heavy fish. Did you prick him?"

I could not answer. Not only did I not understand his question, but when I realized the commotion I wit-

> **"Any living thing that could generate that sort of explosion could pose challenges I was not sure I wanted to test. My knees shook."**

nessed had come from beneath and not from above, I went into shock. Any living thing that could generate that sort of explosion could pose challenges I was not sure I wanted to test. My knees shook.

"Did you prick him?"

"What?"

"Did you feel him on the hook? Did you prick him? Once he feels that hook, he's not coming back."

I began to understand. But I had to try to reconstruct the explosion. I had felt no actual contact through the rod, just my own emotional shock at the sudden eruption. "No, I don't think so. I didn't feel anything."

I stood there in the rain, paralyzed, the line still drifting this way and that in the current behind the canoe. Glenn reached for it and began hauling it in by hand.

"Give him a rest, eh? Have a smoke. Then try him again. He likes the fly, don't he?"

A sign indicating membership to the Miramichi Salmon Association, one of Canada's most active river-watch organizations.

Synchronized casting on the Cains River just upstream of its junction with the Miramichi.

"Seems to," I said, starting to recover, wondering how much further I wanted these developing events to continue.

Glenn took a cigarette from a pack of Players he'd managed to keep dry and lit it with a kitchen match he must have had individually wrapped.

"About halfway into this smoke, and we'll try him again," he said. "Give him a good rest, eh?"

I nodded and sat down, slumping, but never taking my eyes from the spot off the stern where the boulder had fallen.

So this was why we were here. I began to understand. I acknowledged the rain, recognized the reason for my wrinkled, water-soaked fingertips, my saturated underwear, and the chills shuddering along my spine. I had come to hook up with primal force, with a river god.

"Okay," said Glenn. "Try him again."

I stood, and began casting, all but swept away by the anticipation storming within. Those gales subsided with each cast, and when my fly passed the spot

where the fish had first charged, I told myself the episode had ended.

"He's gone," I said.

Glenn shook his head, tossing rain drops from his visor. "Keep casting," he said.

By the time my casts reached the limits of my ability, I was convinced the fish had never existed. About 50 feet of line had collapsed in a heap on the river, and I was grateful, as always, when the current tugged at the loops, straightening and correcting my mistakes.

Then, again just as the fly reached the end of its drift, farther downstream but close enough for me to look into its open jaws, the salmon appeared, head and shoulders out of water, a wreath of white water around its middle as it rushed the Green Butt.

I yelled, and yanked back on the rod at the moment I felt the fish would engulf the hook.

There was a tap, a split second of resistance that bowed the rod tip an inch or two, and then eternity.

Waiting there for contact to be restored, I knew it

wouldn't, and I began wishing I could vanish as totally as the fish.

"You struck too soon," Glenn said. "Took the fly away from him. Pricked him, too."

I needed no such certification of incompetence. The river was there to admonish me. The entire 48 hours of my recent past had been destined to define my shortcomings. Even without a witness, I could never again claim to be a fisherman. There was no recipe for my redemption anywhere, no possibility for forgiveness, amnesty, or amnesia. I knew I was cursed to total recall of this day on the Upsalquitch

for all the rest of my year.

"It's after noon," Glenn said. "We'd best be heading in." Underscoring the finality of those words with a tug on the anchor lie, he freed us from our union with the Upsalquitch and began the short run back to the boathouse.

Yesterday, after a year of bleak flashbacks, I returned to the river of my disaster, and today I continue to hurl myself at its barricades. How many casts have I made? There can be no count. What purpose would it serve to number the times my fly has twitched just beneath the surface, tempting only the

stones on the bottom, as if they could break the bonds of destiny and leap to the sunlight that floods our Upsalquitch.

Perhaps it is the clarity of this day, a flawless blue sky hung over us and the spruce, pine, alder, birch, and poplar that climb the sharp hills shouldering the banks on both sides; or it could be the river's liquid chorus, the lilting melody of falling water that buoys my spirits as easily as it carries a leaf on its journey to the sea. Whatever the elixir of the place it dispels my gloom.

Helped, I'm certain, by my year-long effort to relieve the paralysis of chronic ignorance, I have spent time in libraries seeking the salmon and have come to know something of *Salmo salar*, this creature of open oceans and narrow streams that has woven its own tapestries of fact and fancy since Caesar's legions watched it leap from streams flowing through ravaged Saxon farms.

> " More than any other fish of the Atlantic Old World and New, Salmo salar has captured Man's fancy. "

More than any other fish of the Atlantic Old World and New, *Salmo salar* has captured Man's fancy. Surely the annual return of the silver creatures – a homecoming announced dramatically at every tumbling waterfall laced with gleaming projectiles shot from the foam by the force of their compulsions – had much to do with early deification. Like the northern sun's December struggle to escape its prison of equinoctial darkness, June's returning salmon reassured agrarian cultures of seasonal renewal and supplied them with some of the finest tasting protein the sea has ever bestowed.

They return to reproduce, these fish. To insure the survival of their species. And this river's headwaters are one of the fast-diminishing spawning and nursery grounds left on the globe. From dark waters off Greenland where they spend their maturing years swimming through a steady rainfall of ocean shrimp,

Opposite: *Spring salmon holding in a weedy run of the once-great St Mary's River in Nova Scotia.*

schools of adult salmon begin forming, moving, and finally surging toward their native rivers sometime in late February and early March. By late May, these fish of the Restigouche, Upsalquitch, Miramichi, Kedgewick, Matapedia, and the other salmon waters still singing in New Brunswick and Quebec, are gathered in Chaleur Bay just offshore of Campellton.

As June's long days lengthen, the first, large fish probe the Restigouche delta at Tide Head, their sensors reading trace element combinations locked in some inner, natal memory. So finely tuned are these keys to their heritage that Upsalquitch salmon will swim the Restigouche only as far as the entrance to their home river. Where the rivers meet, the fish will turn and begin the 40-mile journey to the river's headwaters at Upsalquitch Lake.

This morning I wait to meet one of them at Noye Pool, a glacial footprint where fast water and depth combine to oxygenate and restore a salmon on its mission of renewal. To reach this place, an Upsalquitch fish has traveled almost a thousand miles, and come six more against the falling waters of its native river.

Like my understanding of the creature, my equipment has improved. My right hand holds no borrowed rod, but the Fenwick nine-and-a-half-footer given me at Christmas, along with a Pflueger reel and a small, but discriminating, collection of salmon flies: gifts from Jean who purchased them at L.L. Bean after forthright conversation with one of their fishing equipment consultants. It is better outfitting than I deserve; no beginner could ask for more.

It has done little to improve my casting; only practice, and decent instruction, can do that. So I struggle to cover the water, a short stretch at a time; and Bill Murray is ever patient with his sport. I am grateful that yearning is invisible, thankful that the churning of my soul is silent, hopeful that neither Bill, nor Joe, nor the two Hildreth brothers and their pleasant wives can sense the extraordinary dimensions of my anxieties. Landing a salmon, seeing my name in the book of records Joe keeps in such detail, becomes, in this place, an unquenchable flame of competitive desire, searing my insides. If I don't, I tell myself in the warped logic of desperation, I might as well quit.

"Fish rolled there," Bill says evenly, no inflection of excitement, merely a report, like a forecaster saying, "High temperatures in the seventies." Bill has seen fish roll and announced the event a half-dozen times during our two days on the river. I have yet to confirm any such behavior.

"There he is again."

This time Bill points, and I can see the aberrant swirls that a surfacing salmon leaves behind when it moves against the current. They are, I can tell immediately, out of casting range.

"I don't think I can reach him," I say, hedging what each of us knows is obvious.

"I'll slide back a half-drop," Bill says, reaching for the line that runs the length of the canoe and through the pulley on a bracket at the bow. A submerged lead weight as round and smooth as a cheese is at the rope's far end; its weight holds us, its roundness keeps it from fouling in the rocks. As Bill hauls in line, the weight lifts and we drift backward in the current about 30 feet before Bill releases the rope and waits until our anchor holds.

"There," he says. "You think that's about right, do you?"

I'm not sure what "right" means in this situation, but I know even I can cast far enough to reach the place where the fish was – if, in fact, it is still there.

So I say yes and stand to begin casting. One side, then the other. I cover the water. The fish remains invisible. Bill changes my fly. The Orange Blossom comes off, a Cossaboom goes on.

A long cast and a tight loop on the productive Southwest Miramichi, one of that watershed's many great tributaries.

I cover the water again. I might as well do my casting in a bus terminal.

"We'll give him a rest, eh?" Bill says, reaching for my leader to change the fly again. "Try a Silver Rat this time. That's what that fish took yesterday. Ollie told me."

"That fish," I assume, is the 14-pounder Mrs Hildreth had brought into camp, the very one Joe said we would share at today's luncheon. Visions of the gathering shadow the moment. Can I, I wonder, endure more mannered artifice, more polite salt rubbed in the wounds of my fishless history?

My rod jumps in my hand, as if a tree limb had dropped on the line.

"He's on," Bill says.

I am immobilized. I have done nothing new. This cast is as sloppy as any of the others, yet there is pressure, resistance, a forceful presence at the other end.

There was no warning. Now, what do I do?

The fish decides. After a few long seconds (how many? perhaps three) it moves downstream with a Silver Rat in its mouth. I still hold the rod just as I held it when the fish took the fly. Nothing reacts but my pounding heart.

"Sit down," Bill says.

Sit down? Why sit down? But I do as he says, holding the rod high.

"We'll go ashore." He has already lifted the anchor and, as more line departs my reel, Bill paddles us toward a strip of stones and gravel along the river bank.

"Now," he says when the bow scrapes, "step out and land the fish."

I begin to understand. Feet on the gravel, rod in hand, I am in a situation I recognize: As a surf caster, I have beached striped bass on a rocky shore.

This fish uses the river as its ally, swinging side-to-side in the current, putting strain on the line. Then, just as I want to believe I sense the start of surrender, the salmon soars, leaps clear, suspended silver in the sun, the entire force of its being in stunning profile, its impact on my consciousness as direct as a bullet to the brain.

Luck has joined me. Falling to the river in a rose of white water, the fish has not thrown the hook. This is, I know now, my salmon.

Ten minutes later, Bill's net scythes water where the fish waits, held close by my line. When the net surfaces, the salmon leaps again, but now as prisoner of the mesh around it. Brought to the bank, it is cracked twice on the head by Bill's small club, quivers and dies. Even in the arrogance of my 50 years, even after the desperation of my yearning for verification, I regret my witness of the moment.

But only for the moment.

When we return to the boathouse where the eleven-and-a-half-pound fish is weighed, as I walk the gravel drive to the lodge, I hear the roots of the trees grip the stony ground, feel the river's chill embrace, sense the songs of birds I cannot see, and understand the language of the great slabs of rose granite that line this valley like monuments speaking to me for the first time since I arrived at this brilliant center of the earth.

PHOTOGRAPH

by John Engels, 1995

I enclose with this letter
a photograph of the salmon,
and the proud fisherman,
me. You can see

that the fish is better
than average for this stream.
I display him
from a hawthorn branch.

You can see
the harebells and cornflowers
that bloom from his gills:
my ghillie

put them there. It is
apparently a custom
in these parts. And I
am there, at left, attentive

to my kill, although
I am unsmiling, seriously staring
into the lens, for I wish not to seem
boastful, nor in any way

above my station, for this
is a kingly fish. My ghillie holds
my Hardy's celebrated
"Alnwick Greenheart,"

built suitable for salmon
trout and grayling, and he fiddles
with my reel, a brand-new
"Cascapedia." The river

eddies to a shore of daisies
in the background right. The rapids
of the pool are out of sight, but it was there
this great fish had tried to kill

a full-dressed Beauly Snow 3/0
blue-furred and tinseled, orange-headed
winged with peacock herl
that quartered flittering, across

his lie, a roar of color designed
to exasperate him, and it did,
to his lordly death.
But the biggest masterpiece

done by me was when I –
not with this but with another rod,
got a salmon in the Äaro river, in
Sögndal, in

Sögn. The weight
of this greater fish was
forty-three pounds, and I
was three hours

landing him, and you can bet
it was a strain on the rod,
but it was just as good
after as when

I began. I enclose
a second photograph of my
greater fish, and the proud fisherman,
me. The rod in this picture

was made from well-seasoned
greenheart, and my dear friend
for more than twenty-five
years. But now old age has claimed us.

RUSSIA

"At the end of one quiet drift, a salmon took, ran off with the fly line and, well into the backing, cartwheeled into the air. He put up a strong, fast fight and I had to to follow him down to the beach to a small cover, where I tailed him. I looked down at the fish, not a big salmon, but a wonderful, speckled creature of eight pounds, a pure and ancient product of the Russian arctic. I slipped the barbless hook from the corner of his mouth and this brilliantly precise creature, briefly in my hand, faded like an image on film, into the traveling depths of the Ponoi."

From "Fly-Fishing the Evil Empire" by Thomas McGuane, 1995

FLY-FISHING THE
EVIL EMPIRE

by Thomas McGuane, 1995

THE TARMAC AT MURMANSK was under repair and so we were diverted into a military airport. There was a small group of us now, Americans and English. We stood near a plywood shanty, awaiting transport to the Soviet helicopter, red star painted out, that would carry us to 67° North latitude, above the Arctic Circle, to our camp on the Ponoi River, 350 miles of wild Atlantic salmon water springing from a tundra swamp and flowing to the Barents Sea.

We took the time to inspect the very advanced looking pale blue fighter planes parked in front of bulldozed gravel ledges. They looked like state of the art military equipment; but canvas had been thrown over the canopies, there was at least one flat tire. They now belonged to a discarded chapter of world politics and other cerebral fevers. The hearty, cheerful Russian woman who was our translator for the moment gestured to the airplanes and said, "You like some military secrets?"

We boarded the enormous Russian helicopter and put in our earplugs. We sat on benches amid dufflebags and rod cases. The Russian crew nodded in that enthusiastic, mute way that says we don't know your language. The helicopter lifted off to an altitude of about two feet. I looked out the window at the hurricanes of dust stirred by the rotors. Then the helicopter roared down the runway like a fixed wing aircraft and we were on our way.

In very short order, the view from the window was of natural desolation, rolling tundra, wisps of fog and alarming low-level whiteouts. Even through my earplugs came a vast drumming of power from the

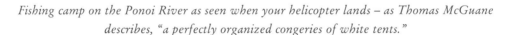

Fishing camp on the Ponoi River as seen when your helicopter lands – as Thomas McGuane describes, "a perfectly organized congeries of white tents."

A ribbon of salmon bliss flowing through an unspoilt Russian wilderness. These rivers have remained isolated from commercial over-fishing and pollution.

helicopter's engine. As I often do when confronted with a barrage of new impressions, I fell asleep, chin on chest, arms dangling between my own knees, like a chimp defeated by shoe laces.

After an hour and half's flight, we stopped at a rural airfield and got out to stretch while the chopper refueled. Parked on this airfield were enormous Antonov biplanes, built in the 1940's. A Russian mechanic told us that some of them had American engines. These were great cargo-hauling workhorses in Siberia and from time to time we would see them flying over the tundra at a snail's pace.

We reboarded. A very pretty Russian girl boarded with us carrying an armload of flowers. She smiled at everyone with the by now familiar mute enthusiasm while the helicopter roared into flight once again. We

all mused on this radiant flower of the Russian north, working up theories about her life and dreams. Everything was so wonderfully foreign that we were later slow to acknowledge that she and her husband were our talented cooks from Minnesota.

We landed on a bluff above the Ponoi River. From here we could see both the camp and the river. The camp was a perfectly organized congeries of white tents of varying sizes and when I was installed in mine, I briefly stretched out on my bunk to take in that bright sense of nomadic domesticity that a well-appointed tent produces. In this far north latitude, I knew that the sun would be beaming through my tent day and night. In one corner was the small Finnish wood stove that, in our sustained spell of warmth, we would never use.

We were briefed about the angling at the first dinner. An amusing and slightly imperious Englishman named Nicholas Hood picked the first pause between syllables during the official briefing to forgo dessert and descend to the river with his 16-foot Spey rod. I was impressed by his deftness in effecting a warp-speed fisherman's exit without getting caught at it. I had just given an old household toast of ours, "Over the lips, over the gums, look out stomach, here it comes." And Hood said, "Cerebral lot, your family," and was out of there. One of my companions, Doug Larsen, a superb outdoorsman, remarked that Hood slept with one leg in his waders. I do like to hit the ground running in these situations, but by the time I could disentangle myself, Hood was stationed midway down the Home Pool cracking out long casts and covering water like one who'd bent to this work before. "Any sense of the protocol on fishing through here?" I asked.

"Go anywhere you like," said Nick Hood, far too busy to get into this with me. So I went, I thought, a polite distance below him and began measuring several long casts onto the tea-colored water. English salmon anglers think that our single-handed rods are either ridiculous, inadequate or simply bespeak, especially when combined with baseball hats, the hyperkinetic, sawed-off spiritual nature of the people who use them. One Englishman fishing here earlier in the season had stated plainly that he didn't think Americans should be allowed to fish for salmon at all.

At the end of one quiet drift, a salmon took, ran off with the fly line and, well into the backing, cartwheeled into the air. He put up a strong, fast fight and I had to follow him down to the beach to a small cover, where I tailed him. I looked down at the fish, not a big salmon, but a wonderful, speckled creature of eight pounds, a pure and ancient product of the Russian arctic. I slipped the barbless hook from the

Covering the lies on the famous Home Pool, Ponoi River camp, where salmon anglers fish the sunlit midnight.

corner of his mouth and this brilliantly precise creature, briefly in my hand, faded like an image on film, into the traveling depths of the Ponoi.

When I returned to my spot on the pool, there was Nicholas Hood, beaming and fishing at once. "Well, *done!*" said Hood with surprising pleasure at my catch. As we would see, Hood was much too able a fisherman to be insecure about anyone else's success.

In addition to the talented Doug Larsen, who fascinated me with his expansion of the carp family: the specklebelly geese so popular among Texas gunners, were "sky carp," the grayling with their tall dorsal fins that darted out after our flies were "sail carp." I know he wanted to place the enormous salmonid of the Danube and other waters, the taimen, into some remote branch of the carp family. But it wouldn't go.

The Russians who fished for them, he explained with ill-concealed disgust, waited until the taimen made his first jump then let him have it with a 12-gauge. It was the only way to land them and made esthetic or even polite tackle out of the question. You would be at one with the shark assassins of Montauk and other brutes.

Larsen had brought with him our third companion, a Mr Duff, who listed among his shadowy achievements giving investment tips to Mookie Blaylock. During the course of our week's angling it became clear to me that the suave well-dressed, neatly coiffed Mr Duff, introduced to me as one who had warmed up for Atlantic salmon by float tubing for bluegills on their spawning beds, was a werewolf. His attempts at angling innocence, like asking whether a Near Nuff Frog would be a good fly to tie on, didn't

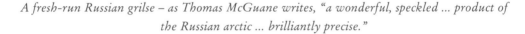

A fresh-run Russian grilse – as Thomas McGuane writes, "a wonderful, speckled ... product of the Russian arctic ... brilliantly precise."

fool me even in the beginning. There was something about the space between his eyes that put me on the *qui vive.* He was into fish all week and stood on the banks of the tundra river at evening and howled like a Russian wolf to commemorate each fish. Not quite physically powerful enough to pinch down the barb on his hook, he had other strengths. Setting off on my middle-of-the-night excursions, I realized that when I reached the river, the wolf would be there. In the end we accepted "Mr Duff" as he was, a wild dog, saliva glistening in the corners of his mouth, chastely marcelled waves of blond over his forehead and a gymnast's ability to fish up to you, around you, past you, nipping continuously at your water, and an unswerving, otherworldly need to catch the most fish. In other words, a werewolf.

Larsen and I were no longer comfortable with our considerable experience in angling for sea-run fish. We were being hunted down by this bluegill jock and had to exhaust our reserves of strength and knowledge to stay ahead of him. And the Ponoi frequently rewarded him as he gazed reflectively through his cigarette smoke. Incidentally, while he always had a cigarette smoldering between his lips, I never saw him light one. This primeval or eternal cigarette ought to be a final clue for any reader who needs one.

After a few days, you imagine you will be on the river forever. This is one of the few places I have ever fished where salmon seemed truly eminent. One fished with ongoing concentration, trying to throw strikes with every cast, mending as exactly as possible, and looking into one's flybook like a fortune teller. The world of the river became more enclosing, the hurtling power of the fish ever more emblematic of the force of wild things and the plenitude of undisturbed nature.

One afternoon I fished in the trance state of repeated casting. The river was so comfortable, I fished without my waders. The clouds were long, thin streamers on a sky of northern summer. On the

cliff face above me was a nest of arctic gyrfalcons; the parents wheeled around the nest bringing food while the pale, fierce youngsters' screams echoed across the canyon.

We had passed a place where villagers had come out and built a fire. There were empty vodka bottles

Renowned photographer Val Atkinson and a big male Russian salmon with a distinctively kyped lower jaw.

" About halfway down the pool, I had a jolting strike. After ripping 40 yards into my backing, a terrific salmon made one crashing jump after another well out in mid-river. "

and pieces of roasted reindeer tongue. The ground was trampled around the fire. The people of that village had been there for thousands of years and had some old habits, not readily discernible to our eyes.

The fish came with a slow rolling motion and started back to his lie with my Green Highlander in the corner of his mouth. I let him tighten against the reel and raised my rod. And now, we were off to the races, running over the round river rocks in wading

shoes, while the fish cartwheeled in mid-river, the thread of dacron backing streaming after it and the reel making its sublime music. We had earlier noted Nick Hood bounding like Nijinski behind a fish, springing from stone to stone, and I felt more than the usual pressure to stay on my feet. But this fish was landed in a slick behind boulders. I released him without ever taking him out of the water and he flickered away into the depths of his ancestral river.

A double hook-up on the generous Ponoi, one of the few salmon rivers in the world where such a thing is likely.

Larsen continued to catch fish steadily while Mr Duff showed some of the deficits of his otherworldly auspices. He would catch fish at a good clip, then become possessed by a "hoodoo." By this time, we had become well enough acquainted that he could share some of the special problems he experienced. A hoodoo evidently is some sort of bird, or possibly a bat. When it settles, imperceptibly, between the shoulderblades of the unsuspecting angler, it becomes impossible to catch a fish. It is possible to *hook* a fish but they always get off. So, for a while, the wolf's echoing howls were less frequent. Sport that he was, though, he finally shook it off. From time to time, the hoodoo settled on Larsen and me. In attempting to provide companionship and sympathy to Mr Duff, we began to acquire some of his problems; by mid-week, for example, Larsen had begun taking great pains to precisely part his hair.

That night, when I left the dining tent with its many pleasures of good food, pleasant companionship, a fly-tying table where the silliest notions may be brought to life, I knew I had to keep fishing. It had been a long day and so a small nap was in order. Larsen and Mr Duff, now transmuted into a *bon vivant*, refilling the drinks of the guests, telling golfing stories and smoking the very cigarette I had watched glow all week, were in the dining tent for the foreseeable future. They were being corrupted by an English farmer, James Keith, who promoted late card games and a general shore-leave atmosphere. I could see that Hood was all in: there was every chance I would have the magnificent Home Pool – one of the great salmon pools in the world – to myself.

I awakened at three and gulped the cup of cold coffee I'd left beside my bunk. I was soon walking through the sleeping camp with my rod over my shoulder. Snores were coming from several tents and the sun was shining merrily. Wagtails had seized this

209

time to hop among the tents looking for food. I noted Hood's 16-foot Spey rod leaned up in front of his tent. I climbed down the path along a small stream, waving away the mosquitoes, and was soon casting out onto the great river and discovering how tired my muscles were.

I caught a small grilse right away, a silver-bright fish only a day or so from the ocean. Then it got still. There were no fish rolling. Sleep kept rising through my mind but I was in the river and the casts were still rolling out. About halfway down the pool, I had a jolting strike. After ripping 40 yards into my backing, a terrific salmon made one crashing jump after another well out in mid-river. Then it started back toward the ocean. I put as deep a bow in the rod as I dared and began following the fish downstream. I beached it on a small point, beyond which I may not have

been able to follow. It was a big male with a lower jaw so hooked it had worn a groove in the upper. I was delighted to make certain this individual made it back to the gene pool. I've always thought that it would be nice after landing an exceptional fish to go straight to bed. This time I did, drifting off in my glowing tent in a dream of sea-run fish.

We stopped in Murmansk for a couple of hours on the way out. I went to a small museum and looked at some wonderful paintings of submarines, some in the open sea, some in remote ocean coves with snow on their decks, portraits of their captains. This glimpse of military glory was at sharp odds with the beleaguered municipality all around us. As I looked at the cheerlessly monolithic public housing towering over raw, bulldozed ground, I remembered that the leading cause of domestic fires in Russia is exploding

1 *Copper Shrimp* **2** *Yellow Ally's Shrimp*
3 *Willie Gunn* **4** *Munroe Killer* **5** *Willie Gunn Variant* **6** *Thunder and Lightning* **7** *Comally* **8** *Ally's Shrimp* **9** *Silver Rat* **10** *Bomber* **11** *Thunder and Lightning Variant* **12** *Mickey Finn*

A final cast into the sunset of Russia's magnificent Ponoi River – the last great Atlantic salmon frontier.

television sets. But no one in the world has wild, open country like the Russians, a possible ace-in-the-hole on a strangling planet. Poets and naturalists could have seen this so much more comprehensively than I did, dragging my fly rod, but without it I would probably never have gotten there, or stood for a week in a tundra river bound for the Barents Sea.

Mr Duff gazed at me with the faintest of smiles as I dragged my duffle to the boarding area. A thin plume of motionless smoke extended vertically from his cigarette. He looked away from me and resumed his scrutiny of a back issue of *Golf Digest*. I was conscious of the weight of my duffle which had come to seem tremendous. I dragged it from boarding area to

boarding area that day and night, in Murmansk, in Helsinki, in New York, in Salt Lake City, in Bozeman. I had apparently become so weak I could barely carry it. Finally home, I dragged it out of my car like a corpse. I hated it so much that I slept a full day before unpacking it. When I did I found beneath the soggy wading shoes and dirty laundry, the most beautiful round river rocks and I remembered a distant howl from the shadows along the far shore of the Ponoi.

CONSERVATION

"The problems facing the Atlantic salmon are daunting. But if 'the King of gamefish' is anything, it's irrepressible, as evidenced by its incredible atavistic journey upstream to spawn and its ability to inspire the arts of man. From the ancient Neolithic cave paintings to the literature in this book, no fish in the world has been so celebrated. And no fish is so equally important to fishermen and those who aren't even aware of its existence... No two rivers hold the same genetic strain of Atlantic salmon. Once we lose a river's population of salmon — and this is happening across the North Atlantic — it is gone for good. These silent deaths may be hard to hear over the din of modern life, but they whisper to us in some universal way — the health of our environment is poor."

From "The Dying of the Light" by Monte Burke, 2001

THE DYING OF THE LIGHT

by Monte Burke, 2001

ON A HOT MIDDAY in the first July of the millennium, Charles Gaines, Bill Taylor, and I sat on the shaded porch of Joseph Cullman 3rd's Two Brooks lodge on the Upsalquitch River in New Brunswick, Canada. Before us, the eddying Home Pool held our gazes like some ancient hearth, and we watched the occasional salmon leap gracefully from the current – a form both ephemeral and timeless that never ceases to flutter a salmon angler's heart. The fishing in the morning had been slow, and the sun showed no signs of abdicating its commanding position in the flawless maritime sky, so we whiled away the afternoon on the porch, discussing fishing theories and fly patterns in the manner and bliss of little old ladies gossiping about tea parties. We were in the fine company of Edward Ringwood Hewitt, whose 1927 book, *Secrets*

of the Salmon, I had pulled from the musty library at Two Brooks, hoping for some insight into our mysterious quarry. I find this practice one of the most endearing aspects of Atlantic salmon fishing, a sport layered with tradition that, more often than not, refers to its own past for techniques that still work today. How many other sports can claim this heritage? It is certainly part of its inimitable charm that each cast for an Atlantic salmon connects us with a vast body of study and story and love. The past raves on in this literature.

Hewitt, as it turned out, had many hints for hot weather fishing – fishing submerged dry flies or using small, sparsely tied wets – all devised during the many summers he and Ambrose Monell and George LaBranche spent on the Upsalquitch, at a time when 20 fish a week was considered merely average. I came across a passage that I found particularly interesting: "We were sitting together on the porch looking over the pool," Hewitt wrote, "when Mr Monell jumped and called out, 'I know how to get those devilish fish.'"

Hewitt, a salmon sage if there ever was one, goes on to describe how he and Monell and LaBranche muddied the water above the pool with rakes and hoes – essentially creating an artificial spate – then cast their flies into the clearing water, catching five salmon. An unorthodox method, and probably illegal today, but you've got to give them credit for creativity.

"What porch were they sitting on, Billy?" I asked Taylor, who as the president of the Atlantic Salmon Federation (ASF) posseses an encyclopedic knowledge of salmon lore.

Part of the future of salmon fishing is releasing hatchery-reared salmon parr as shown here in Connemara, Ireland.

Suspended animation: the amazing aerial power and grace of the "king of gamefish."

"This one," he said, pointing to the worn wooden boards on the porch floor.

I thought about Hewitt, Monell, and LaBranche almost 75 years ago, chewing over their own theories, fishing for the ancestors of the same fish that we were after; about how the entire catch for the 1999 season at Two Brooks was 20 fish; about how the past raves on. "That's amazing," I said.

"It is," said Taylor. Then he added in a somewhat wistful tone: "But it would be even more amazing if 75 years from now, our grandchildren could sit here and do the same thing."

THOUSANDS OF YEARS after the last Ice Age, Atlantic salmon established what is referred to as their historical range, which extended from latitudes 41° to 60° north in North America and 40° to 70° north in Europe. Salmon inhabited rivers as far south as the Douro in Portugal and the Connecticut in the US, and as far north as the Pechora in Russia and the George in Ungava. To say there was plentitude is a mild understatement. In Europe, widespread famines in the Middle Ages were averted thanks to the abundant salmon. In North America, early colonists netted salmon to spread as fertilizer, and they were so myriad in the rivers of eastern Canada that in the 1600's a Jesuit priest wrote, "at night one is unable to sleep, so great is the noise they make falling on water." Even as late as the 19th century, loggers in the Canadian Maritimes stipulated in their contracts that they could only be served salmon at mealtimes six times a week. The fishing wasn't too bad either. On April 9th, 1795, the tenth Lord Home had the all-time red-letter day fishing on the River Dee in Scotland, killing 38 fish ranging in weight from six to 36 pounds.

But each step of progress during the Industrial Revolution and thereafter was taken at the expense of the Atlantic salmon. The list of rivers rendered uninhabitable by industrial and agricultural pollution and hydro-electric dams includes some of the world's most famous – the Connecticut and Merrimack in the US; and in Europe, the Seine, Elbe, Thames, and the Rhine, the latter being once the most productive salmon river in Europe, perhaps the world. In the 1880's, the Rhine yielded millions of pounds of salmon to commercial nets annually, at an average of 17 pounds a fish. By the 1940's, the great river had no more salmon.

Now, at the dawning of the 21st century, there are no more wild salmon in Portugal, Switzerland, and the Low Countries, and they are in danger of extinction in France and Spain. Likewise, the species' future is tenuous in the New Brunswick and Nova Scotia rivers – 33 of them – that empty into Canada's inner Bay of Fundy. The few hundred fish that returned to these rivers in 1999 represent a 15-year decline of more than 99 percent. But no nation has squandered its Atlantic salmon resources as carelessly as the US. There are now more dams in Maine than the 50–100 wild salmon that run the seven Downeast rivers in Maine and Cove Brook, a tributary of the Penobscot River. These fish, which were listed under the Endangered Species Act in November 2000, represent the last in a US population that once numbered in the hundreds of thousands. Sadly, the listing may be too little too late.

The drastic downslide shows no signs of slowing down. In the last 30 years, salmon populations in North America have declined 75 percent, from one-and-a-half million to just 350,000. In Europe, the estimated three million fish returning to its rivers is only half of the historical average. The evidence from Maine, Portugal, and Spain, indicate that we may be

Salmon holding in the turquoise water of Big Indian Pool on the St Jean River.

witnessing extinction on a northward track. Only on Russia's pristine Kola Peninsula are there runs of Atlantic salmon that could be deemed healthy, but the lack of historical data almost makes this a *non sequitur*. Even Iceland's well-managed system – with no commercial netting and extensive hatchery enhancement – has suffered.

How can we save the Atlantic salmon, a species that has inhabited the oceans and rivers of the North Atlantic for millions of years? It is this question that Taylor and his very able contemporaries, Orri Vigfússon of the North Atlantic Salmon Fund (NASF) and Dr Malcolm Windsor of the North Atlantic Salmon Conservation Organization, (NASCO), wrestle with every day in their capacities as the world's leading salmon conservationists. It is not an easy one to answer.

The future for Atlantic salmon is precarious at best, but we have not yet passed the tipping point. There is enough of a foundation left to restore the species to viability, and extinction, even at our present rate of decline, is still a few lifetimes away. However, there are four main problems that stand in the way of full recovery and how we deal with them will ultimately determine the fate of this regal gamefish.

Poor Marine Survival

Historically speaking, the decline of Atlantic salmon populations could be attributed solely to human activities, whether it be dams, polluted watersheds, or, most important, commercial overharvest. In the 1980's and 90's, with the massive publicly – and privately – financed buyout of commercial nets in the northwest Atlantic and off the coast of Greenland, conservationists believed they had solved the biggest problem facing Atlantic salmon – mortality in the ocean. But in the decade since the removal of the nets,

there has been a 66 percent reduction in the number of salmon returning to spawn in North America and a 50 percent reduction in Europe. Just 15 years ago, there was a ten percent chance that a smolt would survive the ocean to become a spawning adult. Now that rate is closer to one percent, a decline that has baffled scientists and disheartened conservationists. Identifying the reasons for this precipitous drop in marine survival has proven a difficult task in an ocean that remains, to a large extent, a mysterious black hole. Theories run the gamut, from an exploding predatory seal population to increased commercial bottom harvesting that's decimating populations of capelin and sandeels, the salmon's primary food source. And global warming – which has actually made waters near the polar ice caps colder – may also play a role in disrupting the feeding grounds. To date, there has been very little done in this critical area. The Atlantic Salmon Federation has embarked on a privately funded acoustic telemetry study of salmon habits in Canada's troubled Bay of Fundy, which has provided data on smolt migration and the impacts seals, birds, and other predators – even acquaculture – have on wild salmon. But it is too great a task for one organization to undertake alone. A postive first step, but more funding is needed from both private and public sources.

> " ... THERE HAS BEEN A 66 PERCENT REDUCTION IN THE NUMBER OF SALMON RETURNING TO SPAWN IN NORTH AMERICA AND A 50 PERCENT REDUCTION IN EUROPE. "

Mixed-Stock Salmon Harvesting

Although the buyout of the commercial fishery was not the silver bullet solution to the salmon problem, it remains one of the great success stories in Atlantic salmon conservation. The work of Dr Wilfred Carter and Bill Taylor at the ASF, Orri Vigfússon at the NASF, and Dr Malcolm Windsor at NASCO, has led to the dramatic reduction in commercial netting in the North Atlantic, ensuring that the Atlantic salmon

A salmon caught in a mackerel trap in Nova Scotia. Traps designed for other species continue to do damage to salmon populations worldwide.

avoided the fate of the cod and haddock, two denizens of the North Atlantic that succumbed to the devastating convergence of modern technology and commercial fishing. And there is reason to believe that their efforts are beginning to bear fruit: The report from the 2000 International Council for Exploration of the Sea indicates that while stocks of Atlantic salmon are still at all-time lows, they seem to have at least stabilized. By 1997 all commercial nets in Canada had been bought out at a cost to the government of $72 million. The harvest off Greenland – the Atlantic salmon's most important feeding grounds – has gone from one million salmon a year in the mid 1970's to a present-day subsistence level of 7,500. There has been no commercial fishery on the Faroe Islands or Iceland for the past decade. And in

December 2000, the British government, on the advice of the UK's Atlantic Salmon Trust, the ASF and the NASF, announced that it had set aside $1.1 million (£750,000) as matching funds for a permanent buyout of England's northeast driftnet fishery. The buyout, which will save some 40,000 salmon a year, is a major step in the cessation of all ocean fisheries for Atlantic salmon, and strengthens the position of conservationists when negotiating the low quotas for Greenland.

But mixed-stock fisheries (which intercept salmon from different rivers) remain in Ireland where 150,000 salmon are harvested each year, and in the fjords of Norway. Not only do these fisheries take a huge number of fish, they also can wipe out a run of salmon in certain rivers, particularly those where diminished runs have made them vulnerable. The Irish harvest, for example, has contributed to the demise of Atlantic salmon rivers in France and Spain.

There is some disagreement among leading Atlantic salmon activists about the solution to this issue. Vigfússon, a tireless Atlantic salmon crusader, has led the charge in raising private money to buy out commercial nets at a fair-market value, mostly on a year-to-year basis. Vigfússon believes that the Greenlanders should be allowed a commensurate share of stock if and when the salmon recover. Taylor (and the ASF) agree, to a point, arguing that buy-outs like the one in Greenland are indeed the answer, but should be permanent, not year-to-year and financed with public monies. The ASF also is in favor of a static quota for the Greenland harvest which would ensure that any increase in salmon abundance one year would not be undermined by an increase in har-

vest the next. Both groups are working together to pressure the Irish, British, and Norwegian governments to buy out their commercial fisheries.

Freshwater Habitat

The problems in rivers, unlike the ocean, are a known quantity. And there is certainly work to be done. Man-made dams impede fish passage; clearcutting near rivers increases siltation and decreases the sylvan ability to absorb water and shade rivers; and agricultural industries – like blueberry farms in Maine – lower the water table and pollute rivers with pesticides. There are signs of hope on this front. The listing of Maine's Atlantic salmon under the *Endangered Species Act* will reduce clearcutting and agricultural run-off in rivers and finally provide these fish clean spawning habitat. Even the Rhine's once-fetid waters are clearing up, thanks to the installation of sewage

David Clark shows off a 12-pound salmon before releasing it back into the Bonaventure River, in Canada.

treatment plants. German fishing groups have worked with their government to construct fish hatcheries on Rhine tributaries and fish ladders at weirs such as the Iffezheim near Baden Baden. Results of an electrofishing survey showed that there were some 200 adult spawners that returned to the river in 2000. There is quite a way to go on the Rhine – smolts must still negotiate turbines in the lower reaches of the river, and Dutch offshore and inland fishing takes its toll – but it's a promising start.

Recreational anglers play a huge role in freshwater habitat by monitoring river conditions, discouraging poachers, and contributing to the local economy. But the single most important contribution an angler can make to the Atlantic salmon on the river is to voluntarily release his catch. The practice is widely adopted in North America and Russia and has begun to take hold in the British Isles, but it must become common practice for every fisherman, even in countries such as Iceland and Norway which have a long entrenched histories of killing their catch. Salmon that are properly caught and released have a better than 98 percent chance of surviving to continue their migration to spawn. And fishing without intent to kill – even for grilse – certainly puts recreational anglers in a better position to argue against commercial harvest.

Catch and release is a weighty issue, and one that every Atlantic salmon angler must come to terms with on his own. There are obvious circumstances in which there should be no fishing at all – in Maine, Canada's Bay of Fundy rivers, Spain, the Rhine. But where viable populations of Atlantic salmon are found, catch and release recreational angling is beneficial. It is axiomatic that those who are in direct contact with a species are far more likely to become

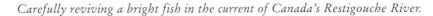

Carefully reviving a bright fish in the current of Canada's Restigouche River.

involved in its preservation. Put simply, without recreational anglers – who contribute 75 percent of Atlantic salmon conservation money – the fight for Atlantic salmon would have been lost long ago.

Aquaculture

The $150 million generated by Atlantic salmon aquaculture in North America accounts for less than five percent of the global market. In 1999, the worldwide production of farmed Atlantic salmon was 758,000 tons (roughly 260 million fish as opposed to the roughly 5 million wild salmon that exist worldwide), with Norway, the United Kingdom, and Chile the top three producers. Ironically, conservationists were among the earliest proponents of aquaculture, which was once viewed as a practice that would lessen worldwide demand for wild Atlantic salmon. It has indeed done just that, but no one could have foreseen the havoc that farmed fish would wreak on wild populations. Parasites and disease, like the devastating infectious salmon anemia, which has been found in wild fish, flourish in overcrowded pens. And when escaped aquaculture fish – which are easily differentiated from wild salmon (it's like comparing couch potatoes to finely tuned, world-class athletes) – run rivers, they interbreed with wild stocks, weakening the gene pool and lowering survival rates. An average of one million farmed fish have escaped pens in each of the last five years in Norway, resulting in the disappearance of wild salmon in 39 rivers. In 2000, an estimated 500,000 farmed fish escaped Scottish pens. In the US and Canada, aquaculturists are not required to report escapees, but a privately funded monitor recorded 40,000 escaped fish from one Nova Scotia site alone. While aquaculturists vehemently deny any negative impact that their fish have on wild stocks, independent studies have shown that the high concentration of pens in the troubled Bay of Fundy have played a role in the loss of its wild salmon. Genetically engineered (or "transgenic") salmon, set to hit the market upon government approval, raise a whole new set of questions, both biological and moral. These farm-raised fish, implanted with ocean pout genes, grow twice as fast as a wild salmon. Their impact on wild populations has yet to be determined.

To date, there is little, if any, regulation in place for aquaculture, a technology that seems to grow as fast as its fish. We must take a precautionary position with transgenic salmon and aquaculture by placing pens at least 20 miles from river mouths and requiring better cage technology (to prevent escapees) and further study on the impacts that these fish have on wild populations, as stipulated by NASCO protocols. The burden of proof, in terms of environmentally detrimental effects, should always be on the producers, not the conservationists.

THE PROBLEMS facing the Atlantic salmon are daunting. But if "the King of gamefish" is anything, it's irrepressible, as evidenced by its incredible atavistic journey upstream to spawn and its ability to inspire the arts of man. From the ancient Neolithic cave paintings to the literature in this book, no fish in the world has been so celebrated. And no fish is so equally important to fishermen and those who aren't even aware of its existence. Why is the Atlantic salmon so important? Why spend so much time and money and energy trying to save them? Surely there are other problems – human problems such as diseases and starvation – that are more pressing. And the loss of this species won't directly compromise our ability to survive, at least not right away. But that's not the point. It's not necessarily what matters more, it's what matters. No two rivers hold the same genetic strain of Atlantic salmon. Once we lose a river's population of salmon – and this is happening across the North Atlantic – it is gone for good. These silent deaths may be hard to hear over the din of modern life, but they whisper to us in some universal way – the health of our environment is poor. Enough of these whispers eventually become a shout that is often heard too late.

The tendency among environmental organizations has been for them to anthropomorphize flora and fauna, to make them matter because they are more like us – like the cuddliness of a panda bear or the "scream" of a felled tree. Attempts have been made for the Atlantic salmon on this front. And although they do have many characteristics that we deem human – courage, tenacity, and an unerring will to procreate – perhaps it is their difference, their utter wildness that makes them so important. Intuitively, we realize that human diversity is important. But diversity in nature – wildness – is equally important in the most fundamental of ways. It is what makes our world vital. Perhaps if we can save salmon – not destroy them – with our progress, we may prove to be as smart as we think we are. Allowing this species to become extinct is a sure sign of a dangerous pathology and immaturity.

You are reading this book because you care about Atlantic salmon. Subjects that inspire good writing – like love and war and, in this case, Atlantic salmon – should never be taken lightly. More likely than not, you've spent hours, days, years, perhaps even decades, casting and casting again, hoping for the eternal tug that pulls you into the salmon's world. For a fleeting moment, that tug leaves in doubt exactly who has been caught and reminds us that at one time, we all came from water. There is hope for the Atlantic salmon, and it lies within each of us. In the end, it is our moral and ethical obligation as humans to save a species that belongs here on earth. And to do that, we must get involved with organizations like the ASF and NASF, and with our governments and "rage, rage against the dying of the light," in the words of Dylan Thomas. It is the best way – perhaps the only way – to ensure that the Atlantic salmon will be accessible in rivers, not just in books; to ensure that their storied past will rave on.

A nudging pair on the York River.

The publishers would like to thank the following authors, copyright holders and publishing houses/magazines for their kind permission to reproduce pieces in this book.

Foreword by Bill Taylor, text copyright © Bill Taylor, 2001.

Introduction by Charles Gaines, text copyright © Charles Gaines, 2001.

"The Lives of the Salmon" by J.D. Bates and P.B. Richards, an extract from the book *Fishing Atlantic Salmon: The Flies and the Patterns* (1996), text copyright © Pamela Bates Richards.

"Fifty Years of Dry-Fly Salmon" by Lee Wulff, text copyright © Joan Wulff, 1983.

"The Lady or the Salmon?" by Andrew Lang, 1891, previously published in *Angling Sketches*, text copyright © Longmans, Green Company, New York.

"An Autumn Fishing" by Romilly Fedden, previously published in *Golden Days – The Fishing Log of a Painter in Brittany* (A & C Black, St Neots, Cambs), text copyright © Romilly Fedden, 1919. Reprinted by permission of A & C Black (Publishers) Ltd.

"The Night of the Gytefisk" by Ernest Schwiebert, which first appeared in *Fishing Moments of Truth*, text copyright © Ernest Schwiebert, 1976.

"One of Our Best Days" by A.H. Chaytor, an extract from *Letters to a Salmon Fisher's Sons*, text copyright © A.H. Chaytor, 1908. Reprinted by permission of John Murray (Publishers) Ltd, London.

"October Salmon" by Ted Hughes, an extract from *River: Poems by Ted Hughes*, text copyright © Ted Hughes, 1980. Reprinted by permission of Faber & Faber Publishers.

"The River God" by Roland Pertwee, previously published in *Fisherman's Bounty* (Lyons Press, 1970), text copyright © the author's estate.

"The Spawning Run" by William Humphrey, 1970, text copyright © Dorothy Humphrey.

"Salmon of the Vatnsdalsa" by Roderick Haig-Brown, which first appeared in *The American Sportsman*, 1969, text copyright © Valerie Haig-Brown.

"Rotation" by Art Lee, text copyright © Art Lee, 2000.

"Spare the Rod" by John Alden Knight, 1942, text copyright © Linda Losch.

"Robinsonville, NB" by John N. Cole, text copyright © John N. Cole, 1989.

"Photograph" by John Engels, previously published in *Big Water*, text copyright © John Engels, 1995.

"Fly-Fishing the Evil Empire" by Thomas McGuane, which first appeared in *Live Water*, text copyright © Thomas McGuane, 1995.

"The Dying of the Light" by Monte Burke, text copyright © Monte Burke, 2001.

The publishers have made every effort to contact the articles' copyright holders. We should like to apologize for any errors or omissions, which we will endeavour to rectify in any future editions of this book.

The publisher would like to thank the following people, museums and photographic libraries for permission to reproduce their material. Every care has been taken to trace copyright holders. However, if we have omitted anyone we apologize and will, if informed, make corrections in any future editions. (b = bottom; t = top)

Pages 36, 50–1 and 125 Andrew Graham-Stewart; Pages 72 and 48 with the very kind permission of Angling Auctions, London; Pages 11, 38b, 40, 46, 60 and 172 The Estate of BB; Pages 1, 14t, 24, 38t, 41, 44t, 52, 53b, 68, 70, 73, 76, 82, 87, 90, 102, 117, 120, 160, 168, 198 and 213 The Estate of C.F. Tunnicliffe; Pages 17, 22, 23, 25, 30, 58, 62, 183, 184, 190, 193 Charles Rangeley-Wilson; Page 44b Christie's Images, London; 45 Corbis/Dewitt Jones; 118 Corbis/Richard Cummins; 150, 152 and 155 Corbis/Phil Schemeister; 165 Corbis/Archive Iconografico, S.A.; 187–7 Corbis/Winslow Homer; Pages 36, 69, 71, 77, 79, 81, 83, 85, 97b, 107, 136, 138, 144, 146, 193 and 221 with the very kind permission of Frontiers International and Tarquin Millington-Drake; Pages 18–9, 174, 194, 212, 219 and 223 Gilbert van Ryckevorsel, Nova Scotia, Canada; Page 145 Giles Pernet; Pages 49 both, 162 and164 both Hulton Getty Images; Pages 89, 121, 123 and 214 John Darling; Page 65 Jon Beer; Pages 16, 100 and 103 Mick Sharp Photography; Pages 2, 14b and 215 NHPA/Laurie Campbell; Page 91 Philips Auction House; Pages 92 and 104 Robin Lowes; Pages 57, 75, 115, 116 and 126 Roger McPhail; Pages 15, 43, 53t, 94, 95 and 111 *British Freshwater Fishes with Illustrations by A.F. Lydon*, The Reverend Houghton, 1879, published by William MacKenzie, London; Pages 7, 9, 10–11, 12, 20, 21, 26, 28–9, 31, 32, 153, 156, 158, 169, 170, 171, 176, 180, 181, 185, 188, 191, 192, 196–7, 216, 220 and 221 Tom Montgomery; Pages 35, 88, 93, 131, 132, 134, 137, 139, 140, 142–3, 148, 161, 166, 173, 200, 202, 203, 204, 206 and 208 R. Valentine Atkinson; Page 55 John Warburton-Lee; Pages 39, 47, 63, 97t, 105 and 149 William Garfit

The Editors would like to give special thanks to: Mary O'Malley; Nancy Moore; Moises Carpio; The Anglers' Club of New York; Jay Cassell; Nick Lyons; Ian Mackintosh; Wilfred Carter; Irene Pohle; Bo Ivanovich; Buby Calvo; Dan Green; Orri Vigfùsson; Dr Malcolm Windsor and Joseph Cullman 3rd.

Duncan Baird Publishers would like to thank for their patient assistance with the compilation of this book: Nicholas Ragonneau; Nick Zoll; John Morgan and the Fly Fishers Club of Great Britain; William Daniel; Neil Freeman and Angling Auctions; Jeremy Reed at the Atlantic Salmon Trust; David Profumo; Edward Barder; Steve Middleton; Dr Anthony Hayter; Derek Mills; and Vicky Rangeley-Wilson. For their assistance, and for supplying the flies photographed in the book, Brian Fratel and Farlows. For the flies tied especially to illustrate Romilly Fedden's story on Brittanny, Yann Le Fèvre, 42 Belbeoch, 29100 Douarnenez, France.